HOLT
SOCIAL
STUDIES

The Americas

Christopher L. Salter

HOLT, RINEHART AND WINSTON

A Harcourt Education Company

Orlando • **Austin** • New York • San Diego • Toronto • London

Author

Dr. Christopher L. Salter

Dr. Christopher L. "Kit" Salter is Professor Emeritus of geography and former Chair of the Department of Geography at the University of Missouri. He did his undergraduate work at Oberlin College and received both his M.A. and Ph.D. degrees in geography from the University of California at Berkeley.

Dr. Salter is one of the country's leading figures in geography education. In the 1980s he helped found the national Geographic Alliance network to promote geography education in all 50 states. In the 1990s Dr. Salter was Co-Chair of the National Geography Standards Project, a group of distinguished geographers who created *Geography for Life* in 1994, the document outlining national standards in geography. In 1990 Dr. Salter received the National Geographic Society's first-ever Distinguished Geography Educator Award. In 1992 he received the George Miller Award for distinguished service in geography education from the National Council for Geographic Education. In 2006 Dr. Salter was awarded Lifetime Achievement Honors by the Association of American Geographers for his transformation of geography education.

Over the years, Dr. Salter has written or edited more than 150 articles and books on cultural geography, China, field work, and geography education. His primary interests lie in the study of the human and physical forces that create the cultural landscape, both nationally and globally.

ISBN-13 978-0-03-099537-8
ISBN-10 0-03-099537-X

2 3 4 5 6 7 8 9 032 13 12 11 10 09 08

Reviewers

Academic Reviewers

Elizabeth Chako, Ph. D.
Department of Geography
The George Washington
    University

Altha J. Cravey, Ph. D.
Department of Geography
University of North Carolina

Eugene Cruz-Uribe, Ph. D.
Department of History
Northern Arizona University

Toyin Falola, Ph.D.
Department of History
University of Texas

Sandy Freitag, Ph.D.
Director, Monterey Bay History
    and Cultures Project
Division of Social Sciences
University of California,
    Santa Cruz

Oliver Froehling, Ph.D.
Department of Geography
University of Kentucky

Reuel Hanks, Ph.D.
Department of Geography
Oklahoma State University

Phil Klein, Ph.D.
Department of Geography
University of Northern Colorado

B. Ikubolajeh Logan, Ph. D.
Department of Geography
Pennsylvania State University

Marc Van De Mieroop, Ph.D.
Department of History
Columbia University
New York, New York

Christopher Merrett, Ph.D.
Department of History
Western Illinois University

Thomas R. Paradise, Ph.D.
Department of Geosciences
University of Arkansas

Jesse P. H. Poon, Ph.D.
Department of Geography
University at Buffalo–SUNY

Robert Schoch, Ph.D.
CGS Division of Natural Science
Boston University

Derek Shanahan, Ph.D.
Department of Geography
Millersville University
Millersville, Pennsylvania

David Shoenbrun, Ph.D.
Department of History
Northwestern University
Evanston, Illinois

Sean Terry, Ph.D.
Department of Interdisciplinary
    Studies, Geography and
    Environmental Studies
Drury University
Springfield, Missouri

Educational Reviewers

Dennis Neel Durbin
Dyersburg High School
Dyersburg, Tennessee

Carla Freel
Hoover Middle School
Merced, California

Tina Nelson
Deer Park Middle School
Randallstown, Maryland

Don Polston
Lebanon Middle School
Lebanon, Indiana

Robert Valdez
Pioneer Middle School
Tustin, California

Teacher Review Panel

Heather Green
LaVergne Middle School
LaVergne, Tennessee

John Griffin
Wilbur Middle School
Wichita, Kansas

Rosemary Hall
Derby Middle School
Birmingham, Michigan

Rose King
Yeatman-Liddell School
St. Louis, Missouri

Mary Liebl
Wichita Public Schools USD 259
Wichita, Kansas

Jennifer Smith
Lake Wood Middle School
Overland Park, Kansas

Melinda Stephani
Wake County Schools
Raleigh, North Carolina

Contents

Reading Social Studies H1

Social Studies and Academic Words H4

Geography and Map Skills H5

Making This Book Work for You H18

Scavenger Hunt H20

The Americas 1

Regional Atlas 2

Facts about Countries 8

Planning Guide 11a

CHAPTER 1 Early History of the Americas
500 BC–AD 1537 12

Geography's Impact Video Series
Impact of Mayan Achievements on Math and Astronomy

Section 1 The Maya 14

Section 2 The Aztecs 20

Section 3 The Incas 25

Geography and History North America's Native Cultures 30

Social Studies Skills Analyzing Information 32

Chapter Review 33

Standardized Test Practice 35

CHAPTER 2 Mexico 36

Geography's Impact Video Series
Impact of Emigration

Section 1 Physical Geography 38

Section 2 History and Culture 42

Social Studies Skills Taking Notes 47

Section 3 Mexico Today 48

Chapter Review 53

Standardized Test Practice 55

CHAPTER 3 Central America and
the Caribbean 56

Geography's Impact Video Series
Impact of Tourism

Section 1 Physical Geography 58

Section 2 Central America 62

Geography and History The Panama Canal 68

Section 3 The Caribbean Islands 70

Social Studies Skills Interpreting a Climate Graph 76

Chapter Review 77

Standardized Test Practice 79

CHAPTER 4 Caribbean South America . . 80

Geography's Impact Video Series
Impact of the Orinoco River

Section 1 Physical Geography 82

Section 2 Colombia 86

Section 3 Venezuela and the Guianas 90

Social Studies Skills Using Latitude and Longitude 96

Chapter Review 97

Standardized Test Practice 99

CHAPTER 5 Atlantic South America...... 100

Geography's Impact Video Series
Impact of Deforestation in the Amazon Basin

Section 1 Physical Geography.................................. 102

Section 2 Brazil... 106

Social Studies Skills Connecting Ideas............................. 111

Section 3 Argentina, Uruguay, and Paraguay............... 112

Literature The Gaucho Martín Fierro............................... 118

Chapter Review... 119

Standardized Test Practice... 121

CHAPTER 6 Pacific South America........ 122

Geography's Impact Video Series
Impact of the Andes Mountains

Section 1 Physical Geography.................................. 124

Social Studies Skills Interpreting an Elevation Profile................ 129

Section 2 History and Culture................................. 130

Section 3 Pacific South America Today...................... 134

Chapter Review... 139

Standardized Test Practice... 141

CHAPTER 7 **The United States** 142

Geography's Impact Video Series
Impact of Immigration

Section 1 Physical Geography 144

Social Studies Skills Using a Political Map 149

Case Study Natural Hazards in the United States 150

Section 2 History and Culture 152

Literature Bearstone 159

Section 3 The United States Today 160

Chapter Review 167

Standardized Test Practice 169

CHAPTER 8 **Canada** 170

Geography's Impact Video Series
Impact of Regionalism

Section 1 Physical Geography 172

Section 2 History and Culture 176

Section 3 Canada Today 182

Social Studies Skills Using Mental Maps and Sketch Maps 188

Chapter Review 189

Standardized Test Practice 191

Reference

Reading Social Studies 194

Atlas 202

Facts about the World 222

Gazetteer 226

Biographical Dictionary 231

English and Spanish Glossary 232

Economics Handbook 236

Index 238

Features

Case Study

Take a detailed look at important topics in geography.

Natural Hazards in the United States........ 150

Geography and History

Explore the connections between the world's places and the past.

North America's Native Cultures 30

The Panama Canal 68

Close-up

See how people live and what places look like by taking a close-up view of geography.

Palenque 16

Tenochtitlán 22

A Market in Guatemala...................... 64

The Amazon Rain Forest 104

Climate Zones in the Andes................ 126

Quebec's Winter Carnival.................. 184

FOCUS ON CULTURE

Learn about some of the world's fascinating cultures.

Day of the Dead............................ 46

The Feast of Corpus Christi................. 92

Soccer in Brazil............................ 107

Vancouver's Chinatown 181

CONNECTING TO . . .

Explore the connections between geography and other subjects.

TECHNOLOGY
Chinampas 43

THE ARTS
Caribbean Music 73

HISTORY
Cartagena's Spanish Fort 87

ECONOMICS
The Informal Economy 135

Satellite View

See the world through satellite images and explore what these images reveal.

The Americas.................................1

Slash-and-Burn Agriculture................. 49

Hurricane Isabel........................... 61

Deforestation in the Amazon.............. 110

Atacama Desert 127

The Mississippi River Delta 146

Agriculture in Ontario 175

Social Studies Skills

Learn, practice, and apply the skills you need to study and analyze geography.

Analyzing Information 32

Taking Notes 47

Interpreting a Climate Graph 76

Using Latitude and Longitude 96

Connecting Ideas 111

Interpreting an Elevation Profile 129

Using a Political Map 149

Using Mental Maps and Sketch Maps 188

Literature

Learn about the world's geography through literature.

The Gaucho Martín Fierro 118

Bearstone 159

BIOGRAPHIES

Meet the people who have influenced the world and learn about their lives.

Pacal 17

Pachacuti 26

Atahualpa 29

Francisco Pizarro 29

Benito Juárez 45

Toussaint-L'Ouverture 71

Simon Bolívar 91

Eva Perón 113

George Washington 153

FOCUS ON READING

Learn and practice skills that will help you read your social studies lessons.

Setting a Purpose 194

Predicting 195

Understanding Comparison-Contrast . . 196

Identifying Supporting Details 197

Using Context Clues 198

Making Inferences 199

Categorizing 200

Understanding Lists 201

FOCUS ON WRITING, VIEWING, SPEAKING

Use writing, viewing, and speaking to reflect on the world and its people.

A Newspaper Article 12

Writing an "I Am" Poem 36

Creating a Travel Guide 56

Writing a Letter 80

Creating a Web Site 100

Interviewing 122

Creating a Collage 142

Creating a Radio Ad 170

Primary Source

Learn about the world through important documents and personal accounts.

Bernardino de Sahagún, on riddles,
    from *Florentine Codex* 23

The Constitution 155

Charts and Graphs

The **World Almanac and Book of Facts** is America's largest-selling reference book of all time, with more than 81 million copies sold since 1868.

FACTS ABOUT THE WORLD
Study the latest facts and figures about the world.

Geographical Extremes: The Americas 3
World's Largest Cities 10
Major Food Exports of the Americas 11
World's Top Oil Exporters 93

FACTS ABOUT COUNTRIES
Study the latest facts and figures about countries.

The Americas 8
Urban Populations in the Americas 10
Languages of the Caribbean 72
Argentina's Largest Cities 114
Languages in Pacific South America 132
Population of Major U.S. Cities 161
Canadian Ethnic Groups 179

Charts and Graphs

Use charts and graphs to analyze geographic information.

Geographical Extremes: The Americas 3
The Americas 8
World's Largest Cities 10
Urban Populations in the Americas 10
Major Food Exports of the Americas 11
Mexico's Trading Partners 55
Languages of the Caribbean 72
Climate Graph: Tegucigalpa, Honduras 76
Climate Graph: Nassau, Bahamas 78
World's Top Oil Exporters 93

Argentina's Largest Cities 114
Brazil's Rural and Urban Population
   (Estimates 1950–2000) 121
Ecuador: Elevation Profile 129
Languages in Pacific South America 132
Chile's Exports to the United States, 2004 141
Population of Major U.S. Cities 161
Trade with the United States 187
Earth Facts 222
World Population 224
Developed and Less Developed Countries 224
World Religions 225
World Languages 225

Quick Facts and Infographics

Analyze visual information to learn about geography.

Geographic Dictionary H14
Palenque 16
Maya Astronomy and Writing 18
Tenochtitlán 22
Aztec Ceremonial Jewelry 23
Inca Arts 28
Early History of the Americas 33
Early Cultures of Mexico 42
Mexico's Culture Regions 50
Mexico 53
A Market in Guatemala 64
Central America and the Caribbean 77

Venezuela's Canaima National Park 84
Daily Life in Colombia 88
Caribbean South America 97
The Amazon Rain Forest 104
Regions of Brazil 108
Atlantic South America 119
Climate Zones in the Andes 126
Pacific South America 139
Tornado 151
The United States 167
Canada's History 176
Quebec's Winter Carnival 184
Canada 189

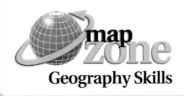

Geography Skills

✦Interactive Maps

Apply geography and interactive map skills to understand the geography and people of the world.

Maya Civilization, c. 900 15
The Inca Empire, 1530. 26
Map Activity: Early History of the Americas 34
Mexico: Political 37
Mexico: Physical 39
Mexico: Climate 40
Mexico's Culture Regions 50
Map Activity: Mexico 54
Central America and the Caribbean: Political 57
Central America and the Caribbean: Physical 59
Volcanic Activity in Central America
  and the Caribbean 60
European Colonies in the Caribbean, 1763 71
Map Activity: Central America and the Caribbean 78
Caribbean South America: Political 81
Caribbean South America: Physical 83
Map Activity: Caribbean South America 98
Atlantic South America: Political. 101

Atlantic South America: Physical 103
Map Activity: Atlantic South America 120
Pacific South America: Political. 123
Pacific South America: Physical 125
Languages in Pacific South America 132
Map Activity: Pacific South America 140
The United States: Political 143
The United States: Physical. 145
The United States: Climate 147
Regions of the United States 161
United States: Land Use and Resources 162
Map Activity: The United States 168
Canada: Political 171
Canada: Physical. 173
Canada's Major Languages 179
Regions of Canada. 183
Map Activity: Canada 190

Maps

Northern Hemisphere H7
Southern Hemisphere H7
Western Hemisphere H7
Eastern Hemisphere. H7
Mercator Projection H8
Conic Projection H9
Flat-plane Projection H9
The First Crusade, 1096. . . . . .H10
Caribbean South America: Political H12
The Indian Subcontinent: Physical. H13
West Africa: Climate. H13
The Americas: Physical. 2
Size Comparison: The United States and the Americas 3
North America: Political. 4
South America: Political. 5
The Americas: Population 6
The Americas: Climate. 7
The Americas: 500 BC–AD 1537 13
The Aztec Empire, 1519. 21
Native Americans 30
Early Civilizations of the Americas 35
Routes Before and After the Panama Canal. 68
Languages of Central America 79
Canaima National Park 84
Venezuela's Major Resources 93
World: Political 96
Volcanoes of Colombia 99
Regions of Brazil. 108

Argentina: Population 114
Paraguay and Uruguay. 116
Bolivia: Resources 128
Settlements around Lima 136
United States, Canada, and Mexico: Political 149
Natural Hazards in the United States. 150
Western Expansion of the United States. 154
Distribution of Selected Ethnic Groups, 2000. 157
Sketch Map of the World. 188
Climate of British Columbia 191
United States: Physical. 202
United States: Political. 204
World: Physical 206
World: Political 208
North America: Physical. 210
North America: Political. 211
South America: Physical 212
South America: Political 213
Europe: Physical 214
Europe: Political 215
Asia: Physical. 216
Asia: Political 217
Africa: Physical 218
Africa: Political. 219
The Pacific: Political 220
The North Pole 221
The South Pole 221

Become an Active Reader

by Dr. Kylene Beers

Did you ever think you would begin reading your social studies book by reading about *reading*? Actually, it makes better sense than you might think. You would probably make sure you knew some soccer skills and strategies before playing in a game. Similarly, you need to know something about reading skills and strategies before reading your social studies book. In other words, you need to make sure you know whatever you need to know in order to read this book successfully.

Tip #1

Read Everything on the Page!

You can't follow the directions on the cake-mix box if you don't know where the directions are! Cake-mix boxes always have directions on them telling you how many eggs to add or how long to bake the cake. But, if you can't find that information, it doesn't matter that it is there.

Likewise, this book is filled with information that will help you understand what you are reading. If you don't study that information, however, it might as well not be there. Let's take a look at some of the places where you'll find important information in this book.

The Chapter Opener
The chapter opener gives you a brief overview of what you will learn in the chapter. You can use this information to prepare to read the chapter.

The Section Openers
Before you begin to read each section, preview the information under What You Will Learn. There you'll find the main ideas of the section and key terms that are important in it. Knowing what you are looking for before you start reading can improve your understanding.

Boldfaced Words
Those words are important and are defined somewhere on the page where they appear—either right there in the sentence or over in the side margin.

Maps, Charts, and Artwork
These things are not there just to take up space or look good! Study them and read the information beside them. It will help you understand the information in the chapter.

Questions at the End of Sections
At the end of each section, you will find questions that will help you decide whether you need to go back and re-read any parts before moving on. If you can't answer a question, that is your cue to go back and re-read.

Questions at the End of the Chapter
Answer the questions at the end of each chapter, even if your teacher doesn't ask you to. These questions are there to help you figure out what you need to review.

Tip #2

Use the Reading Skills and Strategies in Your Textbook

Good readers use a number of skills and strategies to make sure they understand what they are reading. In this textbook you will find help with important reading skills and strategies such as "Predicting," "Making Inferences," and "Using Context Clues."

We teach the reading skills and strategies in several ways. Use these activities and lessons and you will become a better reader.

- First, on the opening page of every chapter we identify and explain the reading skill or strategy you will focus on as you work through the chapter. In fact, these activities are called "Focus on Reading."

- Second, as you can see in the example at right, we tell you where to go for more help. The back of the book has a reading handbook with a full-page practice lesson to match the reading skill or strategy in every chapter.

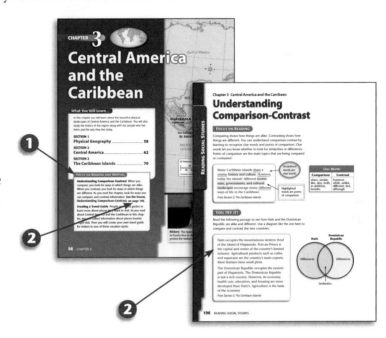

- Third, we give you short practice activities and examples as you read the chapter. These activities and examples show up in the margin of your book. Again, look for the words, "Focus on Reading."

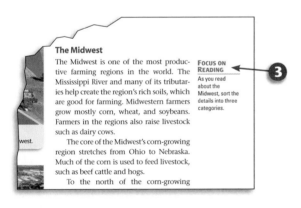

The Midwest

The Midwest is one of the most productive farming regions in the world. The Mississippi River and many of its tributaries help create the region's rich soils, which are good for farming. Midwestern farmers grow mostly corn, wheat, and soybeans. Farmers in the regions also raise livestock such as dairy cows.

The core of the Midwest's corn-growing region stretches from Ohio to Nebraska. Much of the corn is used to feed livestock, such as beef cattle and hogs.

To the north of the corn-growing

FOCUS ON READING
As you read about the Midwest, sort the details into three categories.

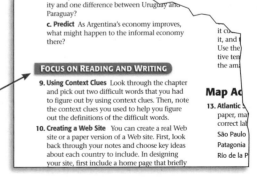

b. Compare and Contrast What is ... ity and one difference between Uruguay and Paraguay?

c. Predict As Argentina's economy improves, what might happen to the informal economy there?

FOCUS ON READING AND WRITING

9. Using Context Clues Look through the chapter and pick out two difficult words that you had to figure out by using context clues. Then, note the context clues you used to help you figure out the definitions of the difficult words.

10. Creating a Web Site You can create a real Web site or a paper version of a Web site. First, look back through your notes and choose key ideas about each country to include. In designing your site, first include a home page that briefly

- Finally, we provide another practice activity in the Chapter Review at the end of every chapter. That activity gives you one more chance to make sure you know how to use the reading skill or strategy.

Tip #3

Pay Attention to Vocabulary

It is no fun to read something when you don't know what the words mean, but you can't learn new words if you only use or read the words you already know. In this book, we know we have probably used some words you don't know. But, we have followed a pattern as we have used more difficult words.

- First, at the beginning of each section you will find a list of key terms that you will need to know. Be on the lookout for those words as you read through the section. You will find that we have defined those words right there in the paragraph where they are used. Look for a word that is in boldface with its definition highlighted in yellow.

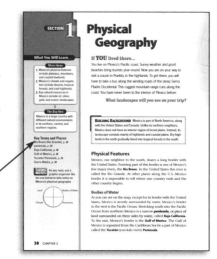

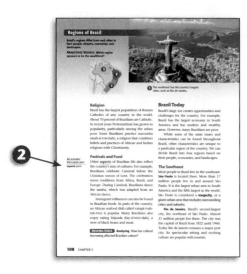

- Second, when we use a word that is important in all classes, not just social studies, we define it in the margin under the heading Academic Vocabulary. You will run into these academic words in other textbooks, so you should learn what they mean while reading this book.

Tip #4

Read Like a Skilled Reader

You won't be able to climb to the top of Mount Everest if you do not train! If you want to make it to the top of Mount Everest then you must start training to climb that huge mountain.

Training is also necessary to become a good reader. You will never get better at reading your social studies book—or any book for that matter—unless you spend some time thinking about how to be a better reader.

Skilled readers do the following:

1. They preview what they are supposed to read before they actually begin reading. When previewing, they look for vocabulary words, titles of sections, information in the margin, or maps or charts they should study.

2. They get ready to take some notes while reading by dividing their notebook paper into two parts. They title one side "Notes from the Chapter" and the other side "Questions or Comments I Have."

3. As they read, they complete their notes.

4. They read like **active readers**. The Active Reading list below shows you what that means.

5. Finally, they use clues in the text to help them figure out where the text is going. The best clues are called signal words. These are words that help you identify chronological order, causes and effects, or comparisons and contrasts.

Chronological Order Signal Words: *first, second, third, before, after, later, next, following that, earlier, subsequently, finally*

Cause and Effect Signal Words: *because of, due to, as a result of, the reason for, therefore, consequently, so, basis for*

Comparison/Contrast Signal Words: *likewise, also, as well as, similarly, on the other hand*

Active Reading

There are three ways to read a book: You can be a turn-the-pages-no-matter-what type of reader. These readers just keep on turning pages whether or not they understand what they are reading. Or, you can be a stop-watch-and-listen kind of reader. These readers know that if they wait long enough, someone will tell them what they need to know. Or, you can be an active reader. These readers know that it is up to them to figure out what the text means. Active readers do the following as they read:

Predict what will happen next based on what has already happened. When your predictions don't match what happens in the text, re-read the confusing parts.

Question what is happening as you read. Constantly ask yourself why things have happened, what things mean, and what caused certain events. Jot down notes about the questions you can't answer.

Summarize what you are reading frequently. Do not try to summarize the entire chapter! Read a bit and then summarize it. Then read on.

Connect what is happening in the section you're reading to what you have already read.

Clarify your understanding. Be sure that you understand what you are reading by stopping occasionally to ask yourself whether you are confused by anything. Sometimes you might need to re-read to clarify. Other times you might need to read further and collect more information before you can understand. Still other times you might need to ask the teacher to help you with what is confusing you.

Visualize what is happening in the text. In other words, try to see the events or places in your mind. It might help you to draw maps, make charts, or jot down notes about what you are reading as you try to visualize the action in the text.

Social Studies and Academic Words

As you read this textbook, you will be more successful if you know the meanings of the words on this page. The first list has social studies words. You will come across these words many times in your social studies classes. The second list contains academic words. These words are important in all of your classes. You will see these words in other textbooks, so you should learn what they mean while reading this book.

Social Studies Words

WORDS ABOUT TIME

AD	refers to dates after the birth of Jesus
BC	refers to dates before Jesus's birth
BCE	refers to dates before Jesus's birth, stands for "before the common era"
CE	refers to dates after Jesus's birth, stands for "common era"
century	a period of 100 years
decade	a period of 10 years
era	a period of time
millennium	a period of 1,000 years

WORDS ABOUT THE WORLD

climate	the weather conditions in a certain area over a long period of time
geography	the study of the world's people, places, and landscapes
physical features	features on Earth's surface, such as mountains and rivers
region	an area with one or more features that make it different from surrounding areas
resources	materials found on Earth that people need and value

WORDS ABOUT PEOPLE

anthropology	the study of people and cultures
archaeology	the study of the past based on what people left behind
citizen	a person who lives under the control of a government
civilization	the way of life of people in a particular place or time

culture	the knowledge, beliefs, customs, and values of a group of people
custom	a repeated practice or tradition
economics	the study of the production and use of goods and services
economy	any system in which people make and exchange goods and services
government	the body of officials and groups that run an area
history	the study of the past
politics	the process of running a government
religion	a system of beliefs in one or more gods or spirits
society	a group of people who share common traditions
trade	the exchange of goods or services

Academic Words

affect	to change or influence
aspects	parts
cause	to make something happen
development	the process of growing or improving
distinct	separate
establish	to set up or create
influence	change or have an effect on
policy	rule, course of action
process	a series of steps by which a task is accomplished
rebel	to fight against authority
traditional	customary, time-honored
vary	to be different

Geography and Map Skills Handbook

Contents

Mapping the Earth H6

Mapmaking H8

Map Essentials H10

Working with Maps H12

Geographic Dictionary H14

Themes and Essential Elements of Geography H16

Throughout this textbook, you will be studying the world's people, places, and landscapes. One of the main tools you will use is the map—the primary tool of geographers. To help you begin your studies, this Geography and Map Skills Handbook explains some of the basic features of maps. For example, it explains how maps are made, how to read them, and how they can show the round surface of Earth on a flat piece of paper. This handbook will also introduce you to some of the types of maps you will study later in this book. In addition, you will learn about the different kinds of features on Earth and about how geographers use themes and elements to study the world.

⭐Interactive Maps

Geography Skills With map zone geography skills, you can go online to find interactive versions of the key maps in this book. Explore these interactive maps to learn and practice important map skills and bring geography to life.

To use map zone interactive maps online:

1. Go to go.hrw.com.
2. Enter the KEYWORD shown on the interactive map.
3. Press return!

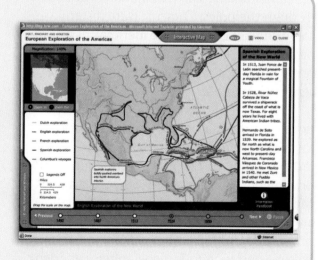

Mapping the Earth
Using Latitude and Longitude

A **globe** is a scale model of the Earth. It is useful for showing the entire Earth or studying large areas of Earth's surface.

To study the world, geographers use a pattern of imaginary lines that circles the globe in east-west and north-south directions. It is called a **grid**. The intersection of these imaginary lines helps us find places on Earth.

The east-west lines in the grid are lines of **latitude**, which you can see on the diagram. Lines of latitude are called **parallels** because they are always parallel to each other. These imaginary lines measure distance north and south of the **equator**. The equator is an imaginary line that circles the globe halfway between the North and South Poles. Parallels measure distance from the equator in **degrees**. The symbol for degrees is °. Degrees are further divided into **minutes**. The symbol for minutes is ´. There are 60 minutes in a degree. Parallels north of the equator are labeled with an N. Those south of the equator are labeled with an S.

The north-south imaginary lines are lines of **longitude**. Lines of longitude are called **meridians**. These imaginary lines pass through the poles. They measure distance east and west of the **prime meridian**. The prime meridian is an imaginary line that runs through Greenwich, England. It represents 0° longitude.

Lines of latitude range from 0°, for locations on the equator, to 90°N or 90°S, for locations at the poles. Lines of longitude range from 0° on the prime meridian to 180° on a meridian in the mid-Pacific Ocean. Meridians west of the prime meridian to 180° are labeled with a W. Those east of the prime meridian to 180° are labeled with an E. Using latitude and longitude, geographers can identify the exact location of any place on Earth.

Lines of Latitude

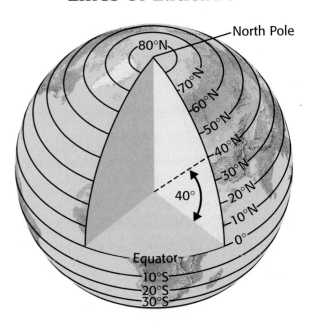

Lines of Longitude

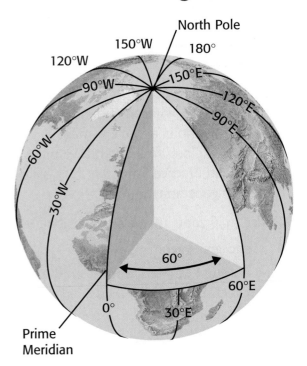

Northern Hemisphere

The equator divides the globe into two halves, called **hemispheres**. The half north of the equator is the Northern Hemisphere. The southern half is the Southern Hemisphere. The prime meridian and the 180° meridian divide the world into the Eastern Hemisphere and the Western Hemisphere. Look at the diagrams on this page. They show each of these four hemispheres.

Earth's land surface is divided into seven large landmasses, called **continents**. These continents are also shown on the diagrams on this page. Landmasses smaller than continents and completely surrounded by water are called **islands**.

Geographers organize Earth's water surface into major regions too. The largest is the world ocean. Geographers divide the world ocean into the Pacific Ocean, the Atlantic Ocean, the Indian Ocean, and the Arctic Ocean. Lakes and seas are smaller bodies of water.

Southern Hemisphere

Western Hemisphere

Eastern Hemisphere

Mapmaking
Understanding Map Projections

A **map** is a flat diagram of all or part of Earth's surface. Mapmakers have created different ways of showing our round planet on flat maps. These different ways are called **map projections**. Because Earth is round, there is no way to show it accurately on a flat map. All flat maps are distorted in some way. Mapmakers must choose the type of map projection that is best for their purposes. Many map projections are one of three kinds: cylindrical, conic, or flat-plane.

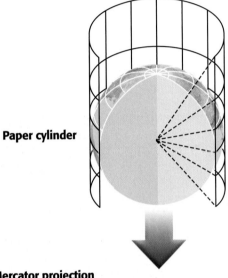

Paper cylinder

Cylindrical Projections

Cylindrical projections are based on a cylinder wrapped around the globe. The cylinder touches the globe only at the equator. The meridians are pulled apart and are parallel to each other instead of meeting at the poles. This causes landmasses near the poles to appear larger than they really arc. The map below is a Mercator projection, one type of cylindrical projection. The Mercator projection is useful for navigators because it shows true direction and shape. However, it distorts the size of land areas near the poles.

Mercator projection

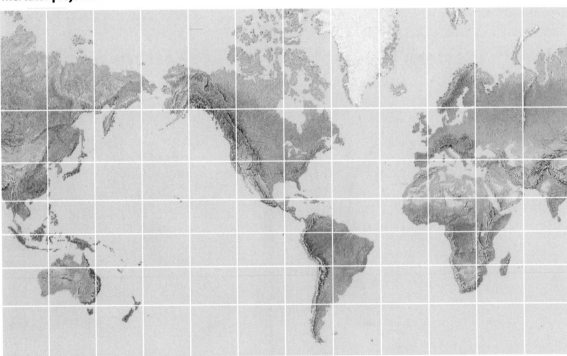

Conic Projections

Conic projections are based on a cone placed over the globe. A conic projection is most accurate along the lines of latitude where it touches the globe. It retains almost true shape and size. Conic projections are most useful for showing areas that have long east-west dimensions, such as the United States.

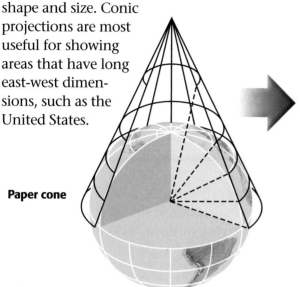

Paper cone

Conic projection

Flat-plane Projections

Flat-plane projections are based on a plane touching the globe at one point, such as at the North Pole or South Pole. A flat-plane projection is useful for showing true direction for airplane pilots and ship navigators. It also shows true area. However, it distorts the true shapes of landmasses.

Flat plane

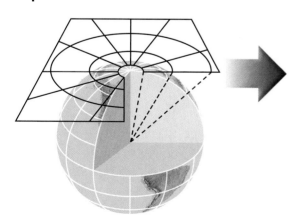

Flat-plane projection

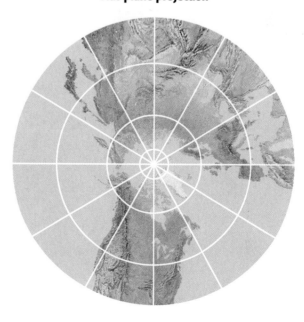

Map Essentials
How to Read a Map

Maps are like messages sent out in code. To help us translate the code, mapmakers provide certain features. These features help us understand the message they are presenting about a particular part of the world. Of these features, almost all maps have a title, a compass rose, a scale, and a legend. The map below has these four features, plus a fifth—a locator map.

❶ Title

A map's **title** shows what the subject of the map is. The map title is usually the first thing you should look at when studying a map, because it tells you what the map is trying to show.

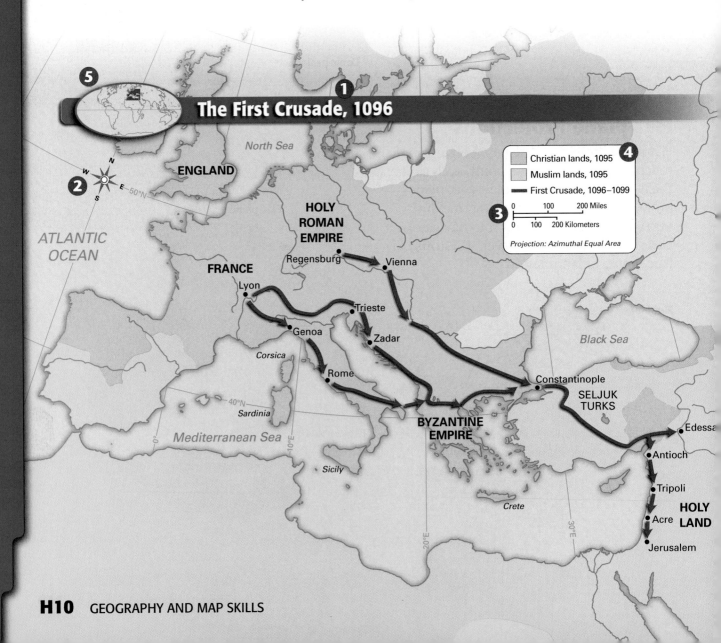

The First Crusade, 1096

Christian lands, 1095
Muslim lands, 1095
First Crusade, 1096–1099

0   100   200 Miles
0   100   200 Kilometers

Projection: Azimuthal Equal Area

North Sea
ENGLAND
ATLANTIC OCEAN
HOLY ROMAN EMPIRE
FRANCE
Lyon
Regensburg
Vienna
Trieste
Genoa
Zadar
Corsica
Rome
Black Sea
Constantinople
SELJUK TURKS
Sardinia
40°N
BYZANTINE EMPIRE
Edessa
Mediterranean Sea
Antioch
Sicily
Tripoli
Crete
HOLY LAND
Acre
Jerusalem
50°N

❷ Compass Rose

A directional indicator shows which way north, south, east, and west lie on the map. Some mapmakers use a "north arrow," which points toward the North Pole. Remember, "north" is not always at the top of a map. The way a map is drawn and the location of directions on that map depend on the perspective of the mapmaker. Most maps in this textbook indicate direction by using a compass rose. A **compass rose** has arrows that point to all four principal directions.

❸ Scale

Mapmakers use scales to represent the distances between points on a map. Scales may appear on maps in several different forms. The maps in this textbook provide a **bar scale**. Scales give distances in miles and kilometers.

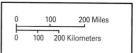

To find the distance between two points on the map, place a piece of paper so that the edge connects the two points. Mark the location of each point on the paper with a line or dot. Then, compare the distance between the two dots with the map's bar scale. The number on the top of the scale gives the distance in miles. The number on the bottom gives the distance in kilometers. Because the distances are given in large intervals, you may have to approximate the actual distance on the scale.

❹ Legend

The **legend**, or key, explains what the symbols on the map represent. Point symbols are used to specify the location of things, such as cities, that do not take up much space on the map. Some legends show colors that represent certain features like empires or other regions. Other maps might have legends with symbols or colors that represent features such as roads. Legends can also show economic resources, land use, population density, and climate.

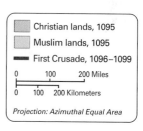

❺ Locator Map

A **locator map** shows where in the world the area on the map is located. The area shown on the main map is shown in red on the locator map. The locator map also shows surrounding areas so the map reader can see how the information on the map relates to neighboring lands.

Working with Maps
Using Different Kinds of Maps

As you study the world's regions and countries, you will use a variety of maps. Political maps and physical maps are two of the most common types of maps you will study. In addition, you will use special-purpose maps. These maps might show climate, population, resources, ancient empires, or other topics.

Political Maps

Political maps show the major political features of a region. These features include country borders, capital cities, and other places. Political maps use different colors to represent countries, and capital cities are often shown with a special star symbol.

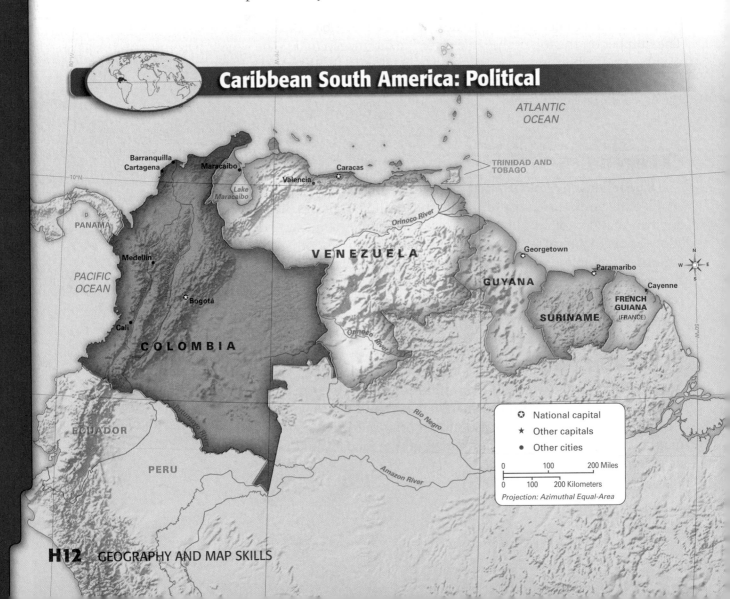

Caribbean South America: Political

ATLANTIC OCEAN

TRINIDAD AND TOBAGO

Barranquilla
Cartagena
Maracaibo
Caracas
Valencia
Lake Maracaibo
Orinoco River

PANAMA

VENEZUELA

Georgetown

Medellín

Paramaribo

PACIFIC OCEAN

GUYANA

Cayenne

Bogotá

SURINAME

FRENCH GUIANA
(FRANCE)

Cali

COLOMBIA

Orinoco River

ECUADOR

Rio Negro

PERU

Amazon River

- ⊗ National capital
- ★ Other capitals
- • Other cities

0   100   200 Miles
0   100   200 Kilometers
Projection: Azimuthal Equal-Area

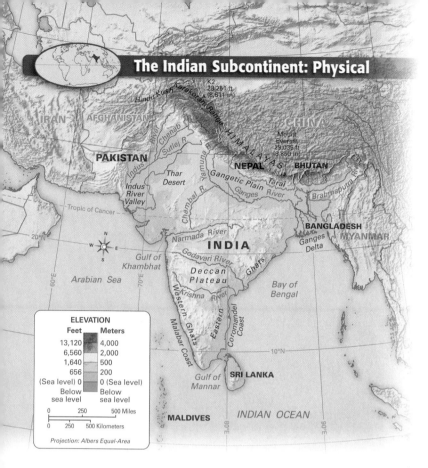

The Indian Subcontinent: Physical

ELEVATION

Feet	Meters
13,120	4,000
6,560	2,000
1,640	500
656	200
(Sea level) 0	0 (Sea level)
Below sea level	Below sea level

0   250   500 Miles
0   250   500 Kilometers
Projection: Albers Equal-Area

Physical Maps

Physical maps show the major physical features of a region. These features may include mountain ranges, rivers, oceans, islands, deserts, and plains. Often, these maps use different colors to represent different elevations of land. As a result, the map reader can easily see which areas are high elevations, like mountains, and which areas are lower.

Special-Purpose Maps

Special-purpose maps focus on one special topic, such as climate, resources, or population. These maps present information on the topic that is particularly important in the region. Depending on the type of special-purpose map, the information may be shown with different colors, arrows, dots, or other symbols.

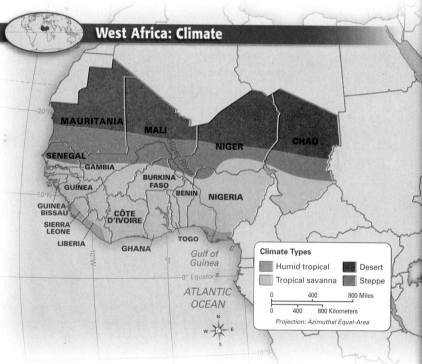

West Africa: Climate

Climate Types

- Humid tropical
- Tropical savanna
- Desert
- Steppe

0   400   800 Miles
0   400   800 Kilometers
Projection: Azimuthal Equal-Area

Using Maps in Geography The different kinds of maps in this textbook will help you study and understand geography. By working with these maps, you will see what the physical geography of places is like, where people live, and how the world has changed over time.

Geographic Dictionary

OCEAN
a large body of water

CORAL REEF
an ocean ridge made up of
skeletal remains of tiny sea animals

GULF
a large part of
the ocean that
extends into land

PENINSULA
an area of land that sticks
out into a lake or ocean

BAY
part of a large
body of water
that is smaller
than a gulf

ISLAND
an area of land
surrounded entirely
by water

ISTHMUS
a narrow piece of land
connecting two larger
land areas

DELTA
an area where a
river deposits soil
into the ocean

STRAIT
a narrow body of
water connecting two
larger bodies of water

SINKHOLE
a circular depression
formed when the roof
of a cave collapses

WETLAND
an area of land
covered by
shallow water

RIVER
a natural flow of
water that runs
through the land

LAKE
an inland body
of water

FOREST
an area of densely
wooded land

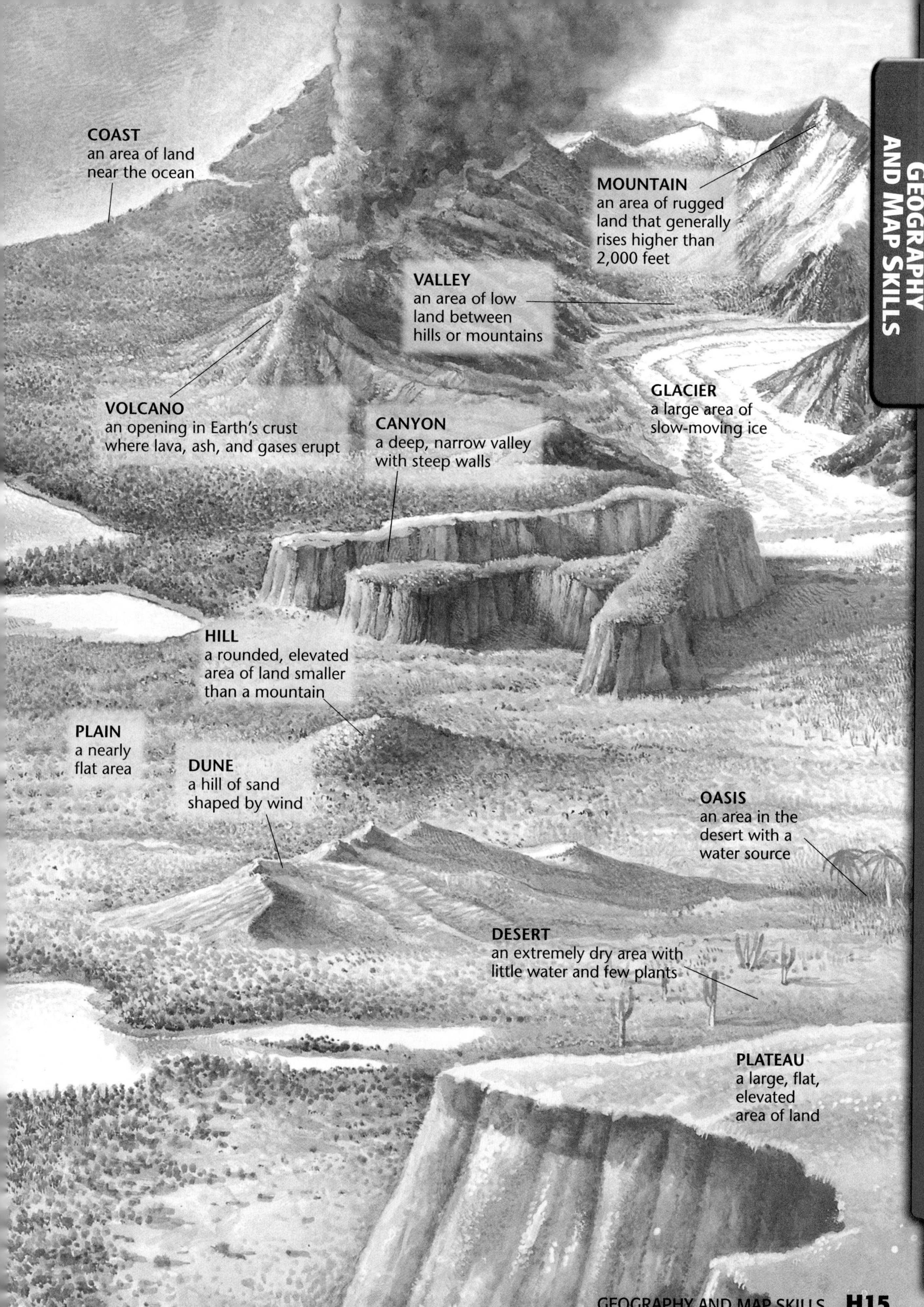

COAST
an area of land
near the ocean

MOUNTAIN
an area of rugged
land that generally
rises higher than
2,000 feet

VALLEY
an area of low
land between
hills or mountains

GLACIER
a large area of
slow-moving ice

VOLCANO
an opening in Earth's crust
where lava, ash, and gases erupt

CANYON
a deep, narrow valley
with steep walls

HILL
a rounded, elevated
area of land smaller
than a mountain

PLAIN
a nearly
flat area

DUNE
a hill of sand
shaped by wind

OASIS
an area in the
desert with a
water source

DESERT
an extremely dry area with
little water and few plants

PLATEAU
a large, flat,
elevated
area of land

Themes and Essential Elements of Geography

by Dr. Christopher L. Salter

To study the world, geographers have identified 5 key themes, 6 essential elements, and 18 geography standards.

"How should we teach and learn about geography?" Professional geographers have worked hard over the years to answer this important question.

In 1984 a group of geographers identified the 5 Themes of Geography. These themes did a wonderful job of laying the groundwork for good classroom geography. Teachers used the 5 Themes in class, and geographers taught workshops on how to apply them in the world.

By the early 1990s, however, some geographers felt the 5 Themes were too broad. They created the 18 Geography Standards and the 6 Essential Elements. The 18 Geography Standards include more detailed information about what geography is, and the 6 Essential Elements are like a bridge between the 5 Themes and 18 Standards.

Look at the chart to the right. It shows how each of the 5 Themes connects to the Essential Elements and Standards. For example, the theme of Location is related to The World in Spatial Terms and the first three Standards. Study the chart carefully to see how the other themes, elements, and Standards are related.

The last Essential Element and the last two Standards cover The Uses of Geography. These key parts of geography were not covered by the 5 Themes. They will help you see how geography has influenced the past, present, and future.

5 Themes of Geography

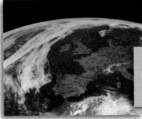

Location The theme of location describes where something is.

Place Place describes the features that make a site unique.

Regions Regions are areas that share common characteristics.

Movement This theme looks at how and why people and things move.

Human-Environment Interaction People interact with their environment in many ways.

6 Essential Elements

18 Geography Standards

I. The World in Spatial Terms

1. How to use maps and other tools
2. How to use mental maps to organize information
3. How to analyze the spatial organization of people, places, and environments

II. Places and Regions

4. The physical and human characteristics of places
5. How people create regions to interpret Earth
6. How culture and experience influence people's perceptions of places and regions

III. Physical Systems

7. The physical processes that shape Earth's surface
8. The distribution of ecosystems on Earth

IV. Human Systems

9. The characteristics, distribution, and migration of human populations
10. The complexity of Earth's cultural mosaics
11. The patterns and networks of economic interdependence on Earth
12. The patterns of human settlement
13. The forces of cooperation and conflict

V. Environment and Society

14. How human actions modify the physical environment
15. How physical systems affect human systems
16. The distribution and meaning of resources

VI. The Uses of Geography

17. How to apply geography to interpret the past
18. How to apply geography to interpret the present and plan for the future

Making This Book Work for You

Studying geography will be easy for you with this textbook. Take a few minutes now to become familiar with the easy-to-use structure and special features of your book. See how it will make geography come alive for you!

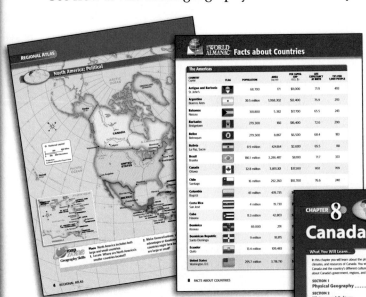

Your book begins with a satellite image, a regional atlas, and a table with facts about each country. Use these pages to get an overview of the region you will study.

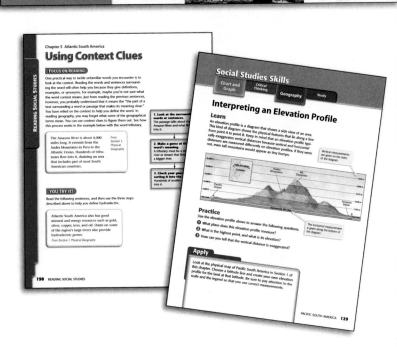

Chapter

Each chapter includes an introduction, a Social Studies Skills activity, Chapter Review pages, and a Standardized Test Practice page.

Reading Social Studies Chapter reading lessons give you skills and practice to help you read the textbook. More help with each lesson can be found in the back of the book. Margin notes and questions in the chapter make sure you understand the reading skill.

Social Studies Skills The Social Studies Skills lessons give you an opportunity to learn, practice, and apply an important skill. Chapter Review questions then follow up on what you learned.

Section

The section opener pages include Main Ideas, an overarching Big Idea, and Key Terms and Places. In addition, each section includes these special features.

If YOU Lived There . . . Each section begins with a situation for you to respond to, placing you in a place that relates to the content you will be studying in the section.

Building Background Building Background connects what will be covered in each section with what you already know.

Short Sections of Content The information in each section is organized into small chunks of text that you can easily understand.

Taking Notes Suggested graphic organizers help you read and take notes on the important ideas in the section.

SECTION 2

History and Culture

What You Will Learn...

Main Ideas

1. Early cultures of Mexico included the Olmec, the Maya, and the Aztec.
2. Mexico's period as a Spanish colony and its struggles since independence have shaped its culture.
3. Spanish and native cultures have influenced Mexico's customs and traditions today.

The Big Idea

Native American cultures and Spanish colonization shaped Mexican history and culture.

Key Terms

empire, p. 43
mestizos, p. 44
missions, p. 44
haciendas, p. 44

TAKING NOTES As you read, use a graphic organizer like the one below to help you organize your notes on Mexico's history and culture.

	Event or Detail
Early Cultures	
Colonial Times and Independence	
Culture	

If YOU lived there...

You belong to one of the native Indian peoples in southern Mexico in the early 1500s. Years ago, the Aztec rulers went to war against your people. They took many captives. They have always treated you cruelly. Now some strangers have come from across the sea. They want your people to help them conquer the Aztecs.

Will you help the strangers fight the Aztecs? Why or why not?

BUILDING BACKGROUND Mexico was home to several of the earliest advanced cultures in the Americas. Early farmers there developed crops that became staples in much of North America. Mexico also has valuable minerals, which drew Spanish conquerors and colonists. Spanish culture blended with native Mexican cultures.

Early Cultures

People first came to Mexico many thousands of years ago. As early as 5,000 years ago, they were growing beans, peppers, and squash. They also domesticated an early form of corn. Farming allowed these people to build the first permanent settlements in the Americas.

Early Cultures of Mexico

Olmec

- The Olmec made sculptures of giant stone heads.
- The heads may have represented rulers or gods.

ACADEMIC VOCABULARY
affect to change or influence

Northern Mexico's closeness to the border has affected the region's culture as well as its economy. American television, music, and other forms of entertainment are popular there. Many Mexicans cross the border to shop, work, or live in the United States. While many people cross the border legally, the U.S. government tries to prevent Mexicans and others from crossing the border illegally.

Southern Mexico

Southern Mexico is the least populated and least industrialized region of the country. Many people in this region speak Indian languages and practice traditional ways of life. Subsistence farming and slash-and-burn agriculture are common.

FOCUS ON READING
What do you think makes southern Mexico vital to the country's economy?

However, southern Mexico is vital to the country's economy. Sugarcane and coffee, two major export crops, grow well in the region's warm, humid climate. Also, oil production along the Gulf coast has increased in recent years. The oil business has brought more industry and population growth to this coastal area of southern Mexico.

Another place in southern Mexico that has grown in recent years is the Yucatán Peninsula. Maya ruins, beautiful sunny beaches, and clear blue water have made tourism a major industry in this area. Many cities that were just tiny fishing villages only 20 years ago are now booming with new construction for the tourist industry.

Mexico will continue to change in the future. Changes are likely to bring more development. However, maintaining the country's unique regional cultures may be a challenge as those changes take place.

READING CHECK Comparing and Contrasting What similarities and differences exist between greater Mexico City and southern Mexico?

SUMMARY AND PREVIEW Mexico has a democratic government and a growing economy. It also has distinct regions with different cultures, economies, and environments. In the next chapter you will learn about the countries to the south of Mexico.

Section 3 Assessment

**go.hrw.com
Online Quiz
KEYWORD: SGB7 HP2**

Reviewing Ideas, Terms, and Places
1. a. Define What is the term for the practice of burning forest in order to clear land for planting?
   b. Compare and Contrast How is Mexico's government similar to and different from the government of the United States?
2. a. Identify What is an environmental problem found in Mexico City?
   b. Make Inferences What conditions in Mexico lead some Mexicans to cross the border into the United States?
   c. Develop If you were to start a business in Mexico, what type of business would you start and where would you start it? Explain your decisions.

Critical Thinking
3. Finding Main Ideas Review your notes on Mexico's economy. Then use a chart like this one to show what parts of the economy are important in each region.

Greater Mexico City	Central Mexico	Northern Mexico	Southern Mexico

FOCUS ON WRITING

4. Describing Mexico Today Write some details about the four culture regions of Mexico. Which details will you include in your poem?

Reading Check Questions end each section of content so you can check to make sure you understand what you just studied.

Summary and Preview The Summary and Preview connects what you studied in the section to what you will study in the next section.

Section Assessment Finally, the section assessment boxes make sure that you understand the main ideas of the section. We also provide assessment practice online!

Scavenger Hunt

Are you ready to explore the world of geography? *Holt Social Studies: The Americas* is your ticket to this exciting world. Before you begin your journey, complete this scavenger hunt to get to know your book and discover what's inside.

On a separate sheet of paper, fill in the blanks to complete each sentence below. In each answer, one letter will be in a yellow box. When you have answered every question, copy these letters in order to reveal the answer to the question at the bottom of the page.

1 According to the Table of Contents, the title of Chapter 4 is ☐☐☐☐☐☐☐☐ South America. What else can you find in the Table of Contents?

2 Section 1 of Chapter 7 is called ☐☐☐☐☐☐☐ Geography. What are the other sections of this chapter?

3 The Connecting to Technology feature on page 43 is called ☐☐☐☐☐☐☐☐☐☐.

4 The first Key Term on page 130 is ☐☐☐☐☐☐☐.

5 In the English and Spanish Glossary, the third word in the definition of megacity is ☐☐☐☐☐.

6 The title of the Geography and History feature in Chapter 3 is The ☐☐☐☐☐☐ ☐☐☐☐☐.

7 The Close-up feature on pages 184–185 is called Quebec's ☐☐☐☐☐☐ Carnival. What other Close-up features can you find in the book?

8 The Social Studies Skills lesson on page 32 is called ☐☐☐☐☐☐☐☐ Information.

Fact!

Venezuela is home to the largest rodent in the world. What is this animal called?

☐☐☐☐☐☐☐☐☐

The Americas

The Great Lakes

Five huge lakes in North America known as the Great Lakes make up the largest group of fresh water lakes on Earth.

The Andes

Stretching along South America's western coast, the Andes are the longest mountain range in the world.

The Amazon

In the heart of South America, the Amazon rain forest is home to millions of plant and animal species.

The Americas

Explore the Satellite Image Forests, mountains, and plains stretch from north to south across the Americas. How do you think the features you can see on this satellite image influence life in the Americas?

The Satellite's Path

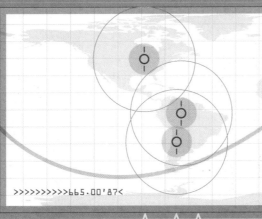

>44'56.08<

>>>>>>>>>665.00'87<

567.476.348   +799   +803   +966   +355

456.094.

The Americas: Physical

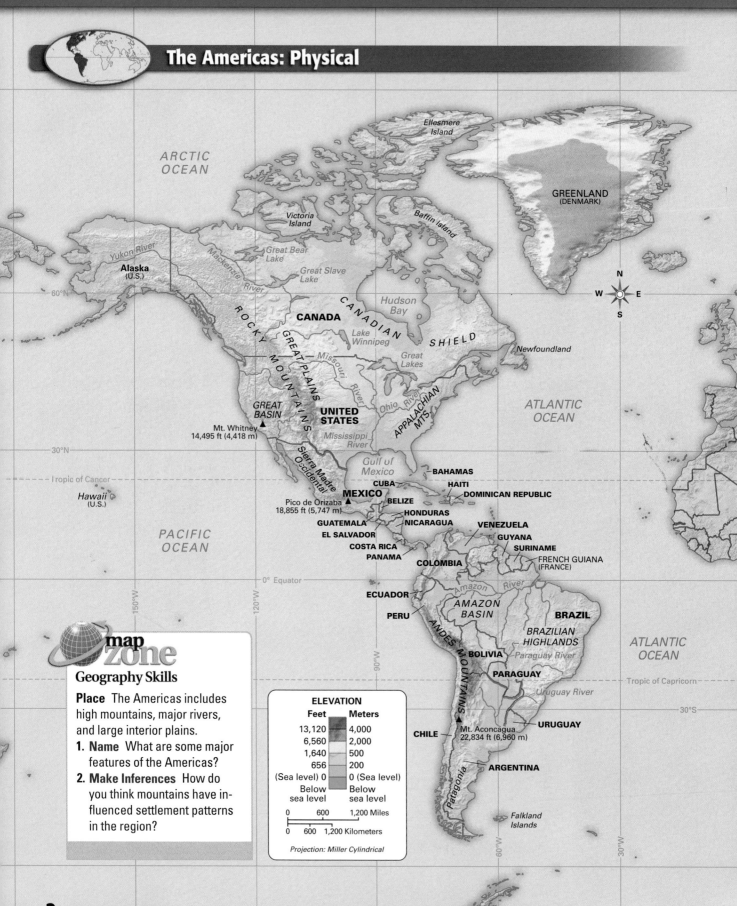

ARCTIC OCEAN

Ellesmere Island

GREENLAND (DENMARK)

Victoria Island

Baffin Island

Yukon River

Alaska (U.S.)

60°N

Mackenzie River

Great Bear Lake

Great Slave Lake

Hudson Bay

R O C K Y   M O U N T A I N S

CANADA

C A N A D I A N   S H I E L D

GREAT PLAINS

Lake Winnipeg

Missouri River

Great Lakes

Newfoundland

GREAT BASIN

UNITED STATES

Mt. Whitney 14,495 ft (4,418 m)

Ohio River

APPALACHIAN MTS.

ATLANTIC OCEAN

N
W   E
S

30°N

Sierra Madre Occidental

Mississippi River

Hawaii (U.S.)

PACIFIC OCEAN

Tropic of Cancer

Gulf of Mexico

Pico de Orizaba 18,855 ft (5,747 m)

MEXICO

BELIZE

GUATEMALA

EL SALVADOR

HONDURAS

NICARAGUA

COSTA RICA

PANAMA

BAHAMAS

CUBA

HAITI

DOMINICAN REPUBLIC

VENEZUELA

GUYANA

SURINAME

FRENCH GUIANA (FRANCE)

COLOMBIA

0° Equator

ECUADOR

PERU

Amazon River

AMAZON BASIN

BRAZIL

BRAZILIAN HIGHLANDS

ATLANTIC OCEAN

A N D E S   M O U N T A I N S

BOLIVIA

Paraguay River

PARAGUAY

Uruguay River

Tropic of Capricorn

30°S

CHILE

Mt. Aconcagua 22,834 ft (6,960 m)

URUGUAY

ARGENTINA

Patagonia

Falkland Islands

150°W   120°W   90°W   60°W   30°W

map zone

Geography Skills

Place The Americas includes high mountains, major rivers, and large interior plains.

1. **Name** What are some major features of the Americas?
2. **Make Inferences** How do you think mountains have influenced settlement patterns in the region?

ELEVATION

Feet	Meters
13,120	4,000
6,560	2,000
1,640	500
656	200
(Sea level) 0	0 (Sea level)
Below sea level	Below sea level

0   600   1,200 Miles

0   600   1,200 Kilometers

Projection: Miller Cylindrical

The Americas

THE WORLD ALMANAC®
Facts about the World — Geographical Extremes: The Americas

Longest River	Amazon River, Brazil/Peru: 4,000 miles (6,435 km)
Highest Point	Mt. Aconcagua, Argentina: 22,834 feet (6,960 m)
Lowest Point	Death Valley, United States: 282 feet (86 m) below sea level
Highest Recorded Temperature	Death Valley, United States: 134˚F (56.6˚C)
Lowest Recorded Temperature	Snag, Canada: -81.4˚F (-63˚C)
Wettest Place	Lloro, Colombia: 523.6 inches (1,329.9 cm) average precipitation per year
Driest Place	Arica, Chile: .03 inches (.08 cm) average precipitation per year
Highest Waterfall	Angel Falls, Venezuela: 3,212 feet (979 m)
Most Tornadoes	United States: More than 1,000 per year

Death Valley, United States

go.hrw.com KEYWORD: SGB7 UN2

Size Comparison: The United States and the Americas

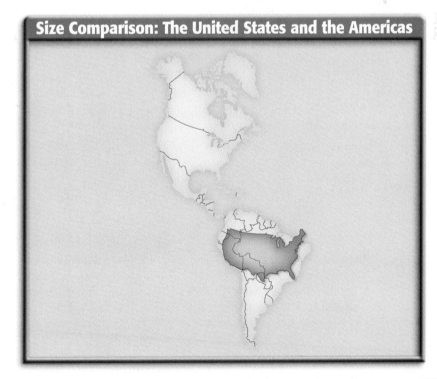

North America: Political

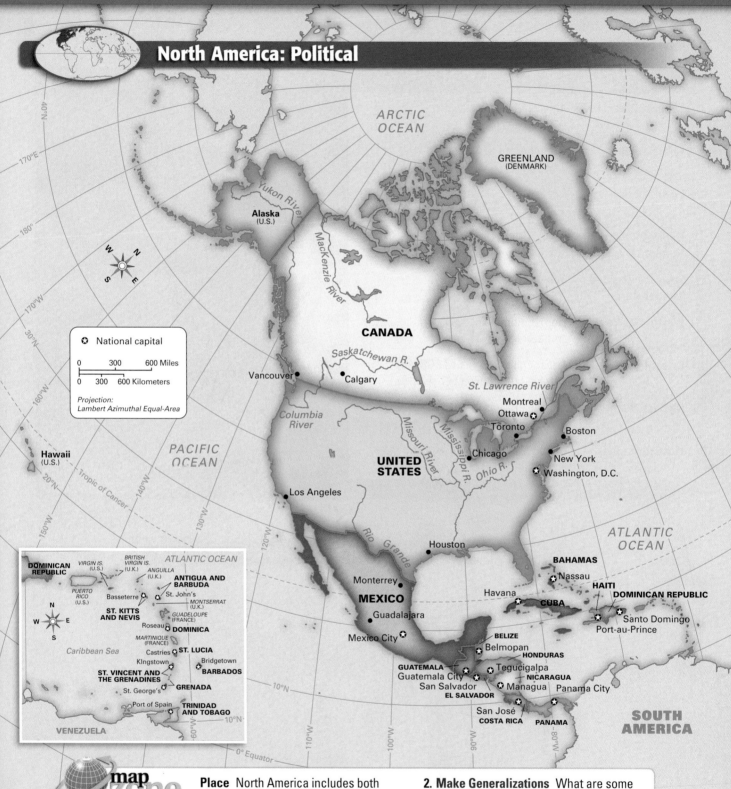

ARCTIC OCEAN

GREENLAND
(DENMARK)

Yukon River

Alaska
(U.S.)

MacKenzie River

CANADA

Saskatchewan R.

St. Lawrence River

Vancouver

Calgary

Montreal
Ottawa ✪
Toronto
Boston

Columbia
River

Missouri River

Mississippi R.

Ohio R.

UNITED
STATES

Chicago

New York
Washington, D.C. ✪

PACIFIC
OCEAN

Hawaii
(U.S.)

Tropic of Cancer

Los Angeles

ATLANTIC
OCEAN

Rio Grande

Houston

BAHAMAS
Nassau ✪

Monterrey

Havana ✪

HAITI
DOMINICAN REPUBLIC

MEXICO

CUBA

Guadalajara

Mexico City ✪

Santo Domingo ✪
Port-au-Prince ✪

BELIZE
Belmopan ✪

GUATEMALA
Guatemala City ✪
San Salvador ✪
EL SALVADOR

HONDURAS
Tegucigalpa ✪
NICARAGUA
Managua ✪
Panama City ✪

San José ✪
COSTA RICA   PANAMA

SOUTH
AMERICA

National capital

0   300   600 Miles
0   300   600 Kilometers

Projection:
Lambert Azimuthal Equal-Area

ATLANTIC OCEAN

DOMINICAN
REPUBLIC

VIRGIN IS.
(U.S.)

BRITISH
VIRGIN IS.
(U.K.)

ANGUILLA
(U.K.)

ANTIGUA AND
BARBUDA

PUERTO
RICO
(U.S.)

Basseterre ✪
St. John's ✪

MONTSERRAT
(U.K.)

ST. KITTS
AND NEVIS

GUADELOUPE
(FRANCE)

Roseau ✪
DOMINICA

MARTINIQUE
(FRANCE)

Caribbean Sea

Castries ✪
ST. LUCIA

Kingstown ✪
Bridgetown ✪
BARBADOS

ST. VINCENT AND
THE GRENADINES

St. George's ✪
GRENADA

Port of Spain ✪
TRINIDAD
AND TOBAGO

VENEZUELA

10°N

Equator

map zone
Geography Skills

Place North America includes both large and small countries.

1. Locate Where are North America's smaller countries located?

2. Make Generalizations What are some advantages or disadvantages that countries might face because they are large or small?

South America: Political

Cartagena
Caracas

VENEZUELA

Georgetown
Paramaribo
French Guiana
(FRANCE)

GUYANA

Bogotá

SURINAME

COLOMBIA

0° Equator

Quito
ECUADOR
Guayaquil

Galápagos
Islands

Manaus

Amazon River

PACIFIC
OCEAN

PERU

BRAZIL

10°S

Lima

Salvador

N
W   E
S

La Paz

Brasília

BOLIVIA

ATLANTIC
OCEAN

Sucre

20°S

Parana River

PARAGUAY

Rio de
Janeiro

Tropic of Capricorn

CHILE

São Paulo

Asunción

National capital

0   300   600 Miles

0   300   600 Kilometers

Projection:
Lambert Azimuthal Equal-Area

Córdoba

URUGUAY

Santiago

Buenos Aires
Montevideo

ARGENTINA

Falkland
Islands

South Georgia
Island

map zone

Geography Skills

Place South America includes 12 countries and one overseas department of France.

1. **Name** Which country is by far the largest in South America?

2. **Compare** Compare this map to the physical map of the Americas. What physical feature separates Chile and Argentina?

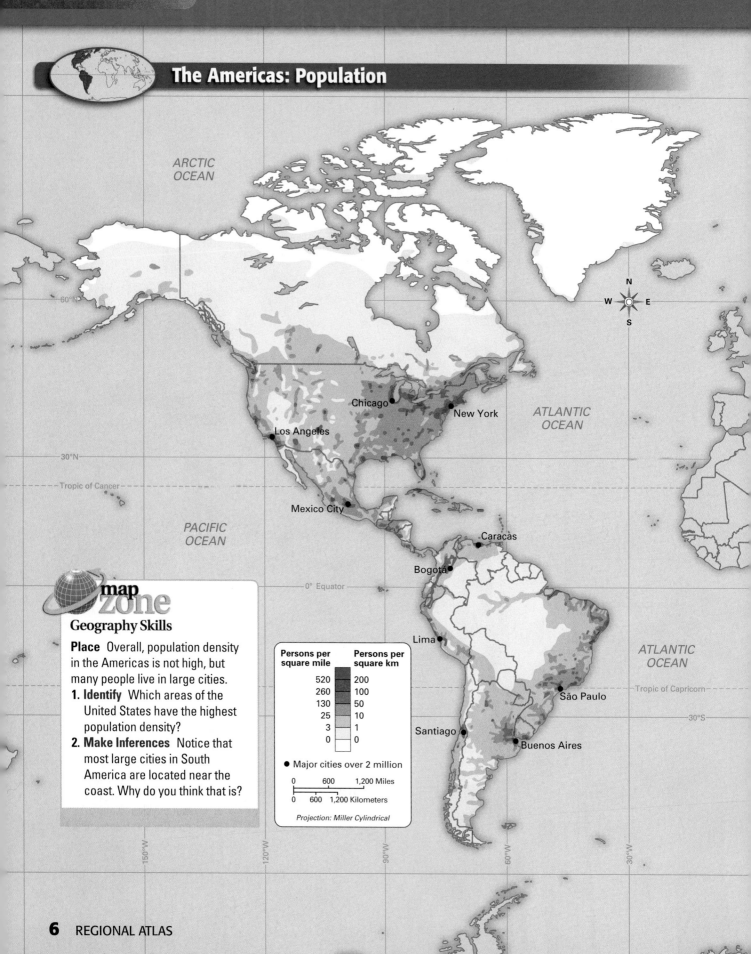

The Americas: Population

ARCTIC OCEAN

ATLANTIC OCEAN

Chicago

New York

Los Angeles

30°N

Tropic of Cancer

Mexico City

PACIFIC OCEAN

0° Equator

Caracas

Bogotá

Lima

ATLANTIC OCEAN

São Paulo

Tropic of Capricorn

Santiago

30°S

Buenos Aires

map zone

Geography Skills

Place Overall, population density in the Americas is not high, but many people live in large cities.

1. **Identify** Which areas of the United States have the highest population density?

2. **Make Inferences** Notice that most large cities in South America are located near the coast. Why do you think that is?

Persons per square mile	Persons per square km
520	200
260	100
130	50
25	10
3	1
0	0

● Major cities over 2 million

0   600   1,200 Miles

0   600   1,200 Kilometers

Projection: Miller Cylindrical

The Americas

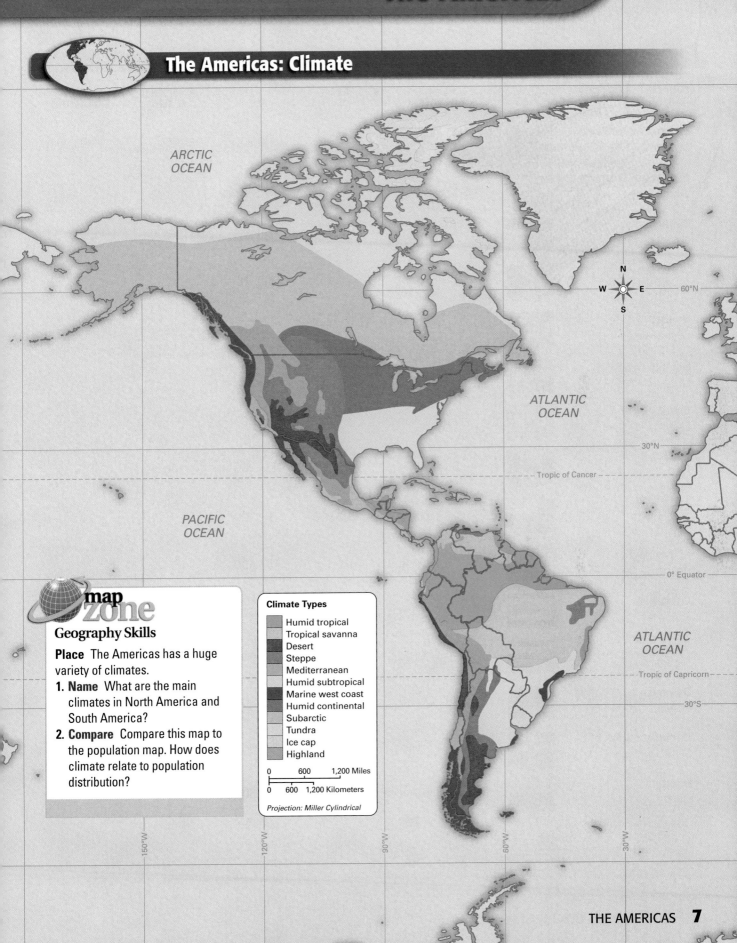

The Americas: Climate

ARCTIC OCEAN

ATLANTIC OCEAN

PACIFIC OCEAN

ATLANTIC OCEAN

60°N

30°N

Tropic of Cancer

0° Equator

Tropic of Capricorn

30°S

150°W   120°W   90°W   60°W   30°W

map zone

Geography Skills

Place The Americas has a huge variety of climates.

1. **Name** What are the main climates in North America and South America?

2. **Compare** Compare this map to the population map. How does climate relate to population distribution?

Climate Types

- Humid tropical
- Tropical savanna
- Desert
- Steppe
- Mediterranean
- Humid subtropical
- Marine west coast
- Humid continental
- Subarctic
- Tundra
- Ice cap
- Highland

0   600   1,200 Miles

0   600   1,200 Kilometers

Projection: Miller Cylindrical

The Americas

COUNTRY Capital	FLAG	POPULATION	AREA (sq mi)	PER CAPITA GDP (U.S. $)	LIFE EXPECTANCY AT BIRTH	TVS PER 1,000 PEOPLE
Antigua and Barbuda St. John's		69,500	171	$10,900	72.4	493
Argentina Buenos Aires		40.3 million	1,068,302	$15,000	76.3	293
Bahamas Nassau		305,600	5,382	$21,300	65.7	243
Barbados Bridgetown		280,900	166	$18,200	73.0	290
Belize Belmopan		294,400	8,867	$8,400	68.4	183
Bolivia La Paz, Sucre		9.1 million	424,164	$3,000	66.2	118
Brazil Brasília		190 million	3,286,487	$8,600	72.2	333
Canada Ottawa		33.4 million	3,855,101	$35,200	80.3	709
Chile Santiago		16.3 million	292,260	$12,700	76.9	240
Colombia Bogotá		44..4 million	439,735	$8,400	72.3	279
Costa Rica San José		4.1 million	19,730	$12,000	77.2	229
Cuba Havana		11.4 million	42,803	$3,900	77.6	248
Dominica Roseau		72,400	291	$3,800	75.1	232
Dominican Republic Santo Domingo		9.4 million	18,815	$8,000	73.1	96
Ecuador Quito		13.8 million	109,483	$4,500	76.6	213
United States Washington, D.C.		301.1 million	3,718,710	$43,500	78.0	844

COUNTRY Capital	FLAG	POPULATION	AREA (sq mi)	PER CAPITA GDP (U.S. $)	LIFE EXPECTANCY AT BIRTH	TVS PER 1,000 PEOPLE
El Salvador San Salvador		6.9 million	8,124	$4,900	71.8	191
Grenada Saint George's		89,900	133	$3,900	65.2	376
Guatemala Guatemala City		12.7 million	42,043	$4,900	69.7	61
Guyana Georgetown		769,100	83,000	$4,700	66.2	70
Haiti Port-au-Prince		8.7 million	10,714	$1,800	57.0	5
Honduras Tegucigalpa		7.5 million	43,278	$3,000	69.4	95
Jamaica Kingston		2.8 million	4,244	$4,600	73.1	191
Mexico Mexico City		108.7 million	761,606	$10,600	75.6	272
Nicaragua Managua		5.7 million	49,998	$3,000	70.9	69
Panama Panama City		3.2 million	30,193	$7,900	75.2	192
Paraguay Asunción		6.7 million	157,047	$4,700	75.3	205
Peru Lima		28.7 million	496,226	$6,400	70.1	147
Saint Kitts and Nevis Basseterre		39,300	101	$8,200	72.7	256
Saint Lucia Castries		170,600	238	$4,800	74.0	368
Saint Vincent and the Grenadines; Kingstown		118,100	150	$3,600	74.1	230
United States Washington, D.C.		301.1 million	3,718,711	$43,500	78.0	844

COUNTRY Capital	FLAG	POPULATION	AREA (sq mi)	PER CAPITA GDP (U.S. $)	LIFE EXPECTANCY AT BIRTH	TVS PER 1,000 PEOPLE
Suriname Paramaribo		470,800	63,039	$7,100	73.2	241
Trinidad and Tobago Port-of-Spain		1.1 million	1,980	$19,700	66.9	337
Uruguay Montevideo		3.5 million	68,039	$10,700	76.5	531
Venezuela Caracas		26 million	352,144	$6,900	74.8	185
United States Washington, D.C.		301.1 million	3,718,710	$43,500	78.0	844

ANALYSIS SKILL ANALYZING TABLES

1. Compare the information for the United States, Canada, Brazil, and Mexico. How do these four countries compare?
2. Which country has the lowest per capita GDP?

Largest Cities and Urban Populations

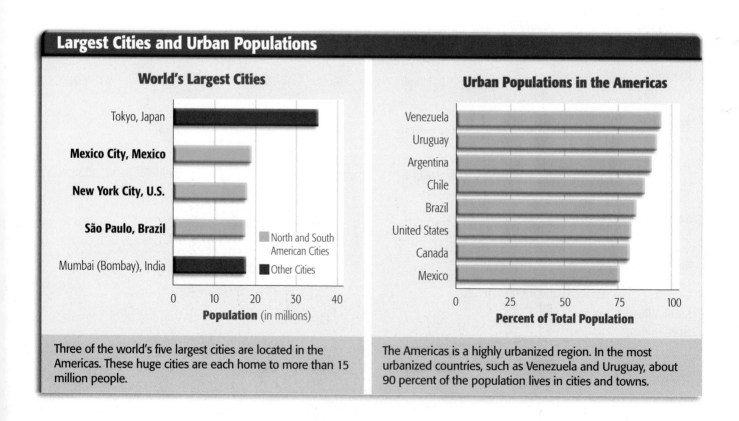

World's Largest Cities

- Tokyo, Japan
- **Mexico City, Mexico**
- **New York City, U.S.**
- **São Paulo, Brazil**
- Mumbai (Bombay), India

North and South American Cities
Other Cities

0 10 20 30 40
Population (in millions)

Urban Populations in the Americas

- Venezuela
- Uruguay
- Argentina
- Chile
- Brazil
- United States
- Canada
- Mexico

0 25 50 75 100
Percent of Total Population

Three of the world's five largest cities are located in the Americas. These huge cities are each home to more than 15 million people.

The Americas is a highly urbanized region. In the most urbanized countries, such as Venezuela and Uruguay, about 90 percent of the population lives in cities and towns.

Major Food Exports of the Americas

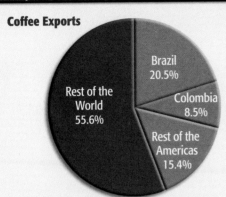

Coffee Exports

Rest of the World 55.6%

Brazil 20.5%

Colombia 8.5%

Rest of the Americas 15.4%

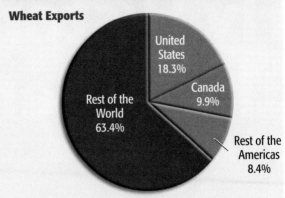

Wheat Exports

United States 18.3%

Canada 9.9%

Rest of the World 63.4%

Rest of the Americas 8.4%

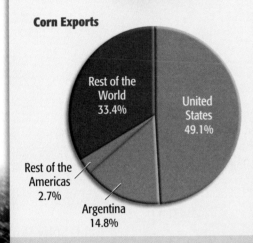

Corn Exports

Rest of the World 33.4%

United States 49.1%

Rest of the Americas 2.7%

Argentina 14.8%

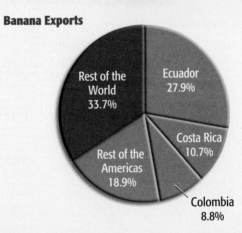

Banana Exports

Rest of the World 33.7%

Ecuador 27.9%

Costa Rica 10.7%

Rest of the Americas 18.9%

Colombia 8.8%

The Americas is a major exporter of some crops, like coffee, wheat, corn, and bananas. While the United States leads in wheat and corn exports, other crops like coffee and bananas are exported from Central and South America.

ANALYSIS SKILL | **ANALYZING GRAPHS**

1. What percentage of the world's corn exports come from the Americas?
2. Which countries in the Americas export the most coffee?

Workers harvest coffee beans in Costa Rica.

CHAPTER 1

Early History of the Americas

500 BC–AD 1537

What You Will Learn...

In this chapter you will learn about the location, growth, and decline of the Maya, Aztec, and Inca civilizations in the Americas.

SECTION 1
The Maya **14**

SECTION 2
The Aztecs **20**

SECTION 3
The Incas **25**

FOCUS ON READING AND WRITING

Setting a Purpose Setting a purpose for your reading can help give you a focus. Before you read, look at pictures and headings to find out what the text is about. Then decide what your purpose in reading the text is. Keep your purpose in mind as you read. **See the lesson, Setting a Purpose, on page 194.**

Writing a Newspaper Article You are a writer for a European newspaper who is traveling with some explorers to the Americas. As you read this chapter, you will decide what you want to share with readers in a newspaper article—the land, the people, or the events that occurred after the explorers arrived.

PACIFIC
OCEAN

140°W   130°W   120°W

map zone Geography Skills

Region Three great civilizations existed in North and South America before 1537.
1. **Identify** Which civilization was located in South America?
2. **Make Inferences** What do you think happened when the Spanish arrived in the Americas?

The Maya The Maya traded jade between their cities in Mesoamerica.

Maya temple

Spanish explorers' ship

Tenochtitlán

Palenque

ATLANTIC OCEAN

Aztec warrior

Inca with llama

Cuzco

HOLT

Geography's Impact
video series
Watch the video to understand the impact of Mayan achievements on math and astronomy.

● Ancient city

0   300   600 Miles

0   300   600 Kilometers

Projection:
Lambert Azimuthal Equal-Area

Tropic of Capricorn

30°N

20°N

10°N

0° Equator

The Aztecs The Aztecs were known for warfare as well as for their arts.

The Incas The Incas built well-crafted stone cities high in the Andes.

13

The Maya

What You Will Learn...

Main Ideas

1. Geography helped shape the lives of the early Maya.
2. During the Classic Age, the Maya built great cities linked by trade.
3. Maya culture included a strict social structure, a religion with many gods, and achievements in science and the arts.
4. The decline of Maya civilization began in the 900s.

The Big Idea

The Maya developed an advanced civilization that thrived in Mesoamerica from about 250 until the 900s.

Key Terms and Places

maize, *p. 14*
Palenque, *p. 15*
observatories, *p. 18*

TAKING NOTES As you read, take notes on the Maya civilization. Use a chart like this one to organize your notes.

Geography and Cities	
Society and Achievements	
Decline	

If YOU lived there...

You are a Maya farmer, growing corn in fields outside a city. Often you enter the city to join in religious ceremonies. You watch the king and his priests standing at the top of a tall pyramid. They wear capes of brightly colored feathers and gold ornaments that glitter in the sun. Far below them, thousands of worshippers crowd into the plaza with you to honor the gods.

How do these ceremonies make you feel?

BUILDING BACKGROUND Religion was very important to the Maya, one of the early peoples in the Americas. The Maya believed the gods controlled everything in the world around them.

Geography and the Early Maya

The region known as Mesoamerica stretches from the central part of Mexico south to include the northern part of Central America. It was in this region that a people called the Maya (MY-uh) developed a remarkable civilization.

Around 1000 BC the Maya began settling in the lowlands of what is now northern Guatemala. Thick tropical forests covered most of the land, but the people cleared areas to farm. They grew a variety of crops, including beans, squash, avocados, and **maize**, or corn. The forests provided valuable resources, too. Forest animals such as deer, rabbits, and monkeys were sources of food. In addition, trees and other forest plants made good building materials. For example, some Maya used wooden poles and vines, along with mud, to build their houses.

The early Maya lived in small, isolated villages. Eventually, though, these villages started trading with one another and with other groups in Mesoamerica. As trade increased, the villages grew. By about AD 200, the Maya had begun to build large cities in Mesoamerica.

READING CHECK Finding Main Ideas How did the early Maya make use of their physical environment?

The Classic Age

The Maya civilization reached its height between about AD 250 and 900. This time in Maya history is known as the Classic Age. During this time, Maya territory grew to include more than 40 large cities. Each had its own government and its own king. No single ruler united the many cities into one empire.

Instead, the Maya cities were linked through trade. People exchanged goods for products that were not available locally. Look at the trade routes on the map to see the goods that were available in different areas of Maya civilization. For example,

the warm lowlands were good for growing cotton and cacao (kuh-KOW), the source of chocolate. But lowland crops did not grow well in the cool highlands. Instead, the highlands had valuable stones, such as jade and obsidian. People carried these and other products along trade routes.

Through trade, the Maya got supplies for construction. Maya cities had grand buildings, such as palaces decorated with carvings and paintings. The Maya also built stone pyramids topped with temples. Some temples honored local kings. For example, in the city of **Palenque** (pah-LENG-kay), the king Pacal (puh-KAHL) had a temple built to record his achievements.

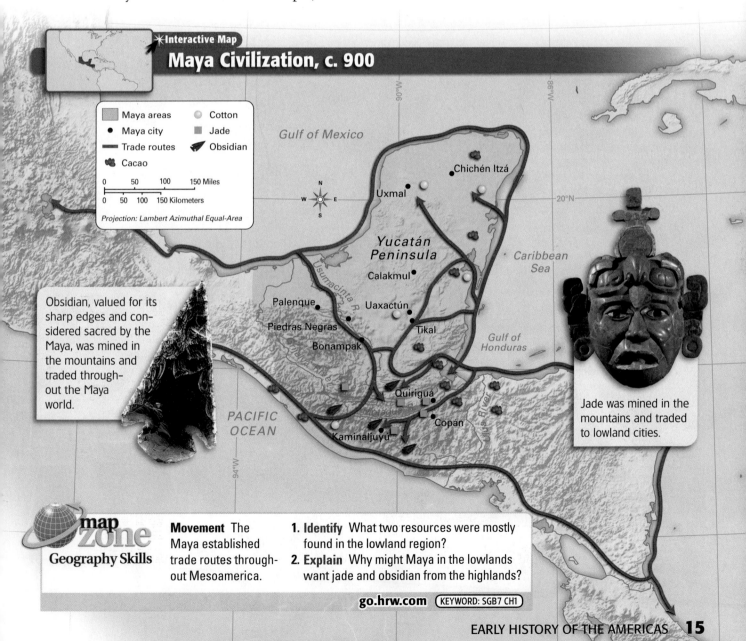

Interactive Map

Maya Civilization, c. 900

Maya areas
Maya city
Trade routes
Cacao
Cotton
Jade
Obsidian

0   50   100   150 Miles
0   50   100   150 Kilometers

Projection: Lambert Azimuthal Equal-Area

Gulf of Mexico

Chichén Itzá
Uxmal

Yucatán Peninsula

Caribbean Sea

Calakmul

Palenque
Uaxactún

Piedras Negras
Bonampak
Tikal

Gulf of Honduras

Quiriguá
Copán
Kaminaljuyú

PACIFIC OCEAN

Obsidian, valued for its sharp edges and considered sacred by the Maya, was mined in the mountains and traded throughout the Maya world.

Jade was mined in the mountains and traded to lowland cities.

map zone
Geography Skills

Movement The Maya established trade routes throughout Mesoamerica.

1. **Identify** What two resources were mostly found in the lowland region?
2. **Explain** Why might Maya in the lowlands want jade and obsidian from the highlands?

go.hrw.com KEYWORD: SGB7 CH1

In addition to palaces and temples, the Maya built canals and paved large plazas, or open squares, for public gatherings. Farmers used stone walls to shape hillsides into flat terraces so they could grow crops on them. Almost every Maya city also had a stone court for playing a special ball game. Using only their heads, shoulders, or hips, players tried to bounce a heavy rubber ball through stone rings attached high on the court walls. The winners of these games received jewels and clothing. The losers were often killed.

READING CHECK Analyzing Why is Maya civilization not considered an empire?

Maya Culture

In Maya society, people's daily lives were heavily influenced by two main forces. One was the social structure, and the other was religion.

Social Structure

The king held the highest position in Maya society. The Maya believed their kings were related to the gods, so Maya kings had religious as well as political authority. Priests, rich merchants, and noble warriors were also part of the upper class. Together with the king, these people held all the power in Maya society.

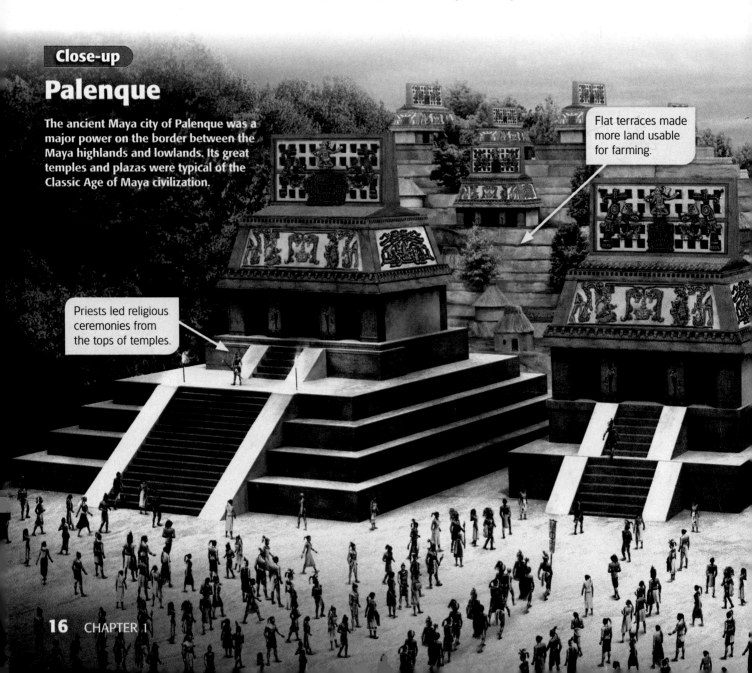

Close-up

Palenque

The ancient Maya city of Palenque was a major power on the border between the Maya highlands and lowlands. Its great temples and plazas were typical of the Classic Age of Maya civilization.

Flat terraces made more land usable for farming.

Priests led religious ceremonies from the tops of temples.

Most Maya, though, belonged to the lower class. This group was made up of farming families who lived outside the cities. The women cared for the children, cooked, made yarn, and wove cloth. The men farmed, hunted, and crafted tools.

Lower-class Maya had to "pay" their rulers by giving the rulers part of their crops and goods such as cloth and salt. They also had to help construct temples and other public buildings. If their city went to war, Maya men had to serve in the army, and if captured in battle, they often became slaves. Slaves carried goods along trade routes or worked for upper-class Maya as servants or farmers.

Religion

The Maya worshipped many gods, such as a creator, a sun god, a moon goddess, and a maize god. Each god was believed to control a different aspect of daily life.

According to Maya beliefs, the gods could be helpful or harmful, so people tried to please the gods to get their help. The Maya believed their gods needed blood to prevent disasters or the end of the world. Every person offered blood to the gods by piercing their tongue or skin. On special occasions, the Maya made human sacrifices. They usually used prisoners captured in battle, offering their hearts to stone carvings of the gods.

Maya temples were shaped like mountains, which the Maya considered sacred because they allowed people to approach the gods.

BIOGRAPHY

Pacal
(603–683)

Pacal became king of the Maya city of Palenque when he was just 12 years old. As king, Pacal led many important community events, such as religious dances and public meetings. When he died, he was buried at the bottom of the Temple of the Inscriptions shown to the near left.

Maya buildings were covered with stucco and painted in bright colors.

ANALYSIS SKILL **ANALYZING VISUALS**

In what ways might Palenque's setting have helped the city? In what ways might it have hurt the city?

Maya Astronomy and Writing

October 28, AD 709

She is letting blood.

Lady Xoc

The Maya studied the stars from their observatory (left) at Chichén Itzá. The stone carving (above) shows a religious ceremony.

ANALYZING VISUALS What is happening in this religious ceremony?

Achievements

FOCUS ON READING

What will be your purpose in reading about Maya achievements?

The Maya's religious beliefs led them to make impressive advances in science. They built large **observatories**, or buildings from which people could study the sky, so their priests could watch the stars and plan the best times for religious festivals. With the knowledge they gained about astronomy, the Maya developed two calendars. One, with 365 days, guided farming activities, such as planting and harvesting. This calendar was more accurate than the one used in Europe at that time. The Maya also had a separate 260-day calendar that they used for keeping track of religious events.

The Maya were able to measure time accurately partly because they were skilled mathematicians. They created a number system that helped them make complex calculations, and they were among the first people with a symbol for zero. The Maya used their number system to record key dates in their history.

The Maya also developed a writing system. Anthropologists, or scholars who study people and cultures, have figured out that symbols used in Maya writing represented both objects and sounds. The Maya carved these symbols into large stone tablets to record their history. They also wrote in bark-paper books and passed down stories and poems orally.

The Maya created amazing art and architecture as well. Their jade and gold jewelry was exceptional. Also, their huge temple-pyramids were masterfully built. The Maya had neither metal tools for cutting nor wheeled vehicles for carrying heavy supplies. Instead, workers used obsidian tools to cut limestone into blocks. Then workers rolled the giant blocks over logs and lifted them with ropes. The Maya decorated their buildings with paintings.

READING CHECK **Categorizing** What groups made up the different classes in Maya society?

Decline of Maya Civilization

Maya civilization began to collapse in the AD 900s. People stopped building temples and other structures. They left the cities and moved back to the countryside. What caused this collapse? Historians are not sure, but they think that a combination of factors was probably responsible.

One factor could have been the burden on the common people. Maya kings forced their subjects to farm for them or work on building projects. Perhaps people didn't want to work for the kings. They might have decided to **rebel** against their rulers' demands and abandon their cities.

Increased warfare between cities could also have caused the decline. Maya cities had always fought for power. But if battles became more widespread or destructive, they would have disrupted trade and cost many lives. People might have fled from the cities for their safety.

A related theory is that perhaps the Maya could not produce enough food to feed everyone. Growing the same crops year after year would have weakened the soil. In addition, as the population grew, the demand for food would have increased. To meet this demand, cities might have begun competing fiercely for new land. But the resulting battles would have hurt more crops, damaged more farmland, and caused even greater food shortages.

Climate change could have played a role, too. Scientists know that Mesoamerica suffered from droughts during the period when the Maya were leaving their cities. Droughts would have made it hard to grow enough food to feed people in the cities.

Whatever the reasons, the collapse of Maya civilization happened gradually. The Maya scattered after 900, but they did not disappear entirely. In fact, the Maya civilization later revived in the Yucatán Peninsula. By the time Spanish conquerors reached the Americas in the 1500s, though, Maya power had faded.

READING CHECK **Summarizing** What factors may have caused the end of Maya civilization?

SUMMARY AND PREVIEW The Maya built a civilization that peaked between about 250 and 900 but later collapsed for reasons still unknown. In Section 2 you will learn about another people who lived in Mesoamerica, the Aztecs.

Section 1 Assessment

go.hrw.com
Online Quiz
KEYWORD: SGB7 HP1

Reviewing Ideas, Terms, and Places

1. **a. Recall** What resources did the Maya get from the forest?
   b. Elaborate How do you think Maya villages grew into large cities?
2. **a. Describe** What features did Maya cities include?
   b. Make Inferences How did trade strengthen the Maya civilization?
3. **a. Identify** Who belonged to the upper class in Maya society?
   b. Explain Why did the Maya build **observatories**?
   c. Rank What do you think was the most impressive cultural achievement of the Maya? Why?
4. **a. Describe** What happened to the Maya after 900?
   b. Evaluate What would you consider to be the key factor in the collapse of Maya civilization? Explain.

Critical Thinking

5. **Evaluating** Draw a diagram like the one to the right. Use your notes to rank Maya achievements, with the most important at the top.

FOCUS ON WRITING

6. **Gathering Information about the Maya** Part of your article will probably be devoted to the Maya. Use the map and pictures in this section to help you decide what to write about. How would you describe the land and the Maya cities? What could you add about the history and culture of the Maya? Take notes on your ideas.

The Aztecs

Main Ideas

1. The Aztecs built a rich and powerful empire in central Mexico.
2. Social structure, religion, and warfare shaped life in the empire.
3. Hernán Cortés conquered the Aztec Empire in 1521.

The Big Idea

The strong Aztec Empire, founded in central Mexico in 1325, lasted until the Spanish conquest in 1521.

Key Terms and Places

Tenochtitlán, *p. 20*
causeways, *p. 20*
conquistadors, *p. 24*

TAKING NOTES As you read, take notes on the founding of the Aztec Empire, life in the empire at its height, and the fall of the Aztec Empire. Use a diagram like the one here to help you organize your notes.

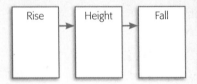

| Rise | Height | Fall |

If YOU lived there...

You live in a village in southeastern Mexico that is ruled by the powerful Aztec Empire. Each year your village must send the emperor many baskets of corn. You have to dig gold for him, too. One day some pale, bearded strangers arrive by sea. They want to overthrow the emperor, and they ask for your help.

Should you help the strangers? Why or why not?

BUILDING BACKGROUND The Aztecs ruled a large empire in Mesoamerica. Each village they conquered had to contribute heavily to the Aztec economy. This system helped create a mighty state, but one that did not inspire loyalty.

The Aztecs Build an Empire

The first Aztecs were farmers who migrated from the north to central Mexico. Finding the good farmland already occupied, they settled on a swampy island in the middle of Lake Texcoco (tays-KOH-koh). There, in 1325, they began building their capital and conquering nearby towns.

War was a key factor in the Aztecs' rise to power. The Aztecs fought fiercely and demanded tribute payments from the people they conquered. The cotton, gold, and food that poured in as a result became vital to their economy. The Aztecs also controlled a huge trade network. Merchants carried goods to and from all parts of the empire. Many merchants doubled as spies, keeping the rulers informed about what was happening in their lands.

War, tribute, and trade made the Aztec Empire strong and rich. By the early 1400s the Aztecs ruled the most powerful state in Mesoamerica. Nowhere was the empire's greatness more visible than in its capital, **Tenochtitlán** (tay-nawch-teet-LAHN).

To build this amazing island city, the Aztecs first had to overcome many geographic challenges. One problem was the difficulty getting to and from the city. The Aztecs addressed this challenge by building three wide **causeways**—raised roads across water or wet ground—to connect the island to the lakeshore.

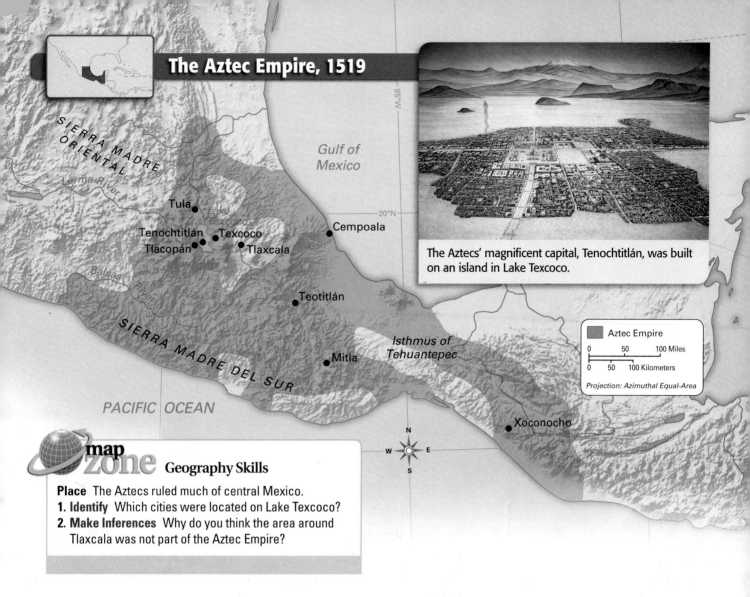

The Aztec Empire, 1519

SIERRA MADRE ORIENTAL

Lerma River

Gulf of Mexico

Tula

Lake Texcoco

Tenochtitlán   Texcoco

Tlacopán   Tlaxcala

Cempoala

20°N

Balsas River

SIERRA MADRE DEL SUR

Teotitlán

Isthmus of Tehuantepec

Mitla

PACIFIC OCEAN

Xoconocho

N
W   E
S

95°W

The Aztecs' magnificent capital, Tenochtitlán, was built on an island in Lake Texcoco.

Aztec Empire

0   50   100 Miles

0   50   100 Kilometers

Projection: Azimuthal Equal-Area

map zone **Geography Skills**

Place The Aztecs ruled much of central Mexico.
1. **Identify** Which cities were located on Lake Texcoco?
2. **Make Inferences** Why do you think the area around Tlaxcala was not part of the Aztec Empire?

They also built canals that crisscrossed the city. The causeways and canals made travel and trade much easier.

Tenochtitlán's island location also limited the amount of land available for farming. To solve this problem, the Aztecs created floating gardens called *chinampas* (chee-NAHM-pahs). They piled soil on top of large rafts, which they anchored to trees that stood in the water.

The Aztecs made Tenochtitlán a truly magnificent city. Home to some 200,000 people at its height, it had huge temples, a busy market, and a grand palace.

READING CHECK **Finding Main Ideas** How did the Aztecs rise to power?

Life in the Empire

The Aztecs' way of life was as distinctive as their capital city. They had a complex social structure, a demanding religion, and a rich culture.

Aztec Society

The Aztec emperor, like the Maya king, was the most important person in society. From his great palace, he attended to law, trade, tribute, and warfare. Trusted nobles helped him as tax collectors, judges, and other government officials. These noble positions were passed down from fathers to sons, and young nobles went to school to learn their responsibilities.

THE IMPACT TODAY

Mexico's capital, Mexico City, is located where Tenochtitlán once stood.

Tenochtitlán

The Aztecs turned a swampy, uninhabited island into one of the largest and grandest cities in the world. The first Europeans to visit Tenochtitlán were amazed. At the time, the Aztec capital was about five times bigger than London.

The Great Temple stood at the heart of the city. On top of the temple were two shrines—a blue shrine for the rain god and a red shrine for the sun god.

Gold, silver, cloaks, and precious stones were among the many items sold at the market.

A network of canals linked different parts of the city.

Aztec farmers grew crops on floating gardens called *chinampas*.

ANALYSIS SKILL **ANALYZING VISUALS**

What is the most important building in this picture? How can you tell?

Aztec Ceremonial Jewelry

Aztec artists were very skilled. They created detailed and brightly colored items. This double-headed serpent was probably worn during religious ceremonies. The man on the right is wearing it on his chest.

ANALYZING VISUALS What are some features of Aztec art that you can see in these pictures?

Just below the emperor and his nobles was a class of warriors and priests. Aztec warriors were highly respected and had many privileges, but priests were more influential. They led religious ceremonies and, as keepers of the calendars, decided when to plant and harvest.

The next level of Aztec society included merchants and artisans. Below them, in the lower class, were farmers and laborers, who made up the majority of the population. Many didn't own their land, and they paid so much in tribute that they often found it tough to survive. Only slaves, at the very bottom of society, struggled more.

Religion and Warfare

Like the Maya, the Aztecs worshipped many gods whom they believed controlled both nature and human activities. To please the gods, Aztec priests regularly made human sacrifices. Most victims were battle captives or slaves. In bloody ritual ceremonies, priests would slash open their victims' chests to "feed" human hearts and blood to the gods. The Aztecs sacrificed as many as 10,000 people a year. To supply enough victims, Aztec warriors often fought battles with neighboring peoples.

Cultural Achievements

As warlike as the Aztecs were, they also appreciated art and beauty. Architects and sculptors created fine stone pyramids and statues. Artisans used gold, gems, and bright feathers to make jewelry and masks. Women embroidered colorful designs on the cloth they wove.

The Aztecs valued learning as well. They studied astronomy and devised a calendar much like the Maya one. They kept detailed written records of historical and cultural events. They also had a strong oral tradition. Stories about ancestors and the gods were passed from one generation to the next. The Aztecs also enjoyed fine speeches and riddles such as these:

*"*What is a little blue-green jar filled with popcorn? Someone is sure to guess our riddle: it is the sky.

What is a mountainside that has a spring of water in it? Our nose.*"*

–Bernardino de Sahagún, from Florentine Codex

Knowing the answers to riddles showed that one had paid attention in school.

READING CHECK **Identifying Cause and Effect** How did Aztec religious practices influence warfare?

Cortés Conquers the Aztecs

FOCUS ON READING

If your purpose is to learn about the end of the Aztecs, how will reading about the Spanish help you?

In the late 1400s the Spanish arrived in the Americas, seeking adventure, riches, and converts to Catholicism. One group of **conquistadors** (kahn-KEES-tuh-dohrz), or Spanish conquerors, reached Mexico in 1519. Led by Hernán Cortés (er-NAHN kawr-TEZ), their motives were to find gold, claim land, and convert the native peoples to Christianity.

The Aztec emperor, Moctezuma II (MAWK-tay-SOO-mah), cautiously welcomed the strangers. He believed Cortés to be the god Quetzalcoatl (ket-suhl-kuh-WAH-tuhl), whom the Aztecs believed had left Mexico long ago. According to legend, the god had promised to return in 1519.

Moctezuma gave the Spanish gold and other gifts, but Cortés wanted more. He took the emperor prisoner, enraging the Aztecs, who attacked the Spanish. They managed to drive out the conquistadors, but Moctezuma was killed in the fighting.

Within a year, Cortés and his men came back. This time they had help from other peoples in the region who resented the Aztecs' harsh rule. In addition, the Spanish had better weapons, including armor, cannons, and swords. Furthermore, the Aztecs were terrified of the enemy's big horses—animals they had never seen before. The Spanish had also unknowingly brought diseases such as smallpox to the Americas. Diseases weakened or killed thousands of Aztecs. In 1521 the Aztec Empire came to an end.

READING CHECK **Summarizing** What factors helped the Spanish defeat the Aztecs?

SUMMARY AND PREVIEW The Aztec Empire, made strong by warfare and tribute, fell to the Spanish in 1521. In the next section you will learn about another empire in the Americas, that of the Incas.

Section 2 Assessment

go.hrw.com
Online Quiz
KEYWORD: SGB7 HP1

Reviewing Ideas, Terms, and Places

1. **a. Recall** Where and when did Aztec civilization develop?
   b. Explain How did the Aztecs in **Tenochtitlán** adapt to their island location?
   c. Elaborate How might Tenochtitlán's location have been both a benefit and a hindrance to the Aztecs?
2. **a. Recall** What did the Aztecs feed their gods?
   b. Rate Consider the roles of the emperor, warriors, priests, and others in Aztec society. Who do you think had the hardest role? Explain.
3. **a. Identify** Who was Moctezuma II?
   b. Make Generalizations Why did allies help Cortés defeat the Aztecs?
   c. Predict The Aztecs vastly outnumbered the **conquistadors**. If the Aztecs had first viewed Cortés as a threat rather than a god, how might history have changed?

Critical Thinking

4. **Evaluating** Draw a diagram like the one shown. Use your notes to identify three factors that contributed to the Aztecs' power. Put the factor you consider most important first and put the least important last. Explain your choices.

1.	2.	3.

FOCUS ON WRITING

5. **Describing the Aztec Empire** Tenochtitlán would certainly be described in your article. Make notes about how you would describe it. Be sure to explain the causeways, chinampas, and other features. What activities went on in the city? Your article should also describe the events that occurred when the Spanish discovered the Aztec capital. Make notes on the fall of the Aztec Empire.

The Incas

If **YOU** lived there...

You live in the Andes Mountains, where you raise llamas. You weave their wool into warm cloth. Last year, soldiers from the powerful Inca Empire took over your village. They brought in new leaders, who say you must all learn a new language and send much of your woven cloth to the Inca ruler. They also promise that the government will provide for you in times of trouble.

How do you feel about living in the Inca Empire?

> **BUILDING BACKGROUND** The Incas built their huge empire by taking over village after village in South America. They brought many changes to the people they conquered before they were themselves conquered by the Spanish.

The Incas Create an Empire

While the Aztecs were ruling Mexico, the Inca Empire arose in South America. The Incas began as a small tribe in the Andes. Their capital was **Cuzco** (KOO-skoh) in what is now Peru.

In the mid-1400s a ruler named Pachacuti (pah-chah-KOO-tee) began to expand Inca territory. Later leaders followed his example, and by the early 1500s the Inca Empire was huge. It stretched from what is now Ecuador south to central Chile. It included coastal deserts, snowy mountains, fertile valleys, and thick forests. About 12 million people lived in the empire. To rule effectively, the Incas formed a strong central government.

The Incas lived in a region of high plains and mountains.

Inca Empire

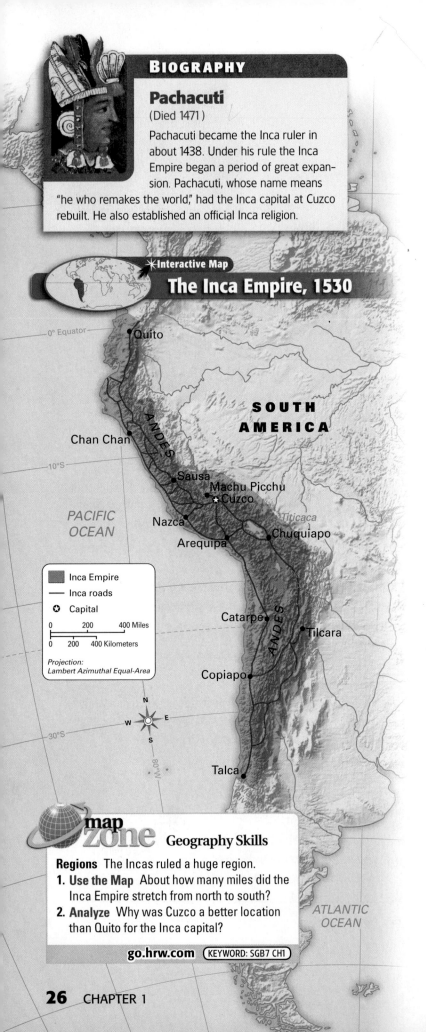

BIOGRAPHY

Pachacuti
(Died 1471)

Pachacuti became the Inca ruler in about 1438. Under his rule the Inca Empire began a period of great expansion. Pachacuti, whose name means "he who remakes the world," had the Inca capital at Cuzco rebuilt. He also established an official Inca religion.

★Interactive Map

The Inca Empire, 1530

Quito

0° Equator

SOUTH AMERICA

ANDES

Chan Chan

10°S

Sausa

Machu Picchu

Cuzco

PACIFIC OCEAN

Nazca

Titicaca

Chuquiapo

Arequipa

Inca Empire

Inca roads

⊙ Capital

0   200   400 Miles

0   200   400 Kilometers

Projection:
Lambert Azimuthal Equal-Area

Catarpe

ANDES

Tilcara

Copiapo

N
W   E
S

30°S

80°W

Talca

ATLANTIC OCEAN

map zone Geography Skills

Regions The Incas ruled a huge region.
1. **Use the Map** About how many miles did the Inca Empire stretch from north to south?
2. **Analyze** Why was Cuzco a better location than Quito for the Inca capital?

go.hrw.com   KEYWORD: SGB7 CH1

Central Rule

Pachacuti did not want the people he conquered to have too much power. He began a policy of removing local leaders and replacing them with new officials whom he trusted. He also made the children of conquered leaders travel to Cuzco to learn about Inca government and religion. When the children were grown, they were sent back to govern their villages, where they taught their people about the Incas' history, traditions, and way of life.

As another way of unifying the empire, the Incas used an official Inca language, **Quechua** (KE-chuh-wuh). Although people spoke many other languages, all official business had to be done in Quechua. Even today, many people in Peru and the other former Inca lands still speak Quechua.

A Well-Organized Economy

The Inca government strictly controlled the economy and told each household what work to do. Most Incas had to spend time working for the government as well as themselves. Farmers tended government land in addition to their own. Villagers made cloth and other goods for the army. Some Incas served as soldiers, worked in mines, or built roads and bridges. In this way the people paid taxes in the form of labor rather than money. This labor tax system was called the *mita* (MEE-tah).

Another feature of the Inca economy was that there were no merchants or markets. Instead, government officials would distribute goods collected through the *mita*. Leftover goods were stored in the capital for emergencies. If a natural disaster struck, or if people simply could not care for themselves, the government provided supplies to help them.

READING CHECK Summarizing How did the Incas control their empire?

Life in the Inca Empire

Because the rulers controlled Inca society so closely, the common people had little personal freedom. At the same time, the government protected the general welfare of all in the empire. But that did not mean everyone was treated equally.

Social Divisions

Inca society had two main social classes. The emperor, government officials, and priests made up the upper class. Members of this class lived in stone houses in Cuzco and wore the best clothes. They did not have to pay the labor tax, and they enjoyed many other privileges. The Inca rulers, for example, could relax in luxury at Machu Picchu (MAH-choo PEEK-choo). This royal retreat lay nestled high in the Andes.

The people of the lower class in Inca society included farmers, artisans, and servants. There were no slaves, however, because the Incas did not practice slavery. Most Incas were farmers. In the warmer valleys they grew crops such as maize and peanuts. In the cooler mountains they carved terraces into the hillsides and grew potatoes. High in the Andes, people raised llamas—South American animals related to camels—for wool and meat.

Lower-class Incas dressed in plain clothes and lived simply. By law, they could not own more goods than just what they needed to survive. Most of what they made went to the mita and the upper class.

Religion

The Inca social structure was partly related to religion. For example, the Incas thought that their rulers were related to the sun god and never really died. As a result, priests brought mummies of former kings to many ceremonies. People gave these royal mummies food and gifts.

Most Incas were farmers. The Incas in this drawing from the mid-1500s are harvesting potatoes.

THE GRANGER COLLECTION, NEW YORK

Inca ceremonies included sacrifices. But unlike the Maya and the Aztecs, the Incas rarely sacrificed humans. They sacrificed llamas, cloth, or food instead.

In addition to practicing the official religion, people outside Cuzco worshipped other gods at local sacred places. The Incas believed certain mountaintops, rocks, and springs had magical powers. Many Incas performed sacrifices at these places as well as at the temple in Cuzco.

Achievements

Inca temples were grand buildings. The Incas were master builders, known for their expert **masonry**, or stonework. They cut stone blocks so precisely that they did not need cement to hold them together. The Incas also built a major network of roads.

The Incas produced works of art as well. Artisans made pottery as well as gold and silver jewelry. They even created a life-sized cornfield of gold and silver, crafting each cob, leaf, and stalk individually. Inca weavers also made some of the finest textiles in the Americas.

FOCUS ON READING
What will be your purpose in reading about Inca achievements?

Inca Arts

Inca arts included beautiful textiles and gold and silver objects.

Inca artisans made many silver offerings to the gods.

The Incas are famous for their textiles. Inca weavers made cloth from cotton and from the wool of llamas.

ANALYSIS SKILL   ANALYZING VISUALS

What are some features of Inca art that you can see in these pictures?

Inca artisans also made many gold objects, such as this mask.

While such artifacts tell us much about the Incas, nothing was written about their empire until the Spanish arrived. Indeed, the Incas had no writing system. Instead, they kept records with knotted cords called *quipus* (KEE-pooz). Knots in the cords stood for numbers. Different colors represented information about crops, land, and other important topics.

The Incas also passed down their stories and history orally. People sang songs and told stories about daily life and military victories. Official "memorizers" learned long poems about Inca legends and history. When the conquistadors arrived, the Inca records were written in Spanish and Quechua. We know about the Incas from these records and from the stories that survive in the songs and religious practices of the people in the region today.

READING CHECK   Contrasting How did daily life differ for upper- and lower-class Incas?

Pizarro Conquers the Incas

The arrival of conquistadors changed more than how the Incas recorded history. In the late 1520s a civil war began in the Inca Empire after the death of the ruler. Two of the ruler's sons, Atahualpa (ah-tah-WAHL-pah) and Huáscar (WAHS-kahr), fought to claim the throne. Atahualpa won the war in 1532, but fierce fighting had weakened the Inca army.

On his way to be crowned as king, Atahualpa got news that a band of about 180 Spanish soldiers had arrived in the Inca Empire. They were conquistadors led by Francisco Pizarro. When Atahualpa came to meet the group, the Spanish attacked. They were greatly outnumbered, but they caught the unarmed Incas by surprise. They quickly captured Atahualpa and killed thousands of Inca soldiers.

To win his freedom, Atahualpa asked his people to fill a room with gold and silver for Pizarro. Incas brought jewelry, statues, and other valuable items from all parts of the empire. Melted down, the gold and silver may have totaled 24 tons. The precious metals would have been worth millions of dollars today. Despite this huge payment, the Spanish killed Atahualpa. They knew that if they let the Inca ruler live, he might rally his people and defeat the smaller Spanish forces.

Some Incas did fight back after the emperor's death. In 1537, though, Pizarro defeated the last of the Incas. Spain took control over the entire Inca Empire and ruled the region for the next 300 years.

READING CHECK Identifying Cause and **Effect** What events ended the Inca Empire?

SUMMARY AND PREVIEW The Incas built a huge empire in South America. But even with a strong central government, they could not withstand the Spanish conquest in 1537. In the next chapters you will learn about how the Americas have changed since the great civilizations of the Maya, Aztecs, and Incas and what these places are like today.

BIOGRAPHY

Atahualpa
(1502–1533)

Atahualpa was the last Inca emperor. He was a popular ruler, but he didn't rule for long. At his first meeting with Pizarro, he was offered a religious book to convince him to accept Christianity. Atahualpa held the book to his ear and listened. When the book didn't speak, Atahualpa threw it on the ground. The Spanish considered this an insult and a reason to attack.

Identifying Bias How do you think the Spanish viewed non-Christians?

BIOGRAPHY

Francisco Pizarro
(1475–1541)

Francisco Pizarro organized expeditions to explore the west coast of South America. His first two trips were mostly uneventful. But on his third trip, Pizarro met the Incas. With only about 180 men, he conquered the Inca Empire, which had been weakened by disease and civil war. In 1535 Pizarro founded Lima, the capital of modern Peru.

Predicting If Pizarro had not found the Inca Empire, what do you think might have happened?

go.hrw.com
Online Quiz
KEYWORD: SGB7 HP1

Section 3 Assessment

Reviewing Ideas, Terms, and Places

1. **a. Identify** Where was the Inca Empire located? What kinds of terrain did it include?
   b. Evaluate Do you think the *mita* system was a good government policy? Why or why not?
2. **a. Describe** What was a unique feature of Inca **masonry**?
   b. Make Inferences How might the Inca road system have helped strengthen the empire?
3. **a. Recall** When did the Spanish defeat the last of the Incas?
   b. Analyze Why do you think Pizarro was able to defeat the much larger forces of the Incas? Name at least two possible reasons.

Critical Thinking

4. **Analyzing** Draw a diagram like the one below. Using your notes, write a sentence in each box about how that topic influenced the next topic.

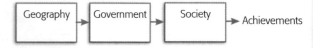

FOCUS ON WRITING

5. **Adding Information about the Inca Empire** Your article would also describe the Inca Empire. Include some comments about how the Incas' building activities related to their environment. Also, note what happened when the Spanish arrived.

North America's Native Cultures

Native Americans once lived all over North America. Their lifestyles varied depending on their local landscapes. Many Native Americans still carry on the traditions of their ancestors.

Bering Sea

Inuit

Inuit

Ingalik

Aleut

Saschutkenne

Beaver

Haida

Nootka

Far West Native Americans in the Far West relied on the sea for food.

Chinook

Columbia

Blackfoot

Plains Cree

Walla Walla

Nez Percé

Crow

Northern Paiute

Cheyenne

Modoc

Northern Shoshone

ROCKY MOUNTAINS

PACIFIC OCEAN

Western Shoshone

Miwok

Ute

Chumash

Hopi (Pueblo)

Apache

Mohave

Navajo

Zuni

Apache

Desert West In the Desert West, Native Americans dealt with their dry, rocky environment by building their homes into the sides of cliffs.

Yaqui

Tarahumara

MESOAMERICA

Arctic and Subarctic Legend:
- Arctic and Subarctic
- Eastern Woodlands
- Great Plains
- Desert West
- Far West

0   150   300 Miles
0   150   300 Kilometers

Projection: Azimuthal Equal-Area

Inuit

Hudson Bay

Inuit

Naskapi

Beothuk

Swampy Cree

Montagnais

Micmac

NORTH AMERICA

Algonquian

Pequot
Mohegan

Great Lakes

Iroquois
Mohawk
Naraganset

Teton Sioux

Omaha

Shawnee

Powhatan

ATLANTIC OCEAN

Cherokee

Osage

Chickasaw

Kiowa

Comanche
Wichita

Caddo

Choctaw

Seminole

Gulf of Mexico

N
W   E
S

Caribbean Sea

Arctic and Subarctic
In the cold north, Native Americans adapted to life in permanent snow and ice.

Eastern Woodlands
The forests of the east provided Native Americans there with good building material.

Great Plains
Native Americans moved around the Great Plains in search of good hunting grounds.

ANALYSIS SKILL **ANALYZING VISUALS**

1. **Regions** In what region did the Osage live?
2. **Human-Environment Interaction** What resources did Native Americans in the Far West use?

Analyzing Information

Learn

An important skill to learn is analyzing information presented in the text you read. One way to do this is to identify main ideas and supporting details. Everything in the paragraph should support the main idea.

After you identify the main idea, watch out for anything that is not related to it or necessary for its understanding. Don't let that extra information distract you from the most important material.

Practice

Look at the paragraph on this page about communication in the Maya civilization. Some unrelated and unnecessary information has been added so that you can learn to identify it. Use the paragraph to answer the questions here.

❶ Which sentence expresses the main idea? What details support it?

❷ What information is unnecessary or unrelated to the main idea?

The Maya

Communication The Maya developed an advanced form of writing that used many symbols. Our writing system uses 26 letters. They recorded information on large stone monuments. Some early civilizations drew pictures on cave walls. The Maya also made books of paper made from the bark of fig trees. Fig trees need a lot of light.

Religion The Maya believed in many gods and goddesses. More than 160 gods and goddesses are named in a single Maya manuscript. Among the gods they worshipped were a corn god, a rain god, a sun god, and a moon goddess. The early Greeks also worshipped many gods and goddesses.

Apply

Use the passage on this page about Maya religion to answer the following questions.

1. What is the main idea of the paragraph?

2. What details support the main idea?

3. What information is unnecessary or unrelated?

Chapter Review

Geography's Impact
video series
Review the video to answer the closing question:
How do archaeologists know the Maya built their pyramids without the aid of metal tools?

Visual Summary

Use the visual summary below to help you review the main ideas of the chapter.

QUICK FACTS

The Maya
The Maya traded valuable goods like jade along trade routes that linked their great cities.

The Aztecs
The Aztec capital, Tenochtitlán, was a huge, bustling city. People came to its marketplace from all over the empire.

The Incas
The Incas are known for their organized empire, impressive stonework, and crafts in gold and silver.

Reviewing Vocabulary, Terms, and Places

For each statement below, write T if it is true and F if it is false. If the statement is false, replace the underlined term with one that would make the sentence a true statement.

1. The main crops of the Maya included **maize** and beans.

2. The **Quechua** came to the Americas to find land, gold, and converts to Catholicism.

3. **Palenque**, located on a swampy island, was the capital of the Aztec Empire.

4. Maya priests studied the sun, moon, and stars from stone **observatories**.

5. The official language of the Inca Empire was **Cuzco**.

6. The Aztecs built raised roads called **masonry** to cross from Tenochtitlán to the mainland.

7. **Tenochtitlán** was the Inca capital.

8. Many people in Mesoamerica died at the hands of the **conquistadors**.

Comprehension and Critical Thinking

SECTION 1 *(Pages 14–19)*

9. **a. Recall** Where did the Maya live, and when was their Classic Age?

   b. Analyze What was the connection between Maya religion and astronomy? How do you think this connection influenced Maya achievements?

   c. Elaborate Why did Maya cities trade with each other? Why did they fight?

SECTION 2 *(Pages 20–24)*

10. **a. Describe** What was Tenochtitlán like? Where was it located?

   b. Make Inferences Why do you think warriors had many privileges and were such respected members of Aztec society?

SECTION 2 *(continued)*

    c. Evaluate What factor do you think played the biggest role in the Aztecs' defeat? Defend your answer.

SECTION 3 *(Pages 25–29)*

11. a. Identify Name two Inca leaders and explain their roles in Inca history.

    b. Draw Conclusions What geographic and cultural problems did the Incas overcome to rule their empire?

    c. Elaborate Do you think most people in the Inca Empire appreciated or resented the *mita* system? Explain your answer.

Using the Internet

go.hrw.com KEYWORD: SGB7 CH1

12. Activity: Making Diagrams In this chapter you learned about the rise and fall of the Maya, Aztecs, and Incas. What you may not know is that the rise and fall of empires is a pattern that occurs again and again throughout history. Enter the activity keyword. Then create a diagram that shows the factors that cause empires to form and the factors that cause empires to fall apart.

FOCUS ON READING AND WRITING

13. Setting a Purpose Look back over the information about the Maya in Section 1. For each blue heading, write down the purpose of reading that text. Then describe how reading the text below each heading achieves your purpose.

14. Writing Your Article Now that you have collected information about the Americas, you are ready to write a newspaper article. Your purpose is to inform readers in Europe about these fascinating civilizations. Write a headline or title and a two- or three-sentence introduction to the civilizations. Then write a short paragraph about one aspect of each civilization. Choose the most interesting topic to discuss. For example, you might discuss their religion, their social structure, or their scientific achievements.

Social Studies Skills

Analyzing Information *In each numbered passage below, the first sentence expresses the main idea. One of the following sentences is irrelevant or nonessential to the main idea. Identify the irrelevant or nonessential sentence in each passage.*

15. Cacao beans had great value to the Maya. Cacao trees are evergreens. They were the source of chocolate, known as a favorite food of rulers and the gods. The Maya also used cacao beans as money.

16. Tenochtitlán was surrounded by water, but the water was undrinkable. As a result, the Aztecs built a stone aqueduct, or channel, to bring fresh water to the city. In many parts of the world, access to clean water is still a problem.

Map Activity ✴Interactive

17. Early History of the Americas On a separate sheet of paper, match the letters on the map with their correct labels.

Palenque   Tenochtitlán

Cuzco

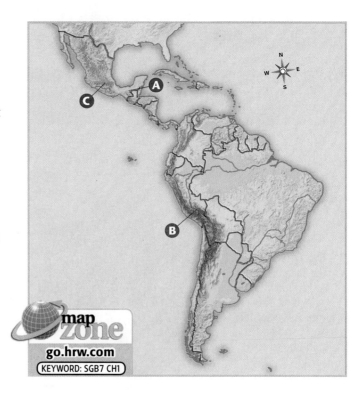

go.hrw.com KEYWORD: SGB7 CH1

Chapter Review

Geography's Impact
video series
Review the video to answer the closing question:
Do you think emigration from Mexico to the United States hurts or helps Mexico? Why?

Visual Summary

Use the visual summary below to help you review the main ideas of the chapter.

QUICK FACTS

The physical geography of Mexico includes a high region of plateaus and mountains.

The Spanish conquered the Aztecs and ruled Mexico for about 300 years until the Mexicans gained independence.

Greater Mexico City, one of Mexico's four culture regions, is the center of Mexico's government and economy.

Reviewing Vocabulary, Terms, and Places

Unscramble each group of letters below to spell a term that matches the given definition.

1. **pmreie**—a land with different territories and peoples under a single ruler

2. **tflinnaoi**—a rise in prices that occurs when currency loses its buying power

3. **mogs**—a mixture of smoke, chemicals, and fog

4. **snipluane**—a piece of land surrounded on three sides by water

5. **ztosemsi**—people of mixed European and Indian ancestry

6. **hacs rpoc**—a crop that farmers grow mainly to sell for a profit

7. **ssnmiosi**—church outposts

8. **dqamiuarsloa**—U.S.- and foreign-owned factories in Mexico

9. **ndhceiasa**—expanses of farm or ranch land

Comprehension and Critical Thinking

SECTION 1 *(Pages 38–41)*

10. **a. Define** What is the Mexican Plateau? What forms its edges?

    b. Contrast How does the climate of Mexico City differ from the climate in the south?

    c. Evaluate What do you think would be Mexico's most important resource if it did not have oil? Explain your answer.

SECTION 2 *(Pages 42–46)*

11. **a. Recall** What early civilization did the Spanish conquer when they came to Mexico?

    b. Analyze How did Spanish rule influence Mexico's culture?

    c. Evaluate Which war—the war for independence, the Mexican War, or the Mexican Revolution—do you think changed Mexico the most? Explain your answer.

SECTION 3 *(Pages 48–52)*

12. a. Describe What are Mexico's four culture regions? Describe a feature of each.

b. Analyze What regions do you think are the most popular with tourists? Explain your answer.

c. Evaluate What are two major drawbacks of slash-and-burn agriculture?

Using the Internet

go.hrw.com
KEYWORD: SGB7 CH2

13. Activity: Writing a Description Colorful textiles, paintings, and pottery are just some of the many crafts made throughout Mexico. Each region in Mexico has its own style of crafts and folk art. Enter the activity keyword to visit some of the different regions of Mexico and explore their arts and crafts. Pick a favorite object from each region. Learn about its use, its design, how it was made, and the people who made it. Then write a brief paragraph that describes each object and its unique characteristics.

Social Studies Skills

14. Taking Notes Look back at the information in Section 3 about Mexico's government and economy. Then use a chart like this one to take notes on the information in your book.

Recall	Notes

15. Predicting Now you can use your skills in predicting to think about events that might happen in the future. Reread the text in your book about Mexico's economy. Write three to four sentences about how you think the economy might change in the future.

16. Writing an "I Am" Poem Now it is time to write your poem. Title your poem "I am Mexico" and make it six lines long. Each line will tell one or more details about the country. For example, one line might state, "I have towering, snow-capped volcanoes." Make sure at least one line deals with physical geography, one line with history and culture, and one line with Mexico today. Your poem does not need to rhyme, but you should try to use vivid language.

Map Activity ★Interactive

17. Mexico On a separate sheet of paper, match the letters on the map with their correct labels.

Gulf of Mexico   Baja California

Río Bravo (Rio Grande)   Tijuana

Yucatán Peninsula   Mexico City

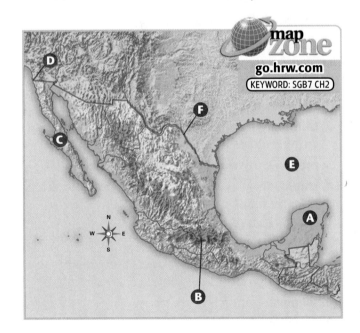

go.hrw.com
KEYWORD: SGB7 CH2

Standardized Test Practice

DIRECTIONS: Read questions 1 through 6 and write the letter of the best response. Then read question 7 and write your own well-constructed response.

1 **What physical features make up much of central Mexico?**

　A plateaus and mountains

　B peninsulas

　C beaches and lowlands

　D sinkholes

2 **What early culture in Mexico did the Spanish conquer?**

　A Olmec

　B Maya

　C Aztec

　D conquistador

3 **Which of the following was a way in which the Spanish affected Mexico during colonial times?**

　A granted land to the native people

　B set up missions and taught about Christianity

　C started the Mexican Revolution

　D gave away half of Mexico to the United States

4 **Where are Mexico's fastest-growing industrial centers?**

　A on the Gulf coast

　B in Mexico City

　C on the Yucatán Peninsula

　D along the U.S. border

5 **What factor helps classify Mexico as a developing country?**

　A high unemployment

　B few political parties

　C an economy based on oil and tourism

　D relatively high living standards

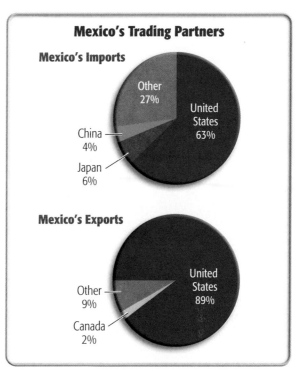

Mexico's Trading Partners

Mexico's Imports

Other 27%
United States 63%
China 4%
Japan 6%

Mexico's Exports

United States 89%
Other 9%
Canada 2%

Source: *World Almanac and Book of Facts,* 2005

6 **Based on the graphs above, which of the following statements is false?**

　A The United States is Mexico's biggest trading partner.

　B The United States imports 63% of its goods from Mexico.

　C 89% of Mexico's exports go to the United States.

　D Imports from Japan make up 6% of Mexico's total imports.

7 **Extended Response** Look at the graphs above and the information in Section 3. Then write a brief essay explaining how NAFTA has influenced Mexico.

CHAPTER 3

Central America and the Caribbean

Gulf of Mexico

MEXICO

Belmopan

BELIZE

GUATEMALA
Guatemala City

HONDURAS
Tegucigalpa

San Salvador

EL SALVADOR

NICARAGUA

PACIFIC OCEAN

Managua

COSTA RICA
San José

Usumacinta River

Motagua R.

Coco River

San Juan River

10°N

90°W

85°W

☼ National capital

0   100   200 Miles
0 100   200 Kilometers

Projection: Azimuthal Equal-Area

What You Will Learn...

In this chapter you will learn about the beautiful physical landscapes of Central America and the Caribbean. You will also study the history of the region along with the people who live there and the way they live today.

SECTION 1
Physical Geography **58**

SECTION 2
Central America **62**

SECTION 3
The Caribbean Islands **70**

FOCUS ON READING AND WRITING

Understanding Comparison-Contrast When you compare, you look for ways in which things are alike. When you contrast, you look for ways in which things are different. As you read the chapter, look for ways you can compare and contrast information. **See the lesson, Understanding Comparison-Contrast, on page 196.**

Creating a Travel Guide People use travel guides to learn more about places they want to visit. As you read about Central America and the Caribbean in this chapter, you will collect information about places tourists might visit. Then you will create your own travel guide for visitors to one of these vacation spots.

History The Spanish built forts like this one in Puerto Rico to defend their islands and protect the harbors from pirates.

One-Crop Economies

The economies of many Central American countries relied on only one crop— bananas. The U.S.-based United Fruit Company was the biggest banana exporter and the largest employer in the region for many years. The old photo below shows the company's hiring hall in Guatemala.

ANALYZING VISUALS Why do workers place cushions between bananas?

Central America Since Independence

The Spanish colonies of Central America declared independence from Spain in 1821, but much of the region remained joined together as the United Provinces of Central America. The countries of Costa Rica, Nicaragua, Honduras, El Salvador, and Guatemala separated from each other in 1838 to 1839. Panama remained part of Colombia until 1903. Belize did not gain independence from Britain until 1981.

For most countries in Central America, independence brought little change. The Spanish officials left, but wealthy landowners continued to run the countries and their economies. The plantation crops of bananas and coffee supported Central American economies.

In the early to mid-1900s, one landowner in particular, the U.S.-based United Fruit Company, controlled most of the banana production in Central America. To help its business, the company developed railroads and port facilities. This kind of development helped transportation and communications in the region.

Many people resented the role of foreign companies, however. They thought it was wrong that only a few people should own so much land while many people struggled to make a living. In the mid- to late 1900s, demands for reforms led to armed struggles in Guatemala, El Salvador, and Nicaragua. Only in recent years have these countries achieved peace.

READING CHECK **Evaluating** How did Spain influence the region's history?

Culture

Central America's colonial history has influenced its culture. The region's people, languages, religion, and festivals reflect both Spanish and native practices.

People and Languages

Most of the people in Central America are mestizos, or people of mixed European and Indian ancestry. Various Indian peoples descended from the ancient Maya live in places such as the Guatemalan Highlands.

People of African ancestry also make up a significant minority in this region. They live mostly along the Caribbean coast.

In some countries in Central America, many people still speak the native Indian languages. In places that were colonized by England, English is spoken. For example, it is the official language of Belize. In most countries, however, Spanish is the official language. The Spanish colonization of Central America left this lasting mark on the region.

Close-up

A Market in Guatemala

Villages in Guatemala and all over Central America hold weekly markets. On market day, people come from all around to buy and sell food and other items. The market is also an important gathering spot for the community. Scenes like this one are typical in the region.

The Catholic church is a major influence in most towns.

Patterns on women's clothing are unique to the village where the woman lives.

Religion, Festivals, and Food

Many Central Americans practice a religion brought to the region by Europeans. Most people are Roman Catholic because Spanish missionaries taught the Indians about Catholicism. However, Indian traditions have influenced Catholicism in return. Also, Protestant Christians are becoming a large minority in places such as Belize.

Religion has influenced celebrations in towns throughout the region. For example, to celebrate special saints' feast days, some people carry images of the saint in parades through the streets. Easter is a particularly important holiday. Some towns decorate whole streets with designs made of flowers and colorful sawdust.

During festivals, people eat **traditional** foods. Central America shares some of its traditional foods, like corn, with Mexico. The region is also known for tomatoes, hot peppers, and cacao (kuh-KOW), which is the source of chocolate.

ACADEMIC VOCABULARY

traditional
customary, time-honored

READING CHECK **Contrasting** How is Belize culturally different from the rest of the region?

Tourists contribute to the local economy when they buy crafts.

People often spend all day at the market and need to eat lunch there.

ANALYSIS SKILL **ANALYZING VISUALS**

How do the contributions of tourists and Guatemalans affect the local economy differently?

Central America Today

The countries of Central America share similar histories and cultures. However, they all face their own economic and political challenges today. In 2005 Costa Rica, the Dominican Republic, El Salvador, Guatemala, Honduras, and Nicaragua signed the Central American Free Trade Agreement (CAFTA) with the United States. The goal of this agreement is to help increase trade among the countries.

Guatemala

Guatemala is the most populous country in Central America. More than 12 million people live there. Although most of the people in Guatemala are mestizos, nearly half of them are Central American Indians. Many speak Maya languages.

Most people in Guatemala live in small villages in the highlands. Fighting between rebels and government forces there killed some 200,000 people between 1960 and 1996. Guatemalans are still recovering from this conflict.

Coffee, which grows well in the cool highlands, is Guatemala's most important crop. The country also is a major producer of cardamom, a spice used in Asian foods.

Belize

Belize has the smallest population in Central America. The country does not have much land for agriculture, either. But **ecotourism**—the practice of using an area's natural environment to attract tourists—has become popular lately. Tourists come to see the country's coral reefs, Maya ruins, and coastal resorts.

Honduras

Honduras is a mountainous country. Most people live in mountain valleys and along the northern coast. The rugged land makes transportation difficult and provides little land where crops can grow. However, citrus fruits and bananas are important exports.

El Salvador

In El Salvador, a few rich families own much of the best land while most people live in poverty. These conditions were a reason behind a long civil war in the 1980s. A **civil war** is a conflict between two or more groups within a country. The war killed many people and hurt the economy.

El Salvador's people have been working to rebuild their country since the end of the war in 1992. One advantage they have in this rebuilding effort is the country's fertile soil. People are able to grow and export crops such as coffee and sugarcane.

Nicaragua

Nicaragua has also been rebuilding since the end of a civil war. In 1979, a group called the Sandinistas overthrew a dictator.

Many Nicaraguans supported the Sandinistas, but rebel forces aided by the United States fought the Sandinistas for power. The civil war ended in 1990 when elections ended the rule of the Sandinistas. Nicaragua is now a democracy.

Costa Rica

Unlike most other Central American countries, Costa Rica has a history of peace. It also has a stable, democratic government. The country does not even have an army. Peace has helped Costa Rica make progress in reducing poverty.

Agricultural products like coffee and bananas are important to Costa Rica's economy. Also, many tourists visit Costa Rica's rich tropical rain forests.

Panama

Panama is the narrowest, southernmost country of Central America. Most people live in areas near the **Panama Canal**. Canal fees and local industries make the canal area the country's most prosperous region.

The Panama Canal provides a link between the Pacific Ocean, the Caribbean Sea, and the Atlantic Ocean. The United States finished building the canal in 1914. For years the Panama canal played an important role in the economy and politics of the region. The United States controlled the canal until 1999. Then, as agreed to in a treaty, Panama finally gained full control of the canal.

READING CHECK **Drawing Inferences** Why do you think Panama might want control of the canal?

FOCUS ON READING
What word in the paragraphs on Costa Rica signals contrast?

SUMMARY AND PREVIEW Native peoples, European colonizers, and the United States have influenced Central America's history and culture. Today most countries are developing stable governments. Their economies rely on tourism and agriculture. In the next section you will learn about the main influences on the Caribbean islands and life there today.

go.hrw.com
Online Quiz
KEYWORD: SGB7 HP3

Section 2 Assessment

Reviewing Ideas, Terms, and Places

1. **a. Recall** What parts of Central America did the British claim?
   b. Analyze How did independence affect most Central American countries?
   c. Elaborate What benefits and drawbacks might there be to the United Fruit Company's owning so much land?
2. **a. Identify** What language do most people in Central America speak?
   b. Explain How have native cultures influenced cultural practices in the region today?
3. **a. Define** What is a **civil war,** and where in Central America has a civil war been fought?
   b. Explain Why might some people practice **ecotourism**?
   c. Elaborate Why is the **Panama Canal** important to Panama? Why is it important to other countries?

Critical Thinking

4. **Summarizing** Copy the graphic organizer below. Using your notes, write at least one important fact about each Central American country today.

Guatemala	
Belize	
Honduras	
El Salvador	
Nicaragua	
Costa Rica	
Panama	

FOCUS ON WRITING

5. **Describing Central America** Note details about the history, culture, and life today of people in Central America. Which details will appeal to people who are thinking of visiting the region?

The Panama Canal

The Panama Canal links the Atlantic and Pacific oceans. Built in the early 1900s, workers on the canal faced tropical diseases and the dangers of blasting through solid rock. The result of their efforts was an amazing feat of engineering. Today some 13,000 to 14,000 ships pass through the canal each year.

Routes Before and After the Panama Canal

map zone

San Francisco
New York
NORTH AMERICA
ATLANTIC OCEAN

5,200 MILES (8,368 KM)

Panama Canal

13,000 MILES (20,921 KM)

PACIFIC OCEAN

SOUTH AMERICA

— Route around South America

— Route through the Panama Canal

0   750   1,500 Miles

0   750   1,500 Kilometers

Projection: Azimuthal Equal-Area

N
W   E
S

The Panama Canal shortens a trip from the east coast of the United States to the west coast by about 8,000 miles (15,000 km).

Caribbean Music

The Caribbean islands have produced many unique styles of music. For example, Jamaica is famous as the birthplace of reggae. Merengue is the national music and dance of the Dominican Republic. Trinidad and Tobago is the home of steel-drum and calypso music.

Here, a band in the Grenadines performs on steel drums. Steel-drum bands can include as few as 4 or as many as 100 musicians. The instruments are actually metal barrels like the kind used for shipping oil. The end of each drum is hammered into a curved shape with multiple grooves and bumps. Hitting different-sized bumps results in different notes.

Drawing Inferences What role might trade have played in the development of steel-drum music?

The Caribbean Islands Today

Many Caribbean islands share a similar history and culture. However, today the islands' different economies, governments, and cultural landscapes encourage many different ways of life in the Caribbean.

Puerto Rico

Puerto Rico was a Spanish colony. Today it is a U.S. commonwealth. A **commonwealth** is a self-governing territory associated with another country. Although Puerto Ricans are U.S. citizens, they have no voting representation in the U.S. Congress. Puerto Ricans debate whether their island should remain a commonwealth. Some want it to become an American state. Others want it to become an independent country.

The link to the United States has been a big influence on Puerto Rico. U.S. aid and investment have helped make Puerto Rico's economy more developed than that of other Caribbean islands. However, wages remain lower and unemployment is still higher in Puerto Rico than in the United States. Many Puerto Ricans have moved to the United States to get better-paying jobs than they can find at home.

Haiti

Haiti occupies the mountainous western third of the island of Hispaniola. Port-au-Prince (pohr-toh-PRINS) is the capital and center of the country's limited industry. Agricultural products such as coffee and sugarcane are the country's main exports. Most Haitians farm small plots.

Haiti is the poorest country in the Americas. Its people have suffered under a string of corrupt governments during the last two centuries. Violence, political unrest, and poverty have created many political refugees. A **refugee** is someone who flees to another country, usually for political or economic reasons. Many Haitian refugees have come to the United States. Also, the United States has sent troops to Haiti on several occasions to help keep the peace.

Dominican Republic

The Dominican Republic occupies the eastern part of Hispaniola. The capital is Santo Domingo. Santo Domingo was the first permanent European settlement in the Western Hemisphere.

The Dominican Republic is not a rich country. However, its economy, health care, education, and housing are more developed than Haiti's. Agriculture is the basis of the economy in the Dominican Republic. The country's tourism industry has also grown in recent years. Beach resorts along the coast are popular with many tourists from Central and South America as well as from the United States.

Cuba

Cuba is the largest and most populous country in the Caribbean. It is located just 92 miles (148 km) south of Florida. **Havana**, the capital, is the country's largest and most important city.

Cuba has been run by a Communist government since Fidel Castro came to power in 1959. At that time, the government took over banks, large sugarcane plantations, and other businesses. Many of these businesses were owned by U.S. companies. Because of the takeovers, the U.S. government banned trade with Cuba and restricted travel there by U.S. citizens.

Today the government still controls the economy. Most of Cuba's farms are organized as cooperatives or government-owned plantations. A **cooperative** is an organization owned by its members and operated for their mutual benefit.

Besides controlling the economy, Cuba's government also controls all the newspapers, television, and radio stations. While many Cubans support these policies, others oppose them. Some people who oppose the government have become refugees in the United States. Many Cuban refugees have become U.S. citizens.

Cubans Divided

Government-sponsored rallies are a part of Cuban life. Meanwhile, some Cubans try to flee their country on tiny rafts.

ANALYZING VISUALS How can you tell that the people in the raft are trying to flee Cuba?

Other Islands

The rest of the Caribbean islands are small countries. Jamaica is the largest of the remaining Caribbean countries. The smallest country is Saint Kitts and Nevis. It is not even one-tenth the size of Rhode Island, the smallest U.S. state!

A number of Caribbean islands are not independent countries but territories of other countries. These territories include the U.S. and British Virgin Islands. The Netherlands and France also still have some Caribbean territories.

Some of these islands have enough land to grow some coffee, sugarcane, or spices. However, most islands' economies are based on tourism. Hundreds of people on the islands work in restaurants and hotels visited by tourists. While tourism has provided jobs and helped economies, not all of its effects have been positive. For example, new construction sometimes harms the same natural environment tourists come to the islands to enjoy.

READING CHECK Contrasting How are the governments of Puerto Rico and Cuba different?

Caribbean Tourism

Tourism has helped Caribbean economies. New developments, like this hotel in Saint Martin, have also changed many islands' landscapes.

SUMMARY AND PREVIEW The Caribbean islands were colonized by European countries, which influenced the culture of the islands. Today the islands have different types of governments but similar economies. Next, you will read about countries in South America that are also located near the Caribbean Sea.

Section 3 Assessment

go.hrw.com
Online Quiz
KEYWORD: SGB7 HP3

Reviewing Ideas, Terms, and Places

1. **a. Describe** What crop was the basis of the colonial economy on the Caribbean islands?
   b. Make Inferences Why do you think most smaller Caribbean countries were able to gain independence peacefully?
2. **a. Define** What is a **dialect**?
   b. Explain In what ways have African influences shaped Caribbean culture?
3. **a. Recall** What is a **refugee**, and from what Caribbean countries have refugees come?
   b. Make Inferences Why do you think many Cubans support their government's policies?
   c. Evaluate What would be the benefits and drawbacks for Puerto Rico if it became a U.S. state?

Critical Thinking

4. **Summarizing** Look over your notes. Then use a diagram like this one to note specific influences on the region and where they came from in each circle. You may add more circles if you need to.

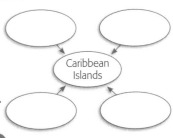

Caribbean Islands

FOCUS ON WRITING

5. **Telling about the Caribbean Islands** These islands have a fascinating history and a rich culture. Take notes about them for your travel guide.

Interpreting a Climate Graph

Learn

A climate graph is a visual representation of the climate in a certain region. The graph shows the average precipitation and average temperature for each month of the year.

Use the following tips to help you interpret a climate graph:

- The months of the year are labeled across the bottom of the graph.
- The measurements for monthly average temperatures are found on the left side of the graph.
- The measurements for monthly average precipitation are found on the right side of the graph.

Practice

Use the climate graph here to answer the following questions.

❶ What four months get the highest amount of precipitation?

❷ What months get fewer than two inches of precipitation?

❸ What is the average temperature in February?

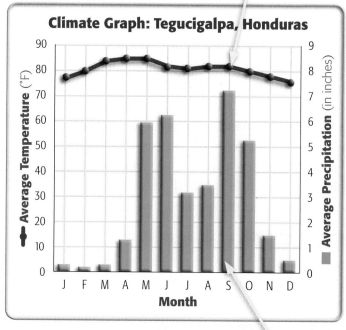

A line shows the average temperature each month.

Climate Graph: Tegucigalpa, Honduras

Source: The Weather Channel Interactive, Inc.

Bars show the average precipitation each month.

Apply

Using the Internet, an almanac, or a newspaper, look up the monthly average temperatures and precipitation for your home town. Then make your own climate graph using that information.

Caribbean South America: Political

National capital
★ Other capitals
• Other cities

0   100   200 Miles
0   100   200 Kilometers
Projection: Azimuthal Equal-Area

ATLANTIC OCEAN

TRINIDAD AND TOBAGO

Valencia
Caracas

Orinoco River

VENEZUELA

Orinoco River

Georgetown

GUYANA

Paramaribo

Cayenne

SURINAME

FRENCH GUIANA
(FRANCE)

Rio Negro

BRAZIL

Amazon River

N
W   E
S

map zone

Geography Skills

Place Most of Caribbean South America is located on the Caribbean Sea.

1. Identify What is the capital of Venezuela?

2. Contrast How is Colombia's location different from Venezuela's location?

go.hrw.com KEYWORD: SGB7 CH4

Culture Cowboys called llaneros work on the plains of Venezuela.

HOLT

Geography's Impact

video series
Watch the video to learn about the impact of the Orinoco River.

Geography Dense rain forest covers much of Suriname.

Physical Geography

What You Will Learn...

Main Ideas

1. Caribbean South America has a wide variety of physical features and wildlife.
2. The region's location and elevation both affect its climate and vegetation.
3. Caribbean South America is rich in resources, such as farmland, oil, timber, and rivers for hydroelectric power.

The Big Idea

Caribbean South America is a region with diverse physical features, wildlife, climates, and resources.

Key Terms and Places

Andes, *p. 82*
cordillera, *p. 82*
Guiana Highlands, *p. 83*
Llanos, *p. 83*
Orinoco River, *p. 84*

TAKING NOTES As you read, take notes on the physical features, wildlife, climates, and resources of Caribbean South America. Use this chart to organize your notes.

Physical Features	Wildlife	Climate	Resources

If YOU lived there...

You live in Caracas, Venezuela, but this is your first visit to the great Orinoco River. You've heard about the fierce creatures that live in the river, so you think your guide is kidding when he says he's going to catch a piranha. You're expecting a monster and are surprised when he pulls up a small orange fish. It has many sharp teeth, but it's only seven inches long!

What other animals might you see in the region?

BUILDING BACKGROUND The narrow Isthmus of Panama joins the continent of South America at its northwestern corner, the country of Colombia. Like the countries of Central America, the five countries in Caribbean South America border the Caribbean Sea. They all vary in landscape, climate, and culture and have large rivers and rugged mountains.

Physical Features and Wildlife

If you were traveling through the region of Caribbean South America, you might see the world's highest waterfall, South America's largest lake, and even the world's largest rodent! As you can see on the map, the geography of this region includes rugged mountains, highlands, and plains drained by huge river systems.

Mountains and Highlands

The highest point in the region is in Colombia, a country larger than California and Texas combined. On the western side of Colombia the **Andes** (AN-deez) reach 18,000 feet (5,490 m). The Andes form a **cordillera** (kawr-duhl-YER-uh), a mountain system made up of roughly parallel ranges. Some of the Andes' snowcapped peaks are active volcanoes. Eruptions and earthquakes shake these mountains frequently.

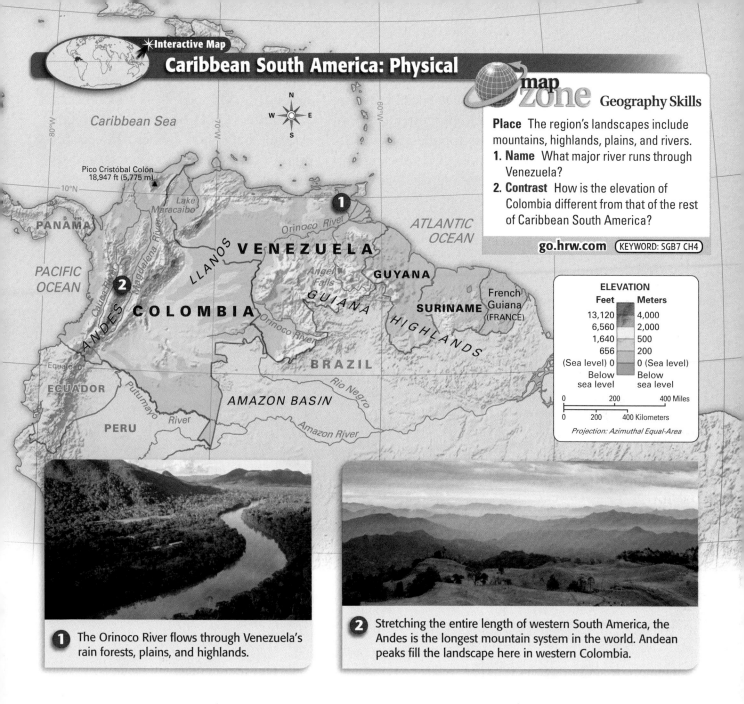

Caribbean South America: Physical

Interactive Map

map zone Geography Skills

Place The region's landscapes include mountains, highlands, plains, and rivers.
1. **Name** What major river runs through Venezuela?
2. **Contrast** How is the elevation of Colombia different from that of the rest of Caribbean South America?

go.hrw.com KEYWORD: SGB7 CH4

ELEVATION

Feet		Meters
13,120		4,000
6,560		2,000
1,640		500
656		200
(Sea level) 0		0 (Sea level)
Below sea level		Below sea level

0   200   400 Miles
0   200   400 Kilometers
Projection: Azimuthal Equal-Area

Caribbean Sea

Pico Cristóbal Colón 18,947 ft (5,775 m)

PANAMA

PACIFIC OCEAN

Lake Maracaibo

Magdalena River

Cauca River

ANDES

LLANOS

COLOMBIA

Orinoco River

VENEZUELA

Angel Falls

GUIANA

Orinoco River

GUYANA

SURINAME

French Guiana (FRANCE)

ATLANTIC OCEAN

HIGHLANDS

BRAZIL

Rio Negro

AMAZON BASIN

Amazon River

ECUADOR

Putumayo River

PERU

1 The Orinoco River flows through Venezuela's rain forests, plains, and highlands.

2 Stretching the entire length of western South America, the Andes is the longest mountain system in the world. Andean peaks fill the landscape here in western Colombia.

Lying on the Caribbean coast, Venezuela is located in the middle of the other countries in the region. Venezuela's highest elevation is in the **Guiana Highlands**, which stretch into Guyana and Suriname. For millions of years, wind and rain have eroded these highlands' plateaus. However, some of the steep-sided plateaus are capped by sandstone layers that have resisted erosion. These unusual flat-topped formations are sometimes called *tepuís* (tay-PWEEZ). The *tepuís* create a dramatic landscape as they rise about 3,000 to 6,000 feet (900 to 1,800 m) above the surrounding plains.

Plains, Rivers, and Wildlife

As you look at the map above, notice how much the elevation drops between the highlands and the Andes. This region of plains is known as the **Llanos** (YAH-nohs). The Llanos is mostly grassland with few trees. At a low elevation and not much vegetation, these plains flood easily.

FOCUS ON
READING
What details in
this paragraph
support this
section's first
main idea?

Flowing for about 1,600 miles (2,575 km), the **Orinoco** (OHR-ee-NOH-koh) **River** is the region's longest river. Snaking its way through Venezuela to the Atlantic Ocean, the Orinoco and its tributaries drain the plains and highlands. Two other important rivers, the Cauca and the Magdalena, drain the Andean region.

Caribbean South America is home to some remarkable wildlife. For example, hundreds of bird species, meat-eating fish called piranhas, and crocodiles live in or around the Orinoco River. Colombia has one of the world's highest concentrations of plant and animal species. The country's wildlife includes jaguars, ocelots, and several species of monkeys.

READING CHECK **Summarizing** What are the region's major physical features?

Venezuela's Canaima National Park

Covering almost 3 million acres of eastern Venezuela, Canaima National Park is one of the largest national parks in the world.

ANALYZING VISUALS What do you think attracts millions of people from around the world to visit Canaima National Park?

Dropping more than 3,200 feet (975 m), Angel Falls is the world's highest waterfall.

A rocky *tepuí* rises from the park's flat plains. Hundreds of these flat-topped mountains are scattered throughout the park.

The red-billed toucan is among the almost 500 species of birds that live in the park.

Climate and Vegetation

Caribbean South America's location near the equator means that most of the region has warm temperatures year-round. However, temperatures do vary with elevation. For example, in the Andes, as you go up in elevation, the temperature can drop rapidly—about four degrees Fahrenheit every 1,000 feet (305 m).

In contrast, the vast, flat landscape of the Llanos region has a tropical savanna climate. Here, both the wet and dry seasons provide favorable conditions for grasslands to grow.

Rain forests, another type of landscape, thrive in the humid tropical climate of southern Colombia. This area is a part of the Amazon Basin. Here, rain falls throughout the year, watering the forest's huge trees. These trees form a canopy where the vegetation is so dense that sunlight barely shines through to the jungle floor.

READING CHECK Analyzing What causes the region's temperatures to vary?

Resources

Good soil and moderate climates help make most of Caribbean South America a rich agricultural region. Major crops include rice, coffee, bananas, and sugarcane.

In addition, the region has other valuable resources, such as oil, iron ore, and coal. Both Venezuela and Colombia have large oil-rich areas. Forests throughout the region provide timber. While the seas provide plentiful fish and shrimp, the region's major rivers are used to generate hydroelectric power.

READING CHECK Summarizing How do geographic factors affect economic activities in Caribbean South America?

SUMMARY AND PREVIEW In this section you learned that the physical geography of Caribbean South America includes mountains, highlands, plains, and rivers. The region's location near the equator and its elevation affect the region's climate. In the next section you will learn about Colombia's history, people, and economy. You will also learn about the challenges Colombia is facing today, which include a civil war.

go.hrw.com
Online Quiz
KEYWORD: SGB7 HP4

Section 1 Assessment

Reviewing Ideas, Terms, and Places

1. **a. Recall** Where are the **Andes** located?
   b. Explain How are the rock formations called *tepuís* unusual?
   c. Elaborate Why do the **Llanos** in Colombia and Venezuela flood easily?
2. **a. Describe** In the Andes, how does the temperature change with elevation?
   b. Make Inferences How does the region's location near the equator affect its climate?
3. **a. Identify** What is a major resource in both Venezuela and Colombia?
   b. Explain Which resource provides hydroelectric power?

Critical Thinking

4. **Categorizing** Use your notes to identify four types of physical features in the region. Write each type in one of the small circles of the diagram.

Physical Features

FOCUS ON WRITING

5. **Describing Physical Geography** Take notes about the physical features, wildlife, climate, vegetation, and resources of the region. After you decide which country you are living in, collect more details about it.

Colombia

If YOU lived there...

You live in the beautiful colonial city of Cartagena, on the coast of the Caribbean. Your family runs a small restaurant there. You're used to the city's wide beaches and old colonial buildings with wooden balconies that overhang the street. Now you are on your way to visit your cousins. They live on a cattle ranch on the inland plains region called the Llanos.

How do you think life on the ranch is different from yours?

BUILDING BACKGROUND Like most of the countries of Central and South America, Colombia was once a colony of Spain. Colombians gained their independence from Spain in 1819. The new country was then named after the explorer Christopher Columbus.

Colombia's History

Giant mounds of earth, mysterious statues, and tombs—these are the marks of the people who lived in Colombia more than 1,500 years ago. Colombia's history begins with these people. It also includes conquest by Spain and, later, independence.

The Chibcha

Have you heard of the legend of El Dorado (el duh-RAH-doh), or the Golden One? That legend about

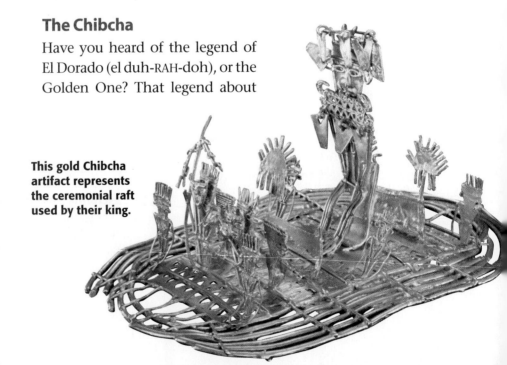

This gold Chibcha artifact represents the ceremonial raft used by their king.

a land rich in gold was inspired by the Chibcha culture in Colombia. The Chibcha covered their new rulers in gold dust. Then they took each ruler to a lake to wash the gold off. As the new ruler washed, the Chibcha threw gold and emerald objects into the water. A well-developed civilization, they practiced pottery making, weaving, and metalworking. Their gold objects were among the finest in ancient America.

Spanish Conquest

In about 1500 Spanish explorers arrived on the Caribbean coast of South America. The Spaniards wanted to expand Spain's new empire. In doing so, the Spanish conquered the Chibcha and seized much of their treasure. Soon after claiming land for themselves, the Spaniards founded a colony and cities along the Caribbean coast.

One colonial city, **Cartagena**, was a major naval base and commercial port in the Spanish empire. By the 1600s Spaniards and their descendants had set up large estates in Colombia. Spanish estate owners forced South American Indians and enslaved Africans to work the land.

Independence

In the late 1700s people in Central and South America began struggling for independence from Spain. After independence was achieved, the republic of Gran Colombia was created. It included Colombia, Ecuador, Panama, and Venezuela. In 1830 the republic dissolved, and New Granada, which included Colombia and Panama, was created.

After independence, two different groups of Colombians debated over how Colombia should be run. One group wanted the Roman Catholic Church to participate in government and education. On the other hand, another group did not want the church involved in their lives.

Outbreaks of violence throughout the 1800s and 1900s killed thousands. Part of the problem had to do with the country's rugged geography, which isolated people in one region from those in another region. As a result, they developed separate economies and identities. Uniting these different groups into one country was hard.

READING CHECK **Drawing Conclusions** How did Spanish conquest shape Colombia's history and culture?

Different regions of Colombia are home to diverse ethnic groups.

ANALYZING VISUALS What are some of the goods sold in this market?

Colombians of African descent unload their goods at a local market near the Pacific coast.

Colombia Today

Colombia is Caribbean South America's most populous country. The national capital is **Bogotá**, a city located high in the eastern Andes. Although Colombia is rich in culture and resources, 40 years of civil war have been destructive to the country's economy.

People and Culture

Most Colombians live in the fertile valleys and river basins among the mountain ranges, where the climate is moderate and good for farming. Rivers, such as the Cauca and the Magdalena, flow down from the Andes to the Caribbean Sea. These rivers provide water and help connect settlements located between the mountains and the coast. Other Colombians live on cattle ranches scattered throughout the Llanos. Few people live in the tropical rainforest regions in the south.

Because the physical geography of Colombia isolates some regions of the country, the people of Colombia are often known by the region where they live. For example, those who live along the Caribbean coast are known for songs and dances influenced by African traditions.

FOCUS ON READING
In the first paragraph under Economy, find at least three details to support the idea stated in the first sentence.

Colombian culture is an interesting mix of influences:

- Music: traditional African songs and dances on the Caribbean coast and South American Indian music in remote areas of the Andes
- Sports: soccer, as well as a traditional Chibcha ring-toss game called *tejo*
- Religion: primarily Roman Catholicism
- Official language: Spanish
- Ethnic groups: 58 percent mestizo; also Spanish, African, and Indian descent

Economy

Colombia's economy relies on several valuable resources. Rich soil, steep slopes, and tall shade trees produce world-famous Colombian coffee. Other major export crops include bananas, sugarcane, and cotton. Many farms in Colombia produce flowers that are exported around the world. In fact, 80 percent of the country's flowers are shipped to the United States.

Colombia's economy depends on the country's valuable natural resources. Recently oil has become Colombia's major export. Other natural resources include iron ore, gold, and coal. Most of the world's emeralds also come from Colombia.

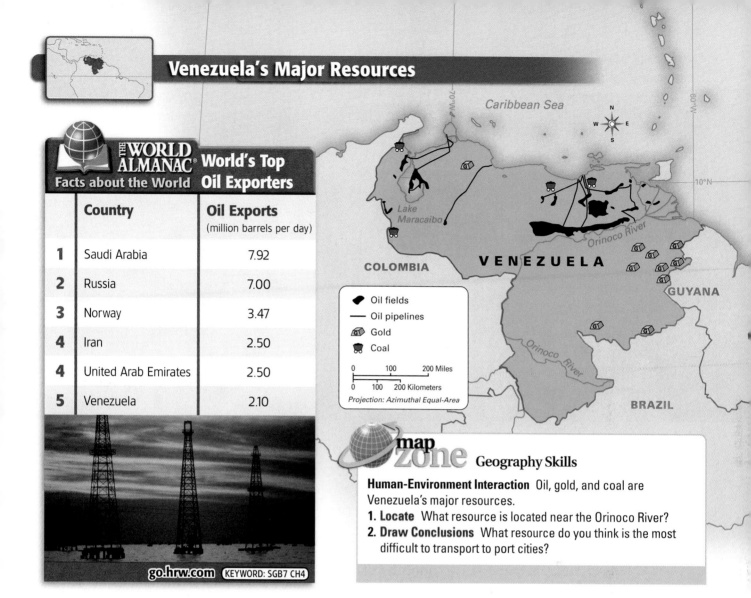

THE WORLD ALMANAC®
Facts about the World
World's Top Oil Exporters

	Country	Oil Exports (million barrels per day)
1	Saudi Arabia	7.92
2	Russia	7.00
3	Norway	3.47
4	Iran	2.50
4	United Arab Emirates	2.50
5	Venezuela	2.10

go.hrw.com KEYWORD: SGB7 CH4

Legend:
- Oil fields
- Oil pipelines
- Gold
- Coal

0   100   200 Miles
0   100   200 Kilometers
Projection: Azimuthal Equal-Area

map zone Geography Skills

Human-Environment Interaction Oil, gold, and coal are Venezuela's major resources.
1. **Locate** What resource is located near the Orinoco River?
2. **Draw Conclusions** What resource do you think is the most difficult to transport to port cities?

Exporting Countries (OPEC). The member countries in this organization attempt to control world oil production and keep oil prices from falling too low.

The Guiana Highlands in the southeast are rich in other minerals, such as iron ore for making steel. Gold is also mined in remote areas of the highlands. Dams on tributaries of the Orinoco River produce hydroelectricity.

Caracas (kah-RAH-kahs) is Venezuela's capital and the economic and cultural center of the country. It is a large city with a modern subway system, busy expressways, and tall office buildings. Still, neither Caracas nor Venezuela has escaped poverty.

Caracas is encircled by slums, and many Venezuelans living in the rural areas of the country are also poor.

Government

After years of suffering under military dictatorships, the people of Venezuela elected their first president in 1959. Since then, Venezuela's government has dealt with economic turmoil and political protests.

In 2002 Venezuela's president, Hugo Chavez, started to distribute the country's oil income equally among all Venezuelans. Before Chavez's presidency, only a small percentage of wealthy Venezuelans benefited from the country's oil income.

Caracas, Venezuela

With a population of more than 4 million, Venezuela's capital city, Caracas, is the country's financial and cultural center.

ANALYZING VISUALS Why do you think Caracas is located in this mountain valley?

Millions of Venezuelans went on strike to protest the president's actions as well as a failing economy. A **strike** is a group of workers stopping work until their demands are met. Some of Venezuela's workers went on strike for about two months. They wanted President Chavez to resign, but he refused. As a result of the strike, the Venezuelan economy suffered and the country's oil exports fell dramatically.

Many Venezuelans opposed to President Chavez called for a **referendum**, or recall vote. In 2004 Venezuelans voted for whether Chavez would remain in office or not. About 58 percent of Venezuelans voted for Chavez. Many of these voters believed he should use the country's oil wealth to help them. In his second term in office, Chavez adopted new **policies** to help end poverty, illiteracy, and hunger.

ACADEMIC VOCABULARY
policy rule, course of action

READING CHECK Identifying Cause and Effect What effect did the workers' strike have on Venezuela's economy?

The Guianas

The countries of Guyana, Suriname, and French Guiana are together known as the Guianas (gee-AH-nuhz). Dense tropical rain forests cover much of this region, which lies east of Venezuela.

Guyana

Guyana (gy-AH-nuh) comes from a South American Indian word that means "land of waters." About one-third of the country's population lives in Georgetown, the capital. Nearly all of Guyana's agricultural lands are located on the flat, fertile plains along the coast. Guyana's most important agricultural products are rice and sugar.

Guyana's population is diverse. About half of its people are descended from people who migrated to Guyana from India. These immigrants came to Guyana to work on the country's sugar plantations. Most Guyanese today farm small plots of land or run small businesses. About one-third of the population is descended from former African slaves. These people operate large businesses and hold most of the government positions.

Suriname

The resources and economy of Suriname (soohr-uh-NAHM) are similar to those of Guyana. Like Guyana, Suriname has a diverse population. The country's population includes South Asians, Africans, Chinese, Indonesians, and Creoles—people of mixed heritage. The capital, Paramaribo (pah-rah-MAH-ree-boh), is home to nearly half of the country's people.

French Guiana

French Guiana (gee-A-nuh) is a territory of France and sends representatives to the government in Paris. French Guiana's roughly 200,000 people live mostly in coastal areas. About two-thirds of the people are of African descent. Other groups include Europeans, Asians, and South American Indians. The country depends heavily on imports for its food and energy.

READING CHECK Contrasting How is French Guiana different from the rest of the Guianas?

Creole women carry gifts to a party in downtown Paramaribo. About 30 percent of Suriname's population is Creole.

SUMMARY AND PREVIEW In this section, you learned that Venezuela's history was largely shaped by Spanish settlement. Today Venezuela's economy is based on oil. You also learned that to the east, the Guianas are home to a diverse population. In the next chapter, you will learn about the history and people of Atlantic South America.

Section 3 Assessment

go.hrw.com
Online Quiz
KEYWORD: SGB7 HP4

Reviewing Ideas, Terms, and Places

1. **a. Recall** What did Spanish settlers hope to find in Venezuela?
   b. Explain Who led Venezuela's revolt against Spain?
2. **a. Describe** What does the landscape of **Caracas** include?
   b. Explain How is oil important to Venezuela's economy?
   c. Elaborate Why did some Venezuelans go on **strike**?
3. **a. Describe** What are Guyana's agricultural lands and products like?
   b. Contrast How is population of the Guianas different from that of Colombia and Venezuela?

Critical Thinking

4. **Identifying Cause and Effect** Using your notes on Venezuela's natural resources and this diagram, list the effects of oil production on Venezuela's people, economy, and government.

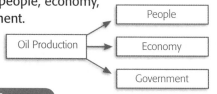

People

Oil Production → Economy

Government

FOCUS ON WRITING

5. **Writing about Venezuela and the Guianas** Collect details about Venezuela and the Guianas for your letter. What is interesting about these cultures?

Chart and Graph

Critical Thinking

Geography

Study

Using Latitude and Longitude

Learn

The pattern of imaginary lines that circle the globe in east-west and north-south directions is called a grid. Geographers measure the distances between the lines of the grid in degrees.

Look at the diagram to the right. As you can see, lines that run east to west are lines of latitude. These lines measure distance north and south of the equator. Lines that run north to south are lines of longitude. These lines measure distance east and west of the prime meridian.

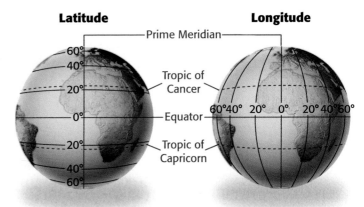

Latitude   Longitude

Prime Meridian
60°
40°
20°
0°
20°
40°
60°

Tropic of Cancer
Equator
Tropic of Capricorn

60° 40° 20° 0° 20° 40° 60°

Practice

Look at the world map to the right. Use these guidelines to read latitude and longitude.

❶ Pick a city on the map.

❷ To find the latitude of the city you picked, first look at the equator. From there, look at the city's location. Then find the closest line of latitude to see how many degrees the city is north or south of the equator.

❸ To find the longitude of the city, first look at the prime meridian. Then find the closest line of longitude to see how many degrees the city is east or west of the prime meridian.

World: Political

Apply

Using an atlas, find a map of the United States and a map of the world. On the map of the United States, find the line of latitude that is located near your hometown. Then look at a world map and follow this line of latitude across the world. Which countries share the same latitude as your hometown?

Chapter Review

Geography's Impact
video series
Review the video to answer the closing question:
What are some advantages and disadvantages of industries along the Orinoco River?

Visual Summary

Use the visual summary below to help you review the main ideas of the chapter.

QUICK FACTS

Caribbean South America's physical features include rivers, plains, mountains, and the world's highest waterfall.

A country rich in history and culture, Colombia is enduring a civil war today.

Venezuela is an oil-rich nation that has a population of mostly mixed Indian and European descent.

Reviewing Vocabulary, Terms, and Places

For each statement below, write T if it is true and F if it is false.

1. The Andes is a river system.

2. The Orinoco River flows 1,300 miles (2,100 km) through Venezuela.

3. Caribbean South America's location near the equator means that the region is very cold.

4. The Chibcha were the first people to settle Colombia.

5. Colombian culture includes traditional African songs and dances.

6. Most Venezuelans are of mixed Indian and European descent.

7. Venezuela gained its independence from France.

8. Venezuela's economy depends on oil production.

Comprehension and Critical Thinking

SECTION 1 *(Pages 82–85)*

9. a. Recall What is the region's longest river?

   b. Analyze How does the temperature vary in the Andes?

   c. Evaluate Why do you think it would be hard to live in the rain forest of Colombia?

SECTION 2 *(Pages 86–89)*

10. a. Describe How did the Chibcha treat their ruler?

   b. Draw Conclusions What created a problem for all Colombians after independence?

   c. Elaborate Why do most Colombians live in fertile valleys and river basins?

SECTION 3 *(Pages 90–95)*

11. a. Define What is a strike?

SECTION 3 *(continued)*

b. Draw Conclusions Why did people from India immigrate to Guyana?

c. Predict Do you think Venezuela's government will continue to use oil wealth to help the country's people? Explain your answer.

Using the Internet

go.hrw.com
KEYWORD: SGB7 CH4

12. Activity: Writing a Journal Entry Ride with the llaneros! Pack your bags and prepare for a trek through the South American countryside. Explore the vast grasslands, visit villages, and learn about the life and work of the cowboys, or llaneros, of the Venezuelan plains. Enter the activity keyword. Then research and take notes about your adventure. Use the interactive template to write your journal entry. Describe what you have learned about the people and places you visited.

Social Studies Skills

13. Using Latitude and Longitude Look at the physical map in Section 1. Find the lines of latitude and longitude. What line of latitude, shown on the map, runs through both Venezuela and Colombia? Which country in Caribbean South America is partly located on the equator?

14. Identifying Supporting Details Look back over Section 2 on Colombia. Then make a list of details you find to support the section's main ideas. Make sure you include details about the Spanish conquest, independence, culture, resources, and civil war.

15. Writing a Letter By now you have information about the region and the country you have chosen to live in. Begin your letter to your pen pal by describing the most interesting physical and cultural features of the whole region. Then write a second paragraph telling your pen pal about the special physical and cultural features of the country you've chosen to live in. Try to keep your pen pal interested in reading by including fascinating details and descriptions.

Map Activity *Interactive*

16. Caribbean South America On a separate sheet of paper, match the letters on the map with their correct labels.

Llanos   Andes

Guiana Highlands   Orinoco River

Lake Maracaibo

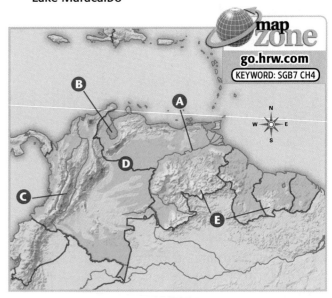

map zone
go.hrw.com
KEYWORD: SGB7 CH4

DIRECTIONS: *Read questions 1 through 7 and write the letter of the best response. Then read question 8 and write your own well-constructed response.*

1 Temperatures in Caribbean South America remain warm year-round because of the region's location near the

A equator.

B Caribbean Sea.

C Amazon Basin.

D Tropic of Cancer.

2 What valuable natural resource were the Chibcha known for using?

A silver

B gold

C copper

D iron

3 What Colombian city was a major naval base and commercial port in the Spanish empire?

A Bogotá

B Cali

C Caracas

D Cartagena

4 Venezuela's economy is based on

A oil production.

B flower exports.

C small farms.

D silver mining.

5 Simon Bolívar helped several South American countries gain independence from

A Britain.

B Brazil.

C Spain.

D Mexico.

Volcanoes of Colombia

6 Based on the map above, active volcanoes are located in Colombia's

A rivers.

B mountains.

C plains.

D coastal areas.

7 The physical geography of the Guianas includes

A dense rain forests.

B deserts.

C the Orinoco River.

D the Andes.

8 Extended Response Look at the table of the world's oil exporters and the map of Venezuela's major resources in Section 3. Write a paragraph explaining why oil is Venezuela's most important resource. Identify at least two reasons.

CHAPTER 5

Atlantic South America

PACIFIC
OCEAN

○ National capital

● Other cities

0   300   600 Miles

0   300   600 Kilometers

Projection:
Lambert Azimuthal Equal-Area

What You Will Learn...

In this chapter you will learn about the plains and rain forest of Atlantic South America. You will also study the histories of the different countries and how different influences have shaped their cultures. In addition, you will learn about life, landscapes, and issues in Brazil, Argentina, Uruguay, and Paraguay today.

SECTION 1
Physical Geography **102**

SECTION 2
Brazil **106**

SECTION 3
Argentina, Uruguay,
and Paraguay.........................**112**

FOCUS ON READING AND WRITING

Using Context Clues As you read, you may find some unknown words. You can usually figure out what a word means by using context clues. Look at the words and sentences around the unknown word—its context—to figure out the definition. **See the lesson, Using Context Clues, on page 198.**

Creating a Web Site You are a Web designer at a travel agency. Read this chapter and then use what you learn to create a Web site about Atlantic South America. The goal of your Web site will be to convince viewers to visit the region.

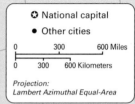

map zone

Geography Skills

Place Brazil and Argentina are South America's largest countries.
1. **Identify** What city lies on the Amazon River?
2. **Analyze** What would be some benefits of the location of Buenos Aires?

go.hrw.com KEYWORD: SGB7 CH5

Culture During Carnival, Brazilians celebrate with music, dancing, and costumes.

COLOMBIA
VENEZUELA
GUYANA
SURINAME
FRENCH GUIANA
(FRANCE)
ECUADOR
Amazon River ●Manaus
PERU
B R A Z I L
●Salvador
BOLIVIA
✴Brasília
PARAGUAY
●Rio de Janeiro
Asunción ✴
São Paulo
CHILE
Paraná River
Córdoba●
URUGUAY
Buenos Aires ✴
✴●Montevideo
ARGENTINA
ATLANTIC
OCEAN

N
W   E
S

Tropic of Capricorn
30°S
40°S
50°S

Equator 0°
10°S
20°S

Falkland
Islands

HOLT
Geography's Impact
video series
Watch the video to understand the impact of deforestation in the Amazon Basin.

Geography The Amazon Basin covers a huge forested region in northern Brazil.

History Colonial buildings, such as the Casa Rosada in Buenos Aires, reflect the region's colonial heritage.

Physical Geography

If YOU lived there...

You live on the coast of Brazil, near the mouth of the Amazon River. Now you are taking your first trip up the river deep into the rain forest. The river is amazingly wide and calm. Trees on the riverbanks seem to soar to the sky. Your boat slows as you pass a small village. You notice that all the houses rest on poles that lift them 8 to 10 feet out of the water.

What would it be like to live in the rain forest?

BUILDING BACKGROUND While rugged mountains and highlands dominate the lansdcape of Caribbean South America, much of the Atlantic region is made up of broad interior plains. Landscapes in this region range from tropical rain forest to temperate, grassy plains.

Physical Features

The region of Atlantic South America includes four countries: Brazil, Argentina, Uruguay, and Paraguay. This large region covers about two-thirds of South America. Brazil alone occupies nearly half of the continent. Most of the physical features found in South America are found in these four countries.

Major River Systems

The world's largest river system, the Amazon, flows eastward across northern Brazil. The **Amazon River** is about 4,000 miles (6,440 km) long. It extends from the Andes Mountains in Peru to the Atlantic Ocean. Hundreds of tributaries flow into it, draining an area that includes parts of most South American countries.

Because of its huge drainage area, the Amazon carries more water than any other river in the world. About 20 percent of the water that runs off Earth's surface flows down the Amazon. Where it meets the Atlantic, this freshwater lowers the salt level of the Atlantic for more than 100 miles (160 km) from shore.

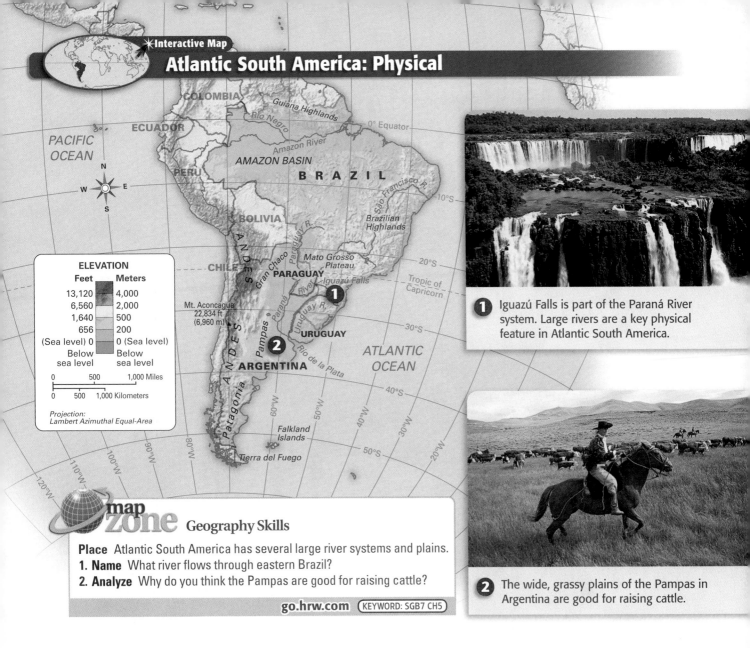

ELEVATION

Feet	Meters
13,120	4,000
6,560	2,000
1,640	500
656	200
(Sea level) 0	0 (Sea level)
Below sea level	Below sea level

0   500   1,000 Miles

0   500   1,000 Kilometers

Projection:
Lambert Azimuthal Equal-Area

Mt. Aconcagua
22,834 ft
(6,960 m)

map zone Geography Skills

Place Atlantic South America has several large river systems and plains.
1. Name What river flows through eastern Brazil?
2. Analyze Why do you think the Pampas are good for raising cattle?

go.hrw.com KEYWORD: SGB7 CH5

1 Iguazú Falls is part of the Paraná River system. Large rivers are a key physical feature in Atlantic South America.

2 The wide, grassy plains of the Pampas in Argentina are good for raising cattle.

The Paraná (pah-rah-NAH) River drains much of the central part of South America. Water from the Paraná River eventually flows into the **Río de la Plata** (REE-oh day lah PLAH-tah) and the Atlantic Ocean beyond. The Río de la Plata is an estuary. An **estuary** is a partially enclosed body of water where freshwater mixes with salty seawater.

Plains and Plateaus

As you can see on the map, this region's landforms mainly consist of plains and plateaus. The Amazon Basin in northern Brazil is a giant, flat floodplain. South of the Amazon Basin are the Brazilian Highlands, a rugged region of old, eroded mountains, and another area of high plains called the Mato Grosso Plateau.

Farther south, a low plains region known as the Gran Chaco (grahn CHAH-koh) stretches across parts of Paraguay and northern Argentina. In central Argentina are the wide, grassy plains of the **Pampas**. South of the Pampas is Patagonia—a region of dry plains and plateaus. All of these southern plains rise in the west to form the high Andes Mountains.

READING CHECK **Summarizing** What are the region's major landforms and rivers?

FOCUS ON READING

Where can you find the definition of Pampas?

Close-up
The Amazon Rain Forest

The Amazon rain forest covers more than one-third of South America. Seen from the air, it looks like a big, green carpet. The top level of tree branches is called the canopy. Most action in the forest takes place in the canopy, but plenty of life also exists below.

Animals such as monkeys and sloths can spend their entire lives in the canopy.

People have cleared parts of the rain forest for farming, ranching, and logging.

Parts of the forest are flooded for half the year, and trees stand in water up to 40 feet (12 m) deep.

ANALYSIS SKILL **ANALYZING VISUALS**

What kinds of animals could not survive living in the canopy?

Climate and Vegetation

Atlantic South America has many climates. Generally, cool climates in southern and highland areas give way to tropical, moist climates in northern and coastal areas.

In southern Argentina Patagonia has a cool, desert climate. North of Patagonia, rich soils and a humid subtropical climate make parts of the Pampas good for farming. Farther north in Argentina, the Gran Chaco has a humid tropical climate. There, summer rains can turn some parts of the plains into marshlands.

North of Argentina, in Brazil, a large part of the central region has a tropical savanna climate with warm grasslands. The northeastern part of the country has a hot, dry climate, while the southeast is cooler and more humid.

In northern Brazil the Amazon Basin's humid tropical climate supports the world's largest tropical rain forest. Rain falls almost every day in this region. The Amazon rain forest contains the world's greatest variety of plant and animal life.

READING CHECK **Finding Main Ideas** What is the climate like in the rain forest?

Natural Resources

The Amazon rain forest is one of the region's greatest natural resources. It provides food, wood, rubber, plants for medicines, and other products. In recent years **deforestation**, or the clearing of trees, has become an issue in the forest.

The region's land is also a resource for commercial farming, which is found near coastal areas of Atlantic South America. In some areas, however, planting the same crop every year has caused **soil exhaustion**, which means the soil is infertile because it has lost nutrients needed by plants.

Atlantic South America also has good mineral and energy resources such as gold, silver, copper, iron, and oil. Dams on some of the region's large rivers also provide hydroelectric power.

READING CHECK **Summarizing** What resources does the rain forest provide?

SUMMARY AND PREVIEW Physical features of Atlantic South America include great river systems and plains. The Amazon rain forest makes up a huge part of the region. Next you will learn about Brazil, the country of the Amazon.

Section 1 Assessment

go.hrw.com
Online Quiz
KEYWORD: SGB7 HP5

Reviewing Ideas, Terms, and Places

1. **a. Define** What is an **estuary**?
   b. Explain How does the **Amazon River** affect the Atlantic Ocean at the river's mouth?
   c. Elaborate What benefits do you think the rivers might bring to Atlantic South America?
2. **a. Recall** What kind of climate does Patagonia have?
   b. Make Inferences Why are temperatures in the south generally cooler than temperatures in the north?
3. **a. Identify** What resources does the rain forest provide?
   b. Analyze What is one benefit and one drawback of practicing commercial agriculture in the rain forest?
   c. Elaborate **Soil exhaustion** might lead to what kinds of additional problems?

Critical Thinking

4. **Categorizing** Look back over your notes. Then use a table like this one to organize the physical geography of Atlantic South America by country.

	Geography
Brazil	
Argentina	

FOCUS ON WRITING

5. **Describing Physical Geography** Jot down notes about the physical features, climate and vegetation, landscapes, and resources of this area. Identify one or two images you could use for your Web site.

Brazil

If YOU lived there...

You live in Rio de Janeiro, Brazil's second-largest city. For months your friends have been preparing for Carnival, the year's biggest holiday. During Carnival, people perform in glittery costumes and there is dancing all day and all night in the streets. The city is packed with tourists. It can be fun, but it is hectic! Your family is thinking of leaving Rio during Carnival so they can get some peace and quiet, but you may stay in Rio with a friend if you like.

Would you stay for Carnival? Why or why not?

BUILDING BACKGROUND Carnival is a tradition that is not unique to Brazil, but it has come to symbolize certain parts of Brazilian culture. Brazilian culture differs from cultures in the rest of South America in many ways. Brazil's unique history in the region is responsible for most of the culture differences.

History

Brazil is the largest country in South America. Its population of more than 188 million is larger than the population of all of the other South American countries combined. Most Brazilians are descended from three groups of people who contributed in different ways throughout Brazil's history.

Colonial Brazil

The first people in Brazil were American Indians. They arrived in the region many thousands of years ago and developed a way of life based on hunting, fishing, and small-scale farming.

In 1500 Portuguese explorers became the first Europeans to find Brazil. Soon Portuguese settlers began to move there. Good climates and soils, particularly in the northeast, made Brazil a large sugar-growing colony. Colonists brought a third group of people—Africans—to work as slaves on the plantations. Sugar plantations made Portugal rich, but they also eventually replaced forests along the Atlantic coast.

What You Will Learn...

Main Ideas

1. Brazil's history has been affected by Brazilian Indians, Portuguese settlers, and enslaved Africans.
2. Brazil's society reflects a mix of people and cultures.
3. Brazil today is experiencing population growth in its cities and new development in rain forest areas.

The Big Idea

The influence of Brazil's history can be seen all over the country in its people and culture.

Key Terms and Places

São Paulo, *p. 108*
megacity, *p. 108*
Rio de Janeiro, *p. 108*
favelas, *p. 109*
Brasília, *p. 109*
Manaus, *p. 109*

 TAKING NOTES As you read, use a graphic organizer like this to take notes on Brazil's history, culture, and four different regions.

Other parts of Brazil also contributed to the colonial economy. Inland, many Portuguese settlers created cattle ranches. In the late 1600s and early 1700s, people discovered gold and precious gems in the southeast. A mining boom drew people to Brazil from around the world. Finally, in the late 1800s southeastern Brazil became a major coffee-producing region.

Brazil Since Independence

Brazil gained independence from Portugal without a fight in 1822. However, independence did not change Brazil's economy much. For example, Brazil was the last country in the Americas to end slavery.

Since the end of Portuguese rule, Brazil has been governed at times by dictators and at other times by elected officials. Today the country has an elected president and legislature. Brazilians can participate in politics through voting.

READING CHECK **Summarizing** What was Brazil's colonial economy like?

People and Culture

The people who came to Brazil over the years brought their own traditions. These traditions blended to create a unique Brazilian culture.

People

More than half of Brazilians consider themselves of European descent. These people include descendants of original Portuguese settlers along with descendants of more recent immigrants from Spain, Germany, Italy, and Poland. Nearly 40 percent of Brazil's people are of mixed African and European descent. Brazil also has the largest Japanese population outside of Japan.

Because of its colonial heritage, Brazil's official language is Portuguese. In fact, since Brazil's population is so huge, there are more Portuguese-speakers in South America than there are Spanish-speakers, even though Spanish is spoken in almost every other country on the continent. Other Brazilians speak Spanish, English, French, Japanese, or native languages.

FOCUS ON READING
What context clues in this paragraph help you understand the meaning of *descent*?

FOCUS ON CULTURE

Soccer in Brazil

To Brazilians, soccer is more than a game. It is part of being Brazilian. Professional stars are national heroes. The national team often plays in Rio de Janeiro, home of the world's largest soccer stadium. Some fans beat drums all through the games. But it is not just professional soccer that is popular. People all over Brazil play soccer—in cleared fields, on the beach, or in the street. Here, boys in Rio practice their skills.

Analyzing Why do you think soccer is so popular in Brazil?

Regions of Brazil

Brazil's regions differ from each other in their people, climates, economies, and landscapes.

ANALYZING VISUALS Which region appears to be the wealthiest?

1 The southeast has the country's largest cities, such as Rio de Janeiro.

Religion

Brazil has the largest population of Roman Catholics of any country in the world. About 75 percent of Brazilians are Catholic. In recent years Protestantism has grown in popularity, particularly among the urban poor. Some Brazilians practice macumba (mah-KOOM-bah), a religion that combines beliefs and practices of African and Indian religions with Christianity.

Festivals and Food

ACADEMIC VOCABULARY
aspects parts

Other **aspects** of Brazilian life also reflect the country's mix of cultures. For example, Brazilians celebrate Carnival before the Christian season of Lent. The celebration mixes traditions from Africa, Brazil, and Europe. During Carnival, Brazilians dance the samba, which was adapted from an African dance.

Immigrant influences can also be found in Brazilian foods. In parts of the country, an African seafood dish called vatapá (vah-tah-PAH) is popular. Many Brazilians also enjoy eating feijoada (fay-ZHWAH-dah), a stew of black beans and meat.

READING CHECK **Analyzing** How has cultural borrowing affected Brazilian culture?

Brazil Today

Brazil's large size creates opportunities and challenges for the country. For example, Brazil has the largest economy in South America and has modern and wealthy areas. However, many Brazilians are poor.

While some of the same issues and characteristics can be found throughout Brazil, other characteristics are unique to a particular region of the country. We can divide Brazil into four regions based on their people, economies, and landscapes.

The Southeast

Most people in Brazil live in the southeast. **São Paulo** is located there. More than 17 million people live in and around São Paulo. It is the largest urban area in South America and the fourth largest in the world. São Paulo is considered a **megacity**, or a giant urban area that includes surrounding cities and suburbs.

Rio de Janeiro, Brazil's second-largest city, lies northeast of São Paulo. Almost 11 million people live there. The city was the capital of Brazil from 1822 until 1960. Today Rio de Janeiro remains a major port city. Its spectacular setting and exciting culture are popular with tourists.

2 The dry northeast is Brazil's poorest region. Here, children attend school in the shade.

3 Rivers provide resources and transportation for people living in the Amazon region.

In addition to having the largest cities, the southeast is also Brazil's richest region. It is rich in natural resources and has most of the country's industries and productive farmland. It is one of the major coffee-growing regions of the world.

Although the southeast has a strong economy, it also has poverty. Cities in the region have huge slums called **favelas** (fah-VE-lahz). Many people who live in favelas have come to cities of the southeast from other regions of Brazil in search of jobs.

The Northeast

Immigrants to Brazil's large cities often come from the northeast, which is Brazil's poorest region. Many people there cannot read, and health care is poor. The region often suffers from droughts, which make farming and raising livestock difficult. The northeast has also had difficulty attracting industry. However, the region's beautiful beaches do attract tourists.

Other tourist attractions in northeastern Brazil are the region's many old colonial cities. These cities were built during the days of the sugar industry. They have brightly painted buildings, cobblestone streets, and elaborate Catholic churches.

The Interior

The interior region of Brazil is a frontier land. Its abundant land and mild climate could someday make it an important area for agriculture. For now, few people live in this region, except for those who reside in the country's capital, **Brasília**.

In the mid-1950s government officials hoped that building a new capital city in the Brazilian interior would help develop the region. Brasília has modern buildings and busy highways. More than 2 million people live in Brasília, although it was originally designed for only 500,000.

The Amazon

The Amazon region covers the northern part of Brazil. **Manaus**, which lies 1,000 miles (1,600 km) from the mouth of the Amazon, is a major port and industrial city. More than 1 million people live there. They rely on the river for transportation and communication.

Isolated Indian villages are scattered throughout the region's dense rain forest. Some of Brazil's Indians had little contact with outsiders until recently. Now, logging, mining, and new roads are bringing more people and development to this region.

Satellite View

Deforestation in the Amazon

Deforestation is changing the landscape of the Amazon rain forest. This satellite image shows new roads and cleared areas where people have taken resources from the forest.

Many people depend on the industries that result in deforestation. For example, people need wood for building and making paper. Also, farmers, loggers, and miners need to make a living. However, deforestation in the Amazon also threatens the survival of many plant and animal species. It also threatens hundreds of unique ecosystems.

Making Inferences What do you think might be some effects of building roads in the rain forest?

This new development provides needed income for some people. But it destroys large areas of the rain forest. It also creates tensions among the Brazilian Indians, new settlers, miners, and the government.

READING CHECK **Contrasting** How does the northeast of Brazil differ from the southeast?

SUMMARY AND PREVIEW In this section you read about Brazil—a huge country of many contrasts. Brazil reflects the mixing of people and cultures from its history. In the next section you will learn about Brazil's neighbors—Argentina, Uruguay, and Paraguay.

go.hrw.com
Online Quiz
KEYWORD: SGB7 HP5

Section 2 Assessment

Reviewing Ideas, Terms, and Places

1. **a. Recall** What European country colonized Brazil?
   b. Make Inferences Why did the colonists bring Africans to work on plantations as slaves?
   c. Elaborate Why do you think the main basis of Brazil's colonial economy changed over the years?
2. **a. Identify** What religion is most common in Brazil?
   b. Explain Why is so much of Brazil's culture influenced by African traditions?
3. **a. Define** What is a **megacity**, and what is an example of a megacity in Brazil?
   b. Make Inferences Why might development in the Amazon cause tensions between Brazilian Indians and new settlers?
   c. Elaborate How might life change for a person who moves from the northeast to the southeast?

Critical Thinking

4. **Finding Main Ideas** Review your notes on Brazil. Then, write a main idea statement about each region. Use a graphic organizer like this one.

	Main Idea
The Southeast	
The Northeast	
The Interior	
The Amazon	

FOCUS ON WRITING

5. **Writing about Brazil** What information about the history, people, and culture of Brazil will draw readers to the country? What regions do you think they would like to visit? List details and ideas for possible images for your Web site.

Social Studies Skills

Chart and Graph

Critical Thinking

Geography

Study

Connecting Ideas

Learn

You have already used several types of graphic organizers in this book. Graphic organizers are drawings that help you organize information and connect ideas.

One type of graphic organizer is a word web. A word web like the one at right helps you organize specific facts and details around a main topic. Notice that information gets more detailed as it gets farther away from the main topic.

Practice

Use the word web here to answer the following questions. You may also want to look back at the information on Brazilian culture in your textbook.

❶ How can a graphic organizer help you connect ideas?

❷ What is the main topic of this word web?

❸ What three main ideas does this graphic organizer connect?

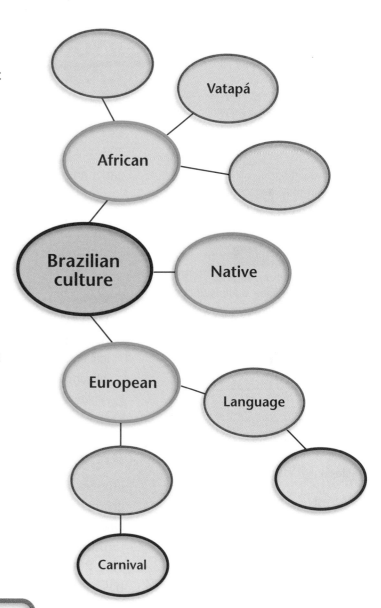

Apply

Copy the graphic organizer shown here in your notebook. Use the information on Brazilian culture in your textbook to fill in the blank circles with additional details about the main topic.

Argentina, Uruguay, and Paraguay

What You Will Learn...

Main Ideas

1. European immigrants have dominated the history and culture of Argentina.
2. Argentina's capital, Buenos Aires, plays a large role in the country's government and economy today.
3. Uruguay has been influenced by its neighbors.
4. Paraguay is the most rural country in the region.

The Big Idea

Argentina, Uruguay, and Paraguay have been influenced by European immigration, a tradition of ranching, and large urban populations.

Key Terms and Places

gauchos, *p. 113*
Buenos Aires, *p. 114*
Mercosur, *p. 114*
informal economy, *p. 115*
landlocked, *p. 116*

TAKING NOTES As you read, use a graphic organizer like the one below to help you organize your notes on Argentina, Uruguay, and Paraguay.

Argentina   Uruguay   Paraguay

If YOU lived there...

You live in Montevideo, the capital of Uruguay. On weekends you like to visit the old part of the city and admire its beautiful buildings. You also enjoy walking along the banks of the Río de la Plata and watching fishers bring in their catch. Sometimes you visit the parks and beaches along the banks of the river.

How do you think the river has influenced Montevideo?

BUILDING BACKGROUND The southern countries of Atlantic South America—Argentina, Uruguay, and Paraguay—have all been influenced by their locations and European culture. Neither Spanish influence nor Indian culture is as strong in the southern part of South America as in other parts of the continent.

Argentina's History and Culture

Like most of South America, Argentina was originally home to groups of Indians. Groups living in the Pampas hunted wild game, while farther north Indians built irrigation systems for farming. However, unlike most of South America, Argentina has very few native peoples remaining. Instead, Argentina's culture has been mostly influenced by Europeans.

Early History

The first Europeans to come to Argentina were the Spanish. In the 1500s Spanish conquerors spread from the northern part of the continent into southern South America in search of silver and gold. They named the region Argentina. *Argentina* means "land of silver" or "silvery one."

Gauchos on the Pampas

Gauchos were a popular subject in Argentine art. In this painting from 1820, gauchos gather to watch a horse race.

ANALYZING VISUALS Why would horses be important to a gaucho?

The Spanish soon built settlements in Argentina. The Spanish monarch granted land to the colonists, who in turn built the settlements. These landowners were also given the right to force the Indians living there to work.

During the colonial era, the Pampas became an important agricultural region. Argentine cowboys, called **gauchos** (GOW-chohz), herded cattle and horses on the open grasslands. Although agriculture is still important on the Pampas, very few people in Argentina live as gauchos today.

In the early 1800s Argentina fought for independence from Spain. A period of violence and instability followed. Many Indians were killed or driven away by fighting during this time.

Modern Argentina

As the Indians were being killed off, more European influences dominated the region. New immigrants arrived from Italy, Germany, and Spain. Also, the British helped build railroads across the country. Railroads made it easier for Argentina to transport agricultural products for export to Europe. Beef exports, in particular, made the country rich.

Argentina remained one of South America's richest countries throughout the 1900s. However, the country also struggled under dictators and military governments during those years.

Some political leaders, like Eva Perón, were popular. But many leaders abused human rights. During the "Dirty War" in the 1970s, they tortured and killed many accused of disagreeing with the government. Both the country's people and its economy suffered. Finally, in the 1980s, Argentina's last military government gave up power to an elected government.

BIOGRAPHY

Eva Perón
(1919–1952)

Known affectionately as Evita, Eva Perón helped improve the living conditions of people in Argentina, particularly the poor. As the wife of Argentina's president, Juan Perón, Evita established thousands of hospitals and schools throughout Argentina. She also helped women gain the right to vote. After years of battling cancer, Evita died at age 33. All of Argentina mourned her death for weeks.

Analyzing Why was Eva Perón able to help many people?

People and Culture

Argentina's historical ties to Europe still affect its culture. Most of Argentina's roughly 40 million people are descended from Spanish, Italian, or other European settlers. Argentine Indians and mestizos make up only about 3 percent of the population. Most Argentines are Roman Catholic.

Beef is still a part of Argentina's culture. A popular dish is parrilla (pah-REE-yah), which includes grilled sausage and steak. Supper is generally eaten late.

READING CHECK **Generalizing** What kind of governments did Argentina have in the 1900s?

Argentina Today

Today many more of Argentina's people live in **Buenos Aires** (BWAY-nohs EYE-rayz) than in any other city. Buenos Aires is the country's capital. It is also the second-largest urban area in South America. Much of Argentina's industry is located in and around Buenos Aires. Its location on the coast and near the Pampas has contributed to its economic development.

The Pampas are the country's most developed agricultural region. About 11 percent of Argentina's labor force works in agriculture. Large ranches and farms there produce beef, wheat, and corn for export to other countries.

Argentina's economy has always been affected by government policies. In the 1990s government leaders made economic reforms to help businesses grow. Argentina joined **Mercosur**—an organization that promotes trade and economic cooperation among the southern and eastern countries of South America. By the late 1900s and early 2000s, however, heavy debt and government spending brought Argentina into an economic crisis.

Argentina: Population

PARAGUAY

San Miguel de Tucumán

CHILE

Tropic of Capricorn

30°S

BRAZIL

Córdoba

Mendoza

Rosario

URUGUAY

Buenos Aires

ATLANTIC OCEAN

PACIFIC OCEAN

ARGENTINA

40°S

N
W E
S

• **10,000 people**

0   300   600 Miles

0   300   600 Kilometers

50°S

Projection:
Lambert Azimuthal Equal-Area

map zone   Geography Skills

Place Buenos Aires is home to nearly a third of all Argentines.

1. **Interpreting Graphs** How many times bigger is Buenos Aires than Argentina's second-largest city?
2. **Analyze** What might be a benefit and a drawback of having most of the country's population in one area?

THE WORLD ALMANAC
Facts about Countries

Argentina's Largest Cities

Population (in millions)

15

10

5

0

Buenos Aires | Córdoba | Rosario | Mendoza | San Miguel de Tucumán

Cities

go.hrw.com **KEYWORD: SGB7 CH5**

At a certain elevation, the climate becomes too cool for trees to grow. This fourth climate zone above the tree line contains alpine meadows with grasslands and hardy shrubs. The altiplano region between the two ridges of the Andes lies mostly in this climate zone.

The fifth climate zone, in the highest elevations, is very cold. No vegetation grows in this zone because the ground is almost always covered with snow and ice.

Deserts

Pacific South America also has some climates that are not typical of any of the five climate zones. Instead of hot and humid climates, some coastal regions have desert climates.

Northern Chile contains the **Atacama Desert**. This desert is about 600 miles (965 km) long. Rain falls there less than five times a century, but fog and low clouds are common. They form when a cold current in the Pacific Ocean chills the warmer air above the ocean's surface. Cloud cover keeps the air near the ground from being warmed by the sun. As a result, coastal Chile is one of the cloudiest—and driest—places on Earth.

In Peru, some rivers cut through the dry coastal region. They bring snowmelt down from the Andes. Because they rely on melting snow, some of these rivers only appear at certain times of the year. The rivers have made some small settlements possible in these dry areas.

El Niño

About every two to seven years, this dry region experiences **El Niño**, an ocean and weather pattern that affects the Pacific coast. During an El Niño year, cool Pacific water near the coast warms. This change may cause extreme ocean and weather events that can have global effects.

As El Niño warms ocean waters, fish leave what is usually a rich fishing area. This change affects fishers. Also, El Niño <u>causes</u> heavy rains, and areas along the coast sometimes experience flooding. Some scientists think that air pollutants have made El Niño last longer and have more damaging effects.

READING CHECK Finding Main Ideas How does elevation affect climate and vegetation?

ACADEMIC VOCABULARY

cause to make something happen

Natural Resources

The landscapes of Pacific South America provide many valuable natural resources. For example, forests in southern Chile and in eastern Peru and Ecuador provide lumber. Also, as you have read, the coastal waters of the Pacific Ocean are rich in fish.

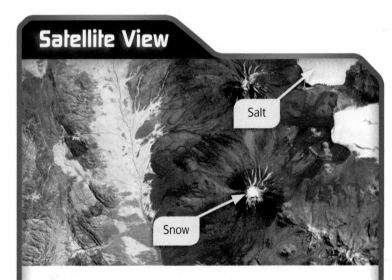

Satellite View

Salt

Snow

Atacama Desert

The Atacama Desert lies between the Pacific coast and the Andes in northern Chile. In this image you can see two snowcapped volcanoes. The salt in the top right part of the image is formed from minerals carried there by rivers that only appear during certain months of the year. These seasonal rivers also support some limited vegetation.

Drawing Conclusions Why do you think there is snow on the volcanoes even though the desert gets hardly any precipitation?

Bolivia: Resources

Gold · Tin · Lead · Zinc · Silver

0   100   200 Miles

0   100   200 Kilometers

Projection: Lambert Azimuthal Equal-Area

BRAZIL

BOLIVIA

Madeira R.

Madre de Dios

Beni River

Guapore River

Lake Titicaca

Mamoré River

Lake Poopó

Pilcomayo River

CHILE   ARGENTINA   PARAGUAY

20°S

map zone Geography Skills

Place Bolivia has many valuable mineral resources.
1. **Locate** Where are most of Bolivia's gold resources found?
2. **Interpret** What do you notice about the location of the mineral resources and the rivers?

In addition, the region has valuable oil and minerals. Ecuador in particular has large oil and gas reserves, and oil is the country's main export. Bolivia has some deposits of tin, gold, silver, lead, and zinc. Chile has copper deposits. In fact, Chile exports more copper than any other country in the world. Chile is also the site of the world's largest open pit mine.

Although the countries of Pacific South America have many valuable resources, one resource they do not have much of is good farmland. Many people farm, but the region's mostly cool, arid lands make it difficult to produce large crops for export.

READING CHECK **Categorizing** What types of resources do the countries of Pacific South America have?

SUMMARY AND PREVIEW The Andes are the main physical feature of Pacific South America. Next, you will learn how the Andes have affected the region's history and how they continue to affect life there today.

Section 1 Assessment

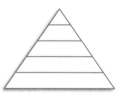

go.hrw.com
Online Quiz
KEYWORD: SGB7 HP6

Reviewing Ideas, Terms, and Places

1. **a. Identify** What is the main physical feature of Pacific South America?
   b. Analyze How is Bolivia's location unique in the region?
2. **a. Define** What is **El Niño**, and what are some of its effects?
   b. Draw Conclusions Why are parts of Ecuador, in the tropics, cooler than parts of southern Chile?
3. **a. Identify** What country in this region has large oil reserves?
   b. Make Inferences Why do you think much of the region is not good for farming?
   c. Elaborate What effects do you think copper mining in Chile might have on the environment?

Critical Thinking

4. **Categorizing** Review your notes on climate. Then use a diagram like this one to describe the climate and vegetation in each of the five climate zones.

FOCUS ON SPEAKING

5. **Describing Physical Geography** Note information about the physical features, climate and vegetation, and resources of Pacific South America. Write two questions and answers you can use in your interview.

Social Studies Skills

Chart and Graph

Critical Thinking

Geography

Study

Interpreting an Elevation Profile

Learn

An elevation profile is a diagram that shows a side view of an area. This kind of diagram shows the physical features that lie along a line from point A to point B. Keep in mind that an elevation profile typically exaggerates vertical distances because vertical and horizontal distances are measured differently on elevation profiles. If they were not, even tall mountains would appear as tiny bumps.

Vertical measurements are given on the sides of the diagram.

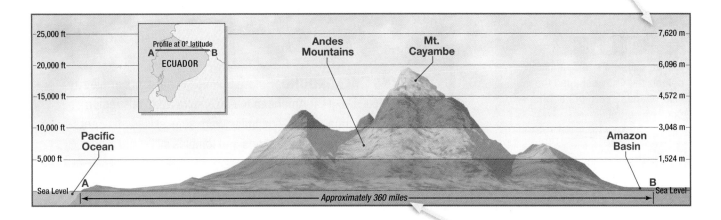

25,000 ft — 7,620 m

Profile at 0° latitude
A   B
ECUADOR

Andes Mountains

Mt. Cayambe

20,000 ft — 6,096 m

15,000 ft — 4,572 m

3,048 m

10,000 ft

Pacific Ocean

Amazon Basin

1,524 m

5,000 ft

Sea Level

A

Approximately 360 miles

B
Sea Level

Practice

Use the elevation profile above to answer the following questions.

The horizontal measurement is given along the bottom of the diagram.

1. What place does this elevation profile measure?

2. What is the highest point, and what is its elevation?

3. How can you tell that the vertical distance is exaggerated?

Apply

Look at the physical map of Pacific South America in Section 1 of this chapter. Choose a latitude line and create your own elevation profile for the land at that latitude. Be sure to pay attention to the scale and the legend so that you use correct measurements.

History and Culture

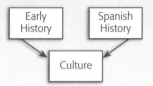

If **YOU** lived there...

You live in Cuzco, the capital of the Inca Empire. You are required to contribute labor to the empire, and you have been chosen to work on a construction project. Hauling the huge stones will be difficult, but the work will be rewarding. You can either choose to help build a magnificent temple to the sun god or you can help build a road from Cuzco to the far end of the empire.

Which project will you choose? Why?

BUILDING BACKGROUND Before Spanish conquerors arrived in the early 1500s, a great American Indian empire ruled this region. Cuzco was the Inca capital. The Incas were such skilled engineers and builders that many of their forts and temples still stand today.

History

Thousands of years ago, people in Pacific South America tried to farm on mountainsides as steep as bleachers. Other people tried to farm where there was almost no rain. These early cultures learned how to adapt to and modify their environments.

Early Cultures

Peru's first advanced civilization reached its height in about 900 BC in the Andes. These people built stone terraces into the steep mountainside so they could raise crops. In coastal areas, people created irrigation systems to store water and control flooding.

Agriculture supported large populations, towns, and culture. In the Bolivian highlands one early culture, the Tiahuanaco (tee-uh-wuh-NAH-koh), made huge stone carvings near a lakeshore. In another civilization on the coast, people scratched outlines of animals and other shapes into the surface of the Peruvian desert. These designs, known as the Nazca lines, are so large they can only be recognized from the sky.

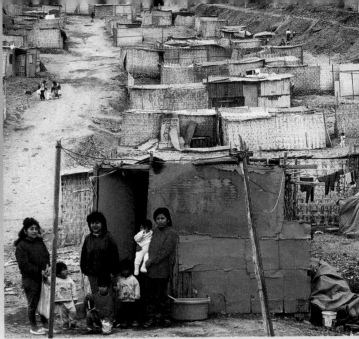

Slums Just outside downtown and near the port area, many people live in slum housing. These buildings are permanent, but run-down.

Young Towns Many poor people in recent years have taken over land on the outskirts of Lima and have built their own shelters.

Government

In the 1980s and 1990s, a terrorist group called the Shining Path was active. This group carried out deadly attacks because it opposed government policies. Some 70,000 people died in violence between the Shining Path and government forces, and Peru's economy suffered. However, after the arrest of the group's leaders, Peru's government began making progress against political violence and poverty. The country has an elected president and congress.

Resources

Peru's resources are key factors in its economic progress. Some mineral deposits are located near the coast, and hydroelectric projects on rivers provide energy. Peru's highlands are less developed than the coastal areas. However, many Peruvian Indians grow potatoes and corn there.

READING CHECK Identifying Cause and **Effect** How did the Shining Path affect Peru?

Chile Today

Like Peru, Chile has ended a long violent period. Chile now has a stable government and a growing economy.

Government

In 1970 Chileans elected a president who had some ideas influenced by communism. A few years later he was overthrown and died in a U.S.-backed military coup (KOO). A **coup** is a sudden overthrow of a government by a small group of people.

In the years after the coup, military rulers tried to crush their political enemies. Chile's military government was harsh and often violent. It imprisoned or killed thousands of people.

In the late 1980s the power of the rulers began to weaken. After more than 15 years, Chileans rejected the military dictatorship and created a new, democratic government. Chileans now enjoy many freedoms. Chile is one of the most stable countries in South America.

FOCUS ON READING

What can you infer about the reason for the end of the military government?

A man in Chile harvests grapes to be made into wine for export.

Mediterranean climate allows farmers to grow many crops. For example, grapes grow well there, and Chilean fruit and wine are exported around the world.

Farming, fishing, forestry, and mining form the basis of Chile's economy. Copper mining is especially important. It accounts for more than one-third of Chile's exports.

Since international trade is key to Chile's economy, Chile wants to expand its trade links. Chile has signed a free trade agreement with the United States, and trade between the two countries has increased. Chile's other important trade partners are Argentina, Brazil, and China.

READING CHECK Identifying Points of View
Why might Chile want to join a free trade group?

Resources and Economy

Chile's economy is the strongest in the region. Poverty rates have decreased, and Chile's prospects for the future seem bright. Small businesses and factories are growing quickly. More Chileans are finding work, and wages are rising.

About one-third of all Chileans live in central Chile. This region includes the capital, **Santiago**, and a nearby seaport, Valparaíso (bahl-pah-rah-EE-soh). Its mild

SUMMARY AND PREVIEW In recent years Ecuador, Peru, Bolivia, and Chile have struggled with political violence and poverty. However, Peru and Chile are recovering. Next, you will study the culture and economy of the United States.

go.hrw.com
Online Quiz
KEYWORD: SGB7 HP6

Section 3 Assessment

Reviewing Ideas, Terms, and Places

1. **a. Identify** What is Ecuador's largest city?
   b. Make Generalizations Why have Ecuadorians been unhappy with their government in recent years?
2. **a. Identify** What are Bolivia's two capital cities?
   b. Analyze Why might Bolivia's economy improve in the future?
3. **a. Recall** Why did many Peruvians move to Lima from the highlands in the 1980s?
   b. Elaborate What challenges do you think people who move to **Lima** from the highlands face?
4. **a. Define** What is a **coup**?
   b. Make Inferences What might happen to Chile's economy if the world price of copper drops?

Critical Thinking

5. **Solving Problems** Review your notes. Then, in a diagram like the one here, write one sentence about each country, explaining how that country is dealing with poverty or government instability.

Ecuador	
Bolivia	
Peru	
Chile	

FOCUS ON SPEAKING

6. **Thinking about Pacific South America Today** Add questions about each country in Pacific South America to your notes. How might you answer these questions in your interview? Write down the answer to each question.

Chapter Review

Geography's Impact
video series
Review the video to answer the closing question:
Why do descendants of the Incas still live in the difficult high altitudes of the Andes?

Visual Summary

Use the visual summary below to help you review the main ideas of the chapter.

QUICK FACTS

The high Andes affect the climates and landscapes of Pacific South America.

Many South American Indians maintain traditional customs and ways of life in the Andes.

Today the countries of Pacific South America are working toward development and improved economies.

Reviewing Vocabulary, Terms, and Places

Write each word defined below, circling each letter that is marked by a star. Then write the word these letters spell.

1. _ _ _ * _ _ _ _ _ _ _ _ _ _ _ _—a desert in northern Chile that is one of the cloudiest and driest places on Earth

2. * _ _ _ _—the capital of Peru

3. _ _ _ _ * _ _—the capital of Ecuador

4. _ * _ _ _ _ _ _—a governor appointed by the king of Spain

5. _ _ * _ _ _—one of the capitals of Bolivia

6. _ _ _ _ _ * _ _—an American-born descendant of Europeans

7. _ _ _ _ * _ _ _—a narrow passageway that connects two large bodies of water

8. _ _ * _ _ _ _—an ocean and weather pattern that affects the Pacific coast

9. _ * _ _ _—a sudden overthrow of a government by a small group of people

Comprehension and Critical Thinking

SECTION 1 *(Pages 124–128)*

10. **a. Describe** What are climate and vegetation like on the altiplano?

 b. Compare and Contrast What are two differences and one similarity between the Atacama Desert and the altiplano?

 c. Evaluate What elevation zone would you choose to live in if you lived in Pacific South America? Why would you choose to live there?

SECTION 2 *(Pages 130–133)*

11. **a. Describe** How did the Incas organize their huge empire?

 b. Analyze How have Spanish and native cultures left their marks on culture in Pacific South America?

 c. Elaborate Why do you think Pizarro killed the Inca king even though he had received riches as ransom?

12. a. Identify What country in Pacific South America has the healthiest economy?

b. Analyze What problems in Ecuador and Bolivia cause political unrest?

c. Evaluate What would be some benefits and drawbacks of moving from the highlands to one of Lima's "young towns"?

FOCUS ON READING AND SPEAKING

Making Inferences *Use the information in this chapter to answer the following questions.*

13. What is an inference?

14. What do you think contributes to people's ability to maintain traditional cultures in Pacific South America?

15. What can you infer about the size of the population in the Atacama Desert? What clues led you to make this inference?

16. Presenting an Interview Now that you have questions and answers, turn them into an interview. You and your partner should decide who will be the interviewer and who will be the expert. Then read through your script several times with your partner so that you both know it well enough to sound natural during the interview. Knowing your script well will allow you to make eye contact with your audience during the interview. Remember to use a lively and authoritative tone as you speak so that members of your audience will pay attention.

Using the Internet

go.hrw.com
KEYWORD: SGB7 CH6

17. Activity: Analyzing Climate Chile has steep mountains, volcanoes, a desert, a rich river valley, and thick forests. These diverse areas contain many different climates. Enter the activity keyword and visit the links given to explore the many climates of Chile. Then test your knowledge by taking an online quiz.

Social Studies Skills

Interpreting an Elevation Profile *Use the elevation profile on the Social Studies Skills page to answer the following questions.*

18. What is the purpose of an elevation profile?

19. Where can you find the vertical measurements on an elevation profile?

20. What horizontal distance does the elevation profile measure?

21. What is the elevation of the Amazon basin?

Map Activity ✴Interactive

22. Pacific South America On a separate sheet of paper, match the letters on the map with their correct labels.

Strait of Magellan	Santiago, Chile
Quito, Ecuador	Atacama Desert
Andes	La Paz, Bolivia

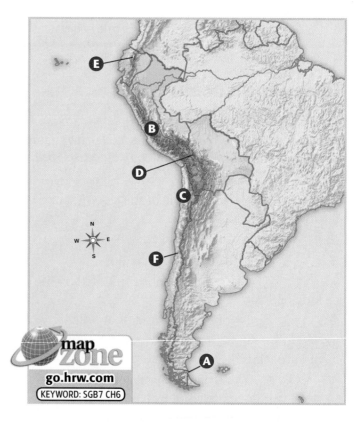

map zone
go.hrw.com
KEYWORD: SGB7 CH6

DIRECTIONS: Read questions 1 through 7 and write the letter of the best response. Then read question 8 and write your own well-constructed response.

1 The main mountain range located in Pacific South America is called the

A altiplano.

B Andes.

C Strait of Magellan.

D Pampas.

2 Which of the following conditions is a result of El Niño?

A increased greenhouse gases

B more fish in a usually poor fishing area

C drought on the Pacific coast

D warmer waters near the Pacific coast

3 What early culture had a huge empire in Pacific South America in the early 1500s?

A Inca

B Aztec

C Tiahuanaco

D Nazca

4 Which of the following statements about culture in Pacific South America is false?

A Most people speak Spanish.

B Chile has a higher percentage of Indians than any other country in South America.

C Religion in the region often combines Catholic and ancient native customs.

D Wooden flutes and drums are traditional instruments.

5 Which country's main export is oil?

A Bolivia

B Chile

C Ecuador

D Peru

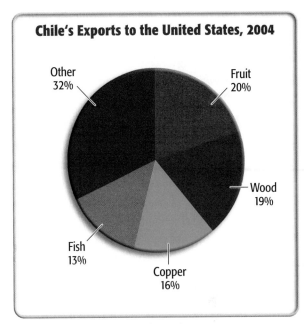

Chile's Exports to the United States, 2004

Other 32%
Fruit 20%
Wood 19%
Copper 16%
Fish 13%

Source: International Trade Administration, TradeStats Express

6 Based on the graph above, what one product is Chile's main export to the United States?

A fish

B wood

C fruit

D copper

7 What has been a major cause of political unrest in the region?

A dissatisfaction with economic policies

B arrest of the leaders of the Shining Path

C development of "young towns" in Peru

D high unemployment in Chile

8 **Extended Response** Using the graph above and your knowledge of Pacific South America today, compare and contrast the economic situations in each of the four countries.

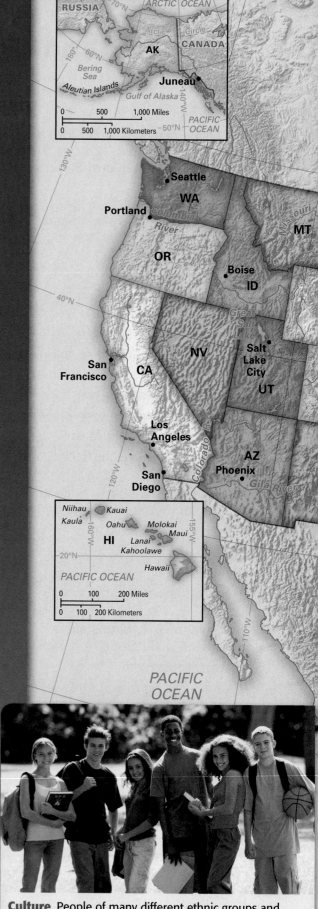

CHAPTER 7

The United States

What You Will Learn...

In this chapter you will learn about the physical features, climates, and resources of the United States. You will also discover how democratic ideas and immigration have shaped the United States. Finally, you will learn about our country's different regions, diverse population, and the challenges we face as a nation.

SECTION 1
Physical Geography **144**

SECTION 2
History and Culture....................**152**

SECTION 3
The United States Today **160**

FOCUS ON READING AND VIEWING

Categorizing A good way to make sense of what you read is to separate facts and details into groups, called categories. For example, you could sort facts about the United States into categories like natural resources, major cities, or rivers. As you read this chapter, look for ways to categorize details under each topic. **See the lesson, Categorizing, on page 200.**

Creating a Collage Artists create collages by gluing art and photographs onto a flat surface, such as a poster board. As you read this chapter, you will collect ideas for a collage about the United States. After you create your own collage, you will view and evaluate the collages of other students in your class.

Culture People of many different ethnic groups and cultures make up the population of the United States.

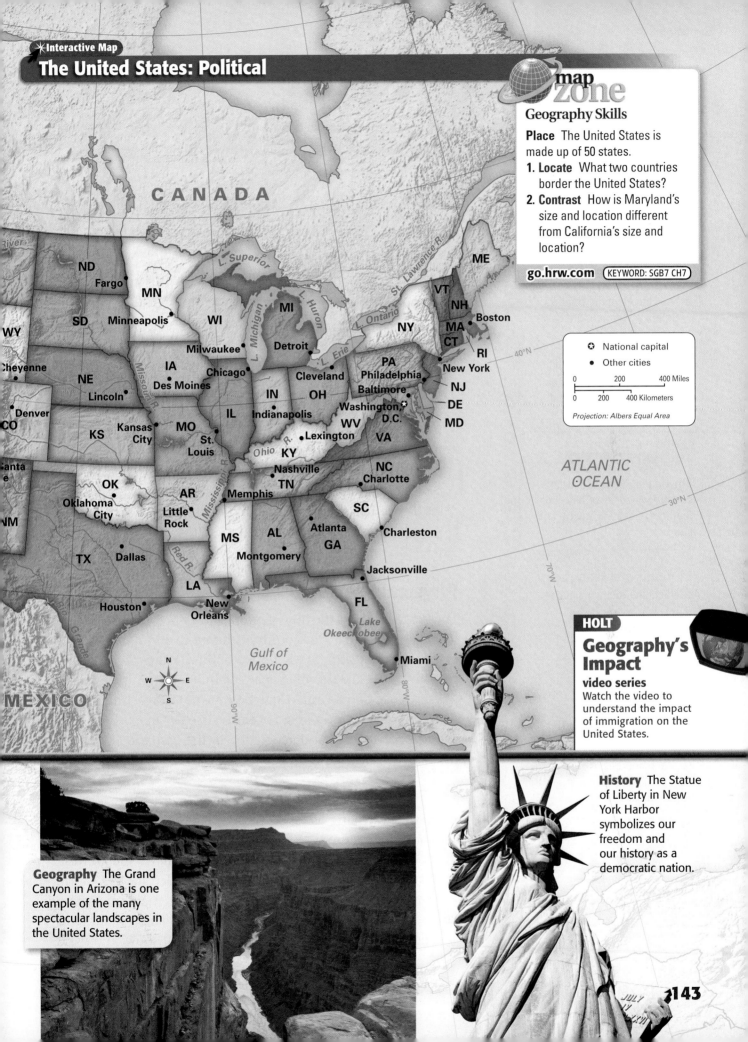

map zone

Geography Skills

Place The United States is made up of 50 states.
1. **Locate** What two countries border the United States?
2. **Contrast** How is Maryland's size and location different from California's size and location?

go.hrw.com KEYWORD: SGB7 CH7

CANADA

L. Superior

St. Lawrence R.

ND
Fargo
MN
MINNEAPOLIS
SD
WI
MI
L. Michigan
L. Huron
Milwaukee
Detroit
L. Erie
Ontario
ME
VT
NH
MA
Boston
NY
CT
RI
New York

WY
Cheyenne
NE
Lincoln
IA
Des Moines
Chicago
Cleveland
OH
PA
Philadelphia
Baltimore
NJ
DE

Denver
CO
KS
Kansas City
MO
St. Louis
IL
Indianapolis
IN
Ohio R.
WV
Washington, D.C.
MD

Santa Fe
Missouri R.
Lexington
KY
VA

OK
Oklahoma City
AR
Little Rock
Memphis
Nashville
TN
NC
Charlotte
SC

NM
TX
Dallas
Red R.
MS
Montgomery
AL
Atlanta
GA
Charleston

Houston
LA
New Orleans
Rio Grande
Mississippi R.
Jacksonville

MEXICO

Gulf of Mexico
Lake Okeechobee
FL
Miami

N W E S

☆ National capital
● Other cities

0   200   400 Miles
0   200   400 Kilometers

Projection: Albers Equal Area

ATLANTIC OCEAN

40°N
30°N
70°W
80°W
90°W

HOLT

Geography's Impact
video series
Watch the video to understand the impact of immigration on the United States.

Geography The Grand Canyon in Arizona is one example of the many spectacular landscapes in the United States.

History The Statue of Liberty in New York Harbor symbolizes our freedom and our history as a democratic nation.

143

Physical Geography

What You Will Learn...

Main Ideas

1. Major physical features of the United States include mountains, rivers, and plains.
2. The climate of the United States is wetter in the East and South and drier in the West.
3. The United States is rich in natural resources such as farmland, oil, forests, and minerals.

The Big Idea

The United States is a large country with diverse physical features, climates, and resources.

Key Terms and Places

Appalachian Mountains, *p. 144*
Great Lakes, *p. 145*
Mississippi River, *p. 145*
tributary, *p. 145*
Rocky Mountains, *p. 146*
continental divide, *p. 146*

TAKING NOTES As you read, look for information about the physical features, climate, and natural resources of the United States. Take notes in a graphic organizer like this one.

Physical Features	Climate	Natural Resources

If YOU lived there...

You live in St. Louis, Missouri, which is located on the Mississippi River. For the next few days, you will travel down the river on an old-fashioned steamboat. The Mississippi begins in Minnesota and flows south through 10 states in the heart of the United States. On your trip, you bring a video camera to film life along this great river.

What will you show in your video about the Mississippi?

BUILDING BACKGROUND The United States stretches from sea to sea across North America. To the north is Canada and to the south lies Mexico. Because it is so large, the United States has a great variety of landscapes and climates.

Physical Features

The United States is the third largest country in the world behind Russia and Canada. Our country is home to an incredible variety of physical features. All but two of the 50 states—Alaska and Hawaii—make up the main part of the country. Look at the physical map of the United States on the next page. It shows the main physical features of our country. Use the map as you read about America's physical geography in the East and South, the Interior Plains, and the West.

The East and South

If you were traveling across the United States, you might start on the country's eastern coast. This low area, which is flat and close to sea level, is called the Atlantic Coastal Plain. As you go west, the land gradually rises higher to a region called the Piedmont. The **Appalachian Mountains**, which are the main mountain range in the East, rise above the Piedmont. These mountains are very old. For many millions of years, rain, snow, and wind

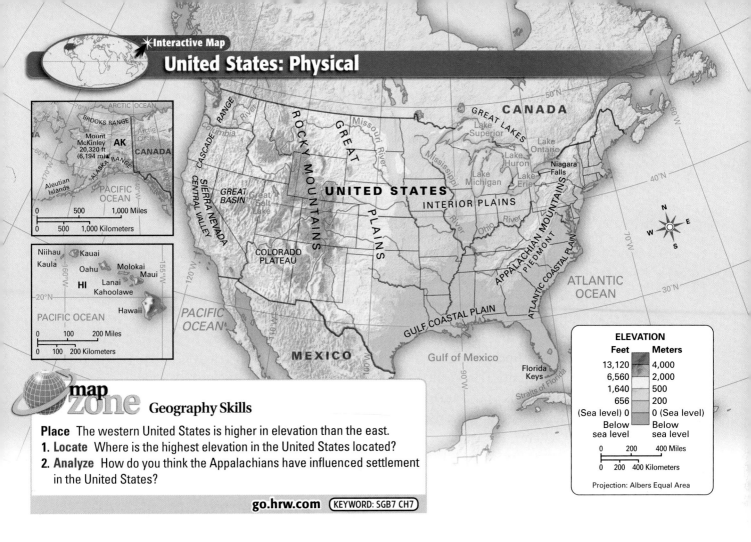

United States: Physical

ELEVATION

Feet		Meters
13,120		4,000
6,560		2,000
1,640		500
656		200
(Sea level) 0		0 (Sea level)
Below sea level		Below sea level

0   200   400 Miles
0   200   400 Kilometers

Projection: Albers Equal Area

map zone Geography Skills

Place The western United States is higher in elevation than the east.
1. **Locate** Where is the highest elevation in the United States located?
2. **Analyze** How do you think the Appalachians have influenced settlement in the United States?

go.hrw.com (KEYWORD: SGB7 CH7)

have eroded and smoothed their peaks. As a result, the highest mountain in the Appalachians is about 6,700 feet (2,040 m).

The Interior Plains

As you travel west from the Appalachians, you come across the vast Interior Plains that stretch to the Great Plains just east of the Rocky Mountains. The Interior Plains are filled with hills, lakes, and rivers. The first major water feature that you see here is called the **Great Lakes**. These lakes make up the largest group of freshwater lakes in the world. The Great Lakes are also an important waterway for trade between the United States and Canada.

West of the Great Lakes lies North America's largest and most important river, the **Mississippi River**. Tributaries in the interior plains flow to the Mississippi. A **tributary** is a smaller stream or river that flows into a larger stream or river.

Appalachians The smooth peaks of the Appalachian Mountains dominate the landscape of western North Carolina.

Along the way, these rivers deposit rich silt. The silt creates fertile farmlands that cover most of the Interior Plains. The Missouri and Ohio rivers are huge tributaries of the Mississippi. They help drain the entire Interior Plains.

Look at the map on the previous page. Notice the land begins to increase in elevation west of the Interior Plains. This higher region is called the Great Plains. Vast areas of grasslands cover these plains.

The West

In the region called the West, several of the country's most rugged mountain ranges make up the **Rocky Mountains**. These enormous mountains, also called the Rockies, stretch as far as you can see. Many of the mountains' jagged peaks rise above 14,000 feet (4,270 m).

In the Rocky Mountains is a line of high peaks called the Continental Divide. A **continental divide** is an area of high ground that divides the flow of rivers towards opposite ends of a continent.

FOCUS ON READING

Into what two categories might you group the details on rivers?

Rivers east of the divide in the Rockies mostly flow eastward and empty into the Mississippi River. Most of the rivers west of the divide flow westward and empty into the Pacific Ocean.

Farther west, mountain ranges include the Cascade Range and the Sierra Nevada. Most of the mountains in the Cascades are dormant volcanoes. One mountain, Mount Saint Helens, is an active volcano. A tremendous eruption in 1980 blew off the mountain's peak and destroyed 150 square miles (390 sq km) of forest.

Mountains also stretch north along the Pacific coast. At 20,320 feet (6,194 m), Alaska's Mount McKinley is the highest mountain in North America.

Far out in the Pacific Ocean are the islands that make up the state of Hawaii. Volcanoes formed these islands millions of years ago. Today, hot lava and ash continue to erupt from the islands' volcanoes.

READING CHECK Summarizing What are the major physical features of the United States?

Satellite View

The river branches out in several places here as it tries to find the shortest way to the ocean.

The Mississippi River Delta

From its source in Minnesota, the Mississippi River flows south across the central United States. It ends at the tip of Louisiana, which is shown here. This satellite image shows the area where the Mississippi River meets the Gulf of Mexico. This area is called a delta. A river's delta is formed from sediment that a river carries downstream to the ocean. Sediment is usually made up of rocks, soil, sand, and dead plants. Each year, the Mississippi dumps more than 400 million tons of sediment into the Gulf of Mexico.

The light blue and green areas in this image are shallow areas of sediment. The deeper water of the Gulf of Mexico is dark blue. Also, notice that much of the delta land looks fragile. This is new land that the river has built up by depositing sediment.

Making Inferences What natural hazards might people living in the Mississippi Delta experience?

United States: Climate

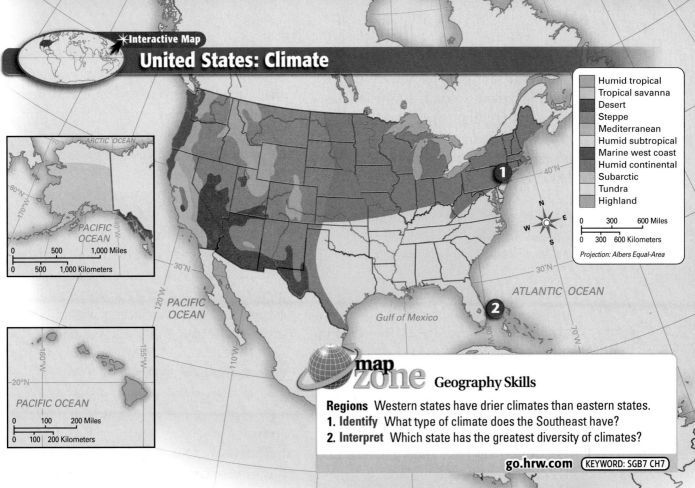

Humid tropical
Tropical savanna
Desert
Steppe
Mediterranean
Humid subtropical
Marine west coast
Humid continental
Subarctic
Tundra
Highland

0   300   600 Miles
0   300   600 Kilometers
Projection: Albers Equal-Area

ARCTIC OCEAN

PACIFIC OCEAN

0   500   1,000 Miles
0   500   1,000 Kilometers

PACIFIC OCEAN

0   100   200 Miles
0   100   200 Kilometers

ATLANTIC OCEAN

Gulf of Mexico

map zone   Geography Skills

Regions Western states have drier climates than eastern states.
1. Identify What type of climate does the Southeast have?
2. Interpret Which state has the greatest diversity of climates?

go.hrw.com   KEYWORD: SGB7 CH7

Climate

Did you know that the United States has a greater variety of climates than any other country? Look at the map above to see the different climates of the United States.

The East and South

The eastern United States has three climate regions. In the Northeast, people live in a humid continental climate with snowy winters and warm, humid summers. Southerners, on the other hand, experience milder winters and the warm, humid summers of a humid subtropical climate. Most of Florida is warm all year.

The Interior Plains

Temperatures throughout the year can vary greatly in the Interior Plains. Summers are hot and dry in the Great Plains. However, most of the region has a humid continental climate with long, cold winters.

1 With a humid continental climate, New York City experiences cold winters with snowfall. In this climate people can ice skate during the winter.

2 With a humid subtropical climate, most of Florida has warm sunny days during most of the year. In this climate people can enjoy the region's beaches.

The West

Climates in the West are mostly dry. The Pacific Northwest coast, however, has a wet, mild coastal climate. The region's coldest climates are in Alaska, which has both subarctic and tundra climates. In contrast, Hawaii is the only state with a warm, tropical climate.

READING CHECK **Identifying** What types of climates are found in the United States?

Natural Resources

The United States is extremely rich in natural resources. Do you know that your life is affected in some way every day by these natural resources? For example, if you ate bread today, it was probably made with wheat grown in the fertile soils of the Interior Plains. If you rode in a car or on a bus recently, it may have used gasoline from Alaska, California, or Louisiana.

The United States is a major oil producer but uses more oil than it produces. In fact, we import more than one half of the oil we need.

Valuable minerals are mined in the Appalachians and Rockies. One mineral, coal, supplies the energy for more than half of the electricity produced in the United States. The United States has about 25 percent of the world's coal reserves and is a major coal exporter.

Other important resources include forests and farmland, which cover much of the country. The trees in our forests provide lumber that is used in constructing buildings. Wood from these trees is also used to make paper. Farmland produces a variety of crops including wheat, corn, soybeans, cotton, fruits, and vegetables.

READING CHECK **Summarizing** What are important natural resources in the U.S.?

SUMMARY AND PREVIEW In this section you learned about the geography, climates, and natural resources of the United States. In the next section, you will learn about the history and culture of the United States.

Section 1 Assessment

go.hrw.com
Online Quiz
KEYWORD: SGB7 HP7

Reviewing Ideas, Terms, and Places

1. a. **Define** What is a **tributary**?
   b. **Contrast** How are the **Appalachian Mountains** different from the **Rocky Mountains**?
   c. **Elaborate** Why are the **Great Lakes** an important waterway?
2. a. **Describe** What is the climate like in the Northeast?
   b. **Draw Conclusions** What would winter be like in Alaska?
3. a. **Recall** What kinds of crops are grown in the United States?
   b. **Explain** Why is coal an important resource?
   c. **Predict** What natural resources might not be as important to your daily life in the future?

Critical Thinking

4. **Categorizing** Copy the graphic organizer below. Use it to organize your notes on physical features, climate, and resources by region of the country.

East and South	Interior Plains	West

FOCUS ON VIEWING

5. **Thinking about Physical Geography** Jot down key words that describe the physical features and climate of the United States. Think of at least three objects or images you might use to illustrate physical features and climate.

Social Studies Skills

Using a Political Map

Learn

Many types of maps are useful in studying geography. Political maps are one of the most frequently used types of maps. These maps show human cultural features such as cities, states, and countries. Look at the map's legend to figure out how these features are represented on the map.

Most political maps show national boundaries and state boundaries. The countries on political maps are sometimes shaded different colors to help you tell where the borders of each country are located.

Practice

Use the political map here to answer the following questions.

❶ What countries does this map show?

❷ How does the map show the difference between state boundaries and national boundaries?

❸ What is the capital of Canada?

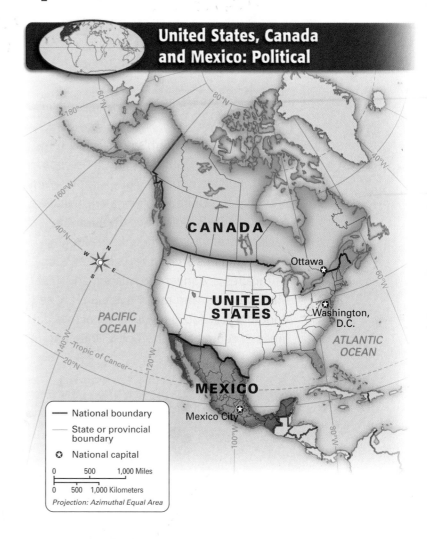

United States, Canada and Mexico: Political

CANADA

Ottawa

UNITED STATES

Washington, D.C.

PACIFIC OCEAN

ATLANTIC OCEAN

MEXICO

Mexico City

— National boundary
— State or provincial boundary
✪ National capital

0   500   1,000 Miles
0 500 1,000 Kilometers
Projection: Azimuthal Equal Area

Apply

Using an atlas or the Internet, find a political map of your state. Use that map to answer the following questions.

1. What is the state capital and where is it located?

2. What other states or countries border your state?

3. What are two other cities in your state besides the capital and the city you live in?

Natural Hazards
in the United States

Essential Elements

The World in Spatial Terms
Places and Regions
Physical Systems
Human Systems
Environment and Society
The Uses of Geography

Background Earth's physical systems create patterns around us, and these patterns influence our lives. For example, every region of the United States has distinctive natural hazards. Volcanoes threaten the Pacific Northwest. Earthquakes rattle California. Wildfires strike forests in the West. Hurricanes endanger the Atlantic and Gulf of Mexico coasts, and major rivers are prone to flooding. Tornadoes regularly rip across flat areas of central and southeast United States.

In fact, the United States lies in danger of getting hit by an average of six hurricanes a year. Formed by the warm waters of the Atlantic Ocean and Caribbean Sea and the collision of strong winds, hurricanes are the most powerful storms on Earth. Most hurricanes look like large doughnuts with a hole, or eye, in the middle of the storm. Around the eye, high winds and rain bands rotate counterclockwise. Once the hurricane moves over land or cold water it weakens.

Natural Hazards in the United States

Tornado Alley

◎ Earthquakes
🔥 Wildfires
◎ Hurricanes
▬ Flood areas

▲ Volcanoes
🔻 Tornadoes

Tornado Risk
▬ Moderate
▬ High

map zone

After Hurricane Katrina hit New Orleans, people escaped the floodwaters by fleeing to rooftops and high-rise apartment buildings like this one.

Using satellite images like this one of Hurricane Katrina, scientists saw how large the storm was and warned people along the Gulf coast to evacuate.

Hurricane Katrina On August 29, 2005, one of the most destructive hurricanes ever hit the United States. Hurricane Katrina devastated coastal regions of Louisiana, the city of New Orleans, and the entire coast of Mississippi.

With winds as high as 145 mph (235 km), Katrina destroyed hundreds of thousands of homes and businesses. In addition, the force of Katrina's storm surge pushed water from the Gulf of Mexico onto land to a height of about two stories tall. As a result, low-lying areas along the Gulf coast experienced massive flooding.

The storm surge also caused several levees that protected New Orleans from the waters of Lake Pontchartrain to break. The loss of these levees caused the lake's waters to flood most of the city. About 150,000 people who did not evacuate before the storm were left stranded in shelters, high-rise buildings, and on rooftops. Using boats and helicopters, emergency workers rescued thousands of the city's people. Total damages from the storm along the Gulf coast was estimated to be nearly $130 billion. More than 1,300 people died and over a million were displaced.

What It Means Natural hazards can influence where we live, how we build our homes, and how we prepare for storms. In addition to hurricanes, other hazards affect the United States. For example, Tornado Alley is a region of the Great Plains that experiences a high number of tornadoes, or "twisters"—rapidly spinning columns of air that stay in contact with the ground. In Tornado Alley, special warning sirens go off when storms develop that might form a dangerous tornado.

Geography for Life Activity

1. How are hurricanes formed?

2. Many people train and volunteer as storm chasers. They may follow storms for hundreds of miles to gather scientific data, take photographs, or file news reports. What might be the risks and rewards of such activity? Would it interest you?

3. **Comparing Windstorms** Do some research to find out how tornadoes and hurricanes differ. Summarize the differences in a chart that includes information about how these storms start, where and when they tend to occur in the United States, and their wind strength.

History and Culture

If YOU lived there...

It is 1803, and President Jefferson just arranged the purchase of a huge area of land west of the Mississippi River. It almost doubles the size of the United States. Living on the frontier in Ohio, you are a skillful hunter and trapper. One day, you see a poster calling for volunteers to explore the new Louisiana Territory. An expedition is heading west soon. You think it would be exciting but dangerous.

Will you join the expedition to the West? Why or why not?

BUILDING BACKGROUND From 13 colonies on the Atlantic coast, the territory of the United States expanded all the way to the Pacific Ocean in about 75 years. Since then, America's democracy has attracted immigrants from almost every country in the world. Looking for new opportunities, these immigrants have made the country very diverse.

First Modern Democracy

Long before Italian explorer Christopher Columbus sailed to the Americas in 1492, native people lived on the land that is now the United States. These Native Americans developed many distinct cultures. Soon after Columbus and his crew explored the Americas, other Europeans began to set up colonies there.

The American Colonies

Europeans began settling in North America and setting up colonies in the 1500s. A **colony** is a territory inhabited and controlled by people from a foreign land. By the mid-1700s the British Empire included more than a dozen colonies along the Atlantic coast. New cities in the colonies such as **Boston** and **New York** became major seaports.

Some people living in the British colonies lived on plantations. A **plantation** is a large farm that grows mainly one crop. Many of the colonial plantations produced tobacco, rice, or cotton. Thousands of enslaved Africans were brought to the colonies and forced to work on plantations.

By the 1770s many colonists in America were unhappy with British rule. They wanted independence from Britain. In July 1776, the colonial representatives adopted the Declaration of Independence. The document stated that "all men are created equal" and have the right to "life, liberty, and the pursuit of happiness." Although not everyone in the colonies was considered equal, the Declaration was a great step toward equality and justice.

To win their independence, the American colonists fought the British in the Revolutionary War. First, colonists from Massachusetts fought in the early battles of the war in and around Boston. As the war spread west and south, soldiers from all the American colonies joined the fight against Britain.

In 1781 the American forces under General George Washington defeated the British army at the Battle of Yorktown in Virginia. With this defeat, Britain recognized the independence of the United States. As a consequence, Britain granted all its land east of the Mississippi River to the new nation.

Expansion and Industrial Growth

After independence, the United States gradually expanded west. Despite the challenges of crossing swift-moving rivers and traveling across rugged terrain and huge mountains, people moved west for land and plentiful resources.

BIOGRAPHY

George Washington
(1732–1799)

As the first president of the United States, George Washington is known as the Father of His Country. Washington was admired for his heroism and leadership as the commanding general during the Revolutionary War. Delegates to the Constitutional Convention chose him to preside over their meetings. Washington was then elected president in 1789 and served two terms.

Drawing Inferences Why do you think Washington was elected president?

Fight for Independence

This painting shows General George Washington leading American troops across the Delaware River to attack British forces.

These first settlers that traveled west were called **pioneers**. Many followed the 2,000-mile Oregon Trail west from Missouri to the Oregon Territory. Groups of families traveled together in wagons pulled by oxen or mules. The trip was harsh. Food, supplies, and water were scarce.

While many pioneers headed west seeking land, others went in search of gold. The discovery of gold in California in the late 1840s had a major impact on the country. Tens of thousands of people moved to California.

By 1850 the population of the United States exceeded 23 million and the country stretched all the way to the Pacific Ocean. As the United States expanded, the nation's economy also grew. By the late 1800s, the country was a major producer of goods like steel, oil, and textiles, or cloth products. The steel industry grew around cities that were located near coal and iron ore deposits. Most of those new industrial cities were in the Northeast and Midwest. The country's economy also benefited from the **development** of waterways and railroads. This development helped industry and people move farther into the interior.

Attracted by a strong economy, millions of people immigrated, or came to, the United States for better jobs and land. Immigration from European countries was especially heavy in the late 1800s and early 1900s. As a result of this historical pattern of immigration, the United States is a culturally diverse nation today.

ACADEMIC VOCABULARY

development the process of growing or improving

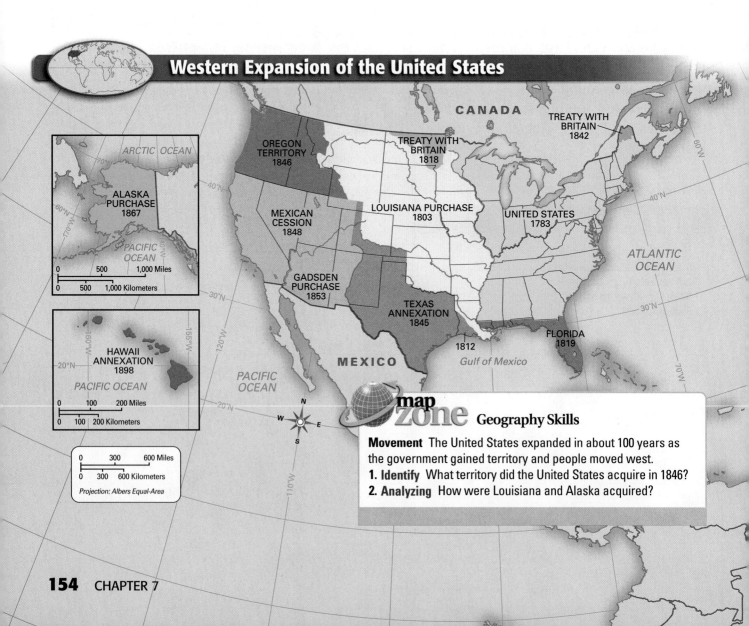

Western Expansion of the United States

map zone Geography Skills

Movement The United States expanded in about 100 years as the government gained territory and people moved west.
1. **Identify** What territory did the United States acquire in 1846?
2. **Analyzing** How were Louisiana and Alaska acquired?

Wars and Peace

The United States fought in several wars during the 1900s. Many Americans died in two major wars, World Wars I and II. After World War II, the United States and the Soviet Union became rivals in what was known as the Cold War. The Cold War lasted until the early 1990s, when the Soviet Union collapsed. U.S. troops also served in long wars in Korea in the 1950s and in Vietnam in the 1960s and 1970s. In 1991, the U.S. fought Iraq in the Persian Gulf War. More recently, the U.S. invaded Iraq in 2003 and is helping Iraqis rebuild their country today.

Today the United States is a member of many international organizations. The headquarters of one such organization, the United Nations (UN), is located in New York City. About 190 countries are UN members. The United States is one of the most powerful members.

Government and Citizenship

The United States has a limited, democratic government based on the U.S. Constitution. This document spells out the powers and functions of the branches of the federal government. The federal government includes an elected president and Congress. In general, the federal government handles issues affecting the whole country, but many powers are left to the 50 state governments. Counties and cities also have their own local governments. Many of these local governments provide services to the community such as trash collection, road building, electricity, and public transportation.

Rights and Responsibilities

American citizens have many rights and responsibilities, including the right to vote. Starting at age 18, U.S. citizens are allowed to vote. They are also encouraged

HISTORIC DOCUMENT
The Constitution

On September 17, 1787, state delegates gathered in Philadelphia to create a constitution, a written statement of the powers and functions of the new government of the United States. The Preamble, or introduction, to the U.S. Constitution is shown below. It states the document's general purpose.

"**We the People** of the United States, in order to form a more perfect Union, establish justice, insure domestic tranquillity, provide for the common defense, promote the general welfare, and secure the blessings of liberty to ourselves and our posterity, do ordain and establish this Constitution for the United States of America."

Americans wanted peace within the United States and a national military force.

They wanted to ensure freedoms for themselves and for future generations.

ANALYSIS SKILL **ANALYZING PRIMARY SOURCES**

How do you think the ideas that appear in the Preamble affect your daily life?

to play an active role in government. For example, Americans can call or write their public officials to ask them to help solve problems in their communities. Without people participating in their government, the democratic process suffers.

READING CHECK **Sequencing** What were some major events in the history of the United States?

People and Culture

About 7 out of 10 Americans are descended from European immigrants. However, the United States is also home to people of many other cultures and ethnic groups. As a result, the United States is a diverse nation where many languages are spoken and different religions and customs are practiced. The blending of these different cultures has helped produce a unique American culture.

Ethnic Groups in the United States

FOCUS ON READING
What details would be included under a category called *ethnic groups*?

Some ethnic groups in the United States include Native Americans, African Americans, Hispanic Americans, and Asian Americans. As you can see on the maps on the next page, higher percentages of these ethnic groups are concentrated in different areas of the United States.

For thousands of years, Native Americans were the only people living in the Americas. Today, most Native Americans live in the western United States. Many Native Americans are concentrated in Arizona and New Mexico.

Even though African Americans live in every region of the country, some areas of the United States have a higher percentage of African Americans. For example, a higher percentage of African Americans live in southern states. Many large cities also have a high percentage of African Americans. On the other hand, descendants of people who came from Asian countries, or Asian Americans, are mostly concentrated in California.

Many Hispanic Americans originally migrated to the United States from Mexico, Cuba, and other Latin American countries. As you can see on the map of Hispanic Americans, a higher percentage of Hispanic Americans live in the southwestern states. These states border Mexico.

Language

What language or languages do you hear as you walk through the hall of your school? Since most people in the United States speak English, you probably hear English spoken every day. However, in many parts of the country, English is just one of many languages you might hear. Are you or is someone you know bilingual? People who speak two languages are **bilingual**.

After English, Spanish is the most widely spoken language in the United States. About 30 million Americans speak Spanish. Many of these people live in areas near Spanish-speaking countries like Mexico and Cuba.

Today more than 50 million U.S. residents speak a language in addition to English. These languages include Spanish, French, Chinese, Russian, Arabic, Navajo, and many others.

Religion

Americans also practice many religious faiths. Most people are Christians. However, some are Jewish or Muslim. A small percentage of Americans are Hindu or Buddhist. What religions are practiced in your community? Your community might have Christian churches, Jewish synagogues, and Islamic mosques, as well as other places of worship. Religious variety adds to our country's cultural diversity.

With so many different religions, many religious holidays are celebrated in the United States. These holidays include the Christian holidays of Christmas and Easter and the Jewish celebrations of Hanukkah, Yom Kippur, and Rosh Hashanah. Some African Americans also celebrate Kwanzaa, a holiday that is based on a traditional African festival. Muslims celebrate the end of the month of Ramadan with a large feast called 'Id al-Fitr.

Distribution of Selected Ethnic Groups, 2000

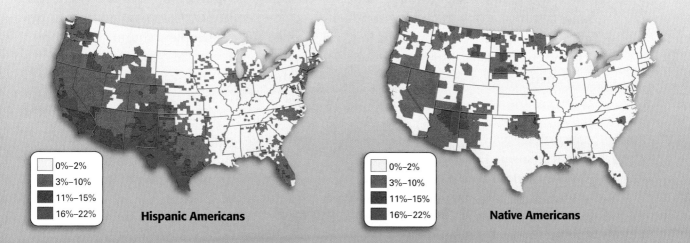

0%–2%
3%–10%
11%–15%
16%–22%

Hispanic Americans

0%–2%
3%–10%
11%–15%
16%–22%

Native Americans

Diverse America

People of different ethnic groups enjoy a concert in Miami, Florida. Like most large American cities, Miami has a very diverse population. More than half of all Hispanic Americans of Cuban descent live in Miami.

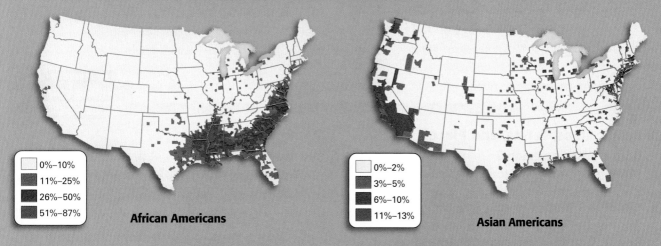

0%–10%
11%–25%
26%–50%
51%–87%

African Americans

0%–2%
3%–5%
6%–10%
11%–13%

Asian Americans

Source: U.S. Census Bureau, 2000

map zone

Geography Skills

Regions These maps show population information from the U.S. Census. Every 10 years, Americans answer census questions about their race or ethnic group.

1. **Locate** In what region of the United States does the highest percentage of African Americans live?
2. **Analyze** Why do you think many Hispanic Americans live in the southwestern United States?

Foods and Music

Diversity shows itself through cultural practices. In addition to language and religion, cultural practices include the food we eat and the music we listen to.

America's food is as diverse as the American people. Think about some of the foods you have eaten this week. You may have eaten Mexican tacos, Italian pasta, or Japanese sushi. These dishes are now part of the American diet.

Different types of music from around the world have also influenced American culture. For example, salsa music from Latin America is popular in the United States today. Many American musicians now combine elements of salsa into their pop songs. However, music that originated in the United States is also popular in other countries. American musical styles include blues, jazz, rock, and hip hop.

American Popular Culture

As the most powerful country in the world, the United States has tremendous influence around the world. American popular culture, such as movies, television programs, and sports, is popular elsewhere. For example, the *Star Wars* movies are seen by millions of people around the world. Other examples of American culture in other places include the popularity of baseball in Japan, Starbucks coffee shops in almost every major city in the world, and an MTV channel available throughout Asia. As you can see, Americans influence the rest of the world in many ways through their culture.

READING CHECK **Generalizing** How has cultural diversity enriched life in the United States?

SUMMARY AND PREVIEW The history of the United States has helped shape the democratic nation it is today. Drawn to the United States because of its democracy, immigrants from around the world have shaped American culture. In the next section, you will learn about the different regions of the United States and the issues the country is facing today.

Section 2 Assessment

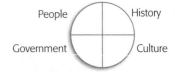

Reviewing Ideas, Terms, and Places

1. **a. Define** What is a **colony**?
   b. Make Inferences Why did the pioneers move west?
   c. Elaborate What is an example of the rights and responsibilities that American citizens have?
2. **a. Recall** What language other than English is widely spoken in the United States?
   b. Summarize What are some religions practiced in the United States?
   c. Predict How do you think American culture will be different in the future, and what influences do you think will bring about the changes?

Critical Thinking

3. **Summarizing** Using your notes, write one descriptive sentence about the history, government, people, and culture of the United States.

   People   History

   Government   Culture

FOCUS ON VIEWING

4. **Thinking about History and Culture** How would you describe the history and culture of the United States? Identify two images for your collage.

from
Bearstone

by Will Hobbs

About the Reading *In* Bearstone, *writer Will Hobbs tells about an orphaned Native American boy named Cloyd who lives on a Colorado farm. While roaming the nearby canyons, Cloyd finds a relic from his ancestors. The relic is a stone in the shape of a turquoise bear, which becomes his Bearstone, the title of this story.*

AS YOU READ Identify what the mountains mean to Cloyd.

. . . This was a shining new world. To the north and east, peaks still covered with snow shone in the cloudless blue sky. He'd never seen mountains so sharp and rugged, so fierce and splendid. Below him, an eagle soared high above the old man's field. It was a good sign.

Then he remembered his grandmother's parting words as he left for Colorado. She told him something he'd never heard before: their band of Weminuche Utes ❶ hadn't always lived at White Mesa. ❷ Colorado, especially the mountains above Durango, had been their home until gold was discovered there and the white men wanted them out of the way. Summers the people used to hunt and fish in the high mountains, she'd said; they knew every stream, places so out of the way that white men still hadn't seen them. 'So don't feel bad about going to Durango,' she told him.

Cloyd regarded the distant peaks with new strength, a fierce kind of pride he'd never felt before. These were the mountains where his people used to live.

In this book, a Native American boy named Cloyd learns more about his ancestors.

GUIDED READING

WORD HELP

band a group of Native American families

❶ Weminuche Utes are a band of Utes, a Native American cultural group.

❷ White Mesa is a Ute community in Utah where Cloyd lived before he moved to Colorado.

Connecting Literature to Geography

1. **Describing** What details in the first paragraph show us that Cloyd feels happy and at home in these mountains? Which details describe the physical features of these mountains?

2. **Making Inferences** Why did Cloyd's grandmother think he shouldn't feel bad about going to Durango? How does this fact affect his feelings about the mountains of Colorado?

The United States Today

What You Will Learn...

Main Ideas

1. The United States has four regions—the Northeast, South, Midwest, and West.
2. The United States has a strong economy and a powerful military but is facing the challenge of world terrorism.

The Big Idea

The United States has four main regions and faces opportunities and challenges.

Key Terms and Places

megalopolis, *p. 161*
Washington, D.C., *p. 161*
Detroit, *p. 163*
Chicago, *p. 163*
Seattle, *p. 164*
terrorism, *p. 166*

TAKING NOTES As you read, take notes on the United States today. Organize your notes in a chart like the one below.

Regions	Economy, Military, and Terrorism

If **YOU** lived there...

You and your family run a small resort hotel in Fort Lauderdale, on the east coast of Florida. You love the sunny weather and the beaches there. Now your family is thinking about moving the business to another region where the tourist industry is important. They have looked at ski lodges in Colorado, lake cottages in Michigan, and hotels on the coast of Maine.

How will you decide among these different regions?

BUILDING BACKGROUND Geography, history, climate, and population give each region of the United States its own style. Some differences between the regions are more visible than others. For example, people in each region speak with different accents and have their favorite foods. Even with some differences, however, Americans are linked by a sense of unity in confronting important issues.

Regions of the United States

Because the United States is such a large country, geographers often divide it into four main regions. These are the Northeast, South, Midwest, and the West. You can see the four regions on the map on the next page. Find the region where you live. You probably know more about your own region than you do the three others. The population, resources, and economies of the four regions are similar in some ways and unique in others.

The Northeast

The Northeast shares a border with Canada. The economy in this region is heavily dependent on banks, investment firms, and insurance companies. Education also contributes to the economy. The area's respected universities include Harvard and Yale.

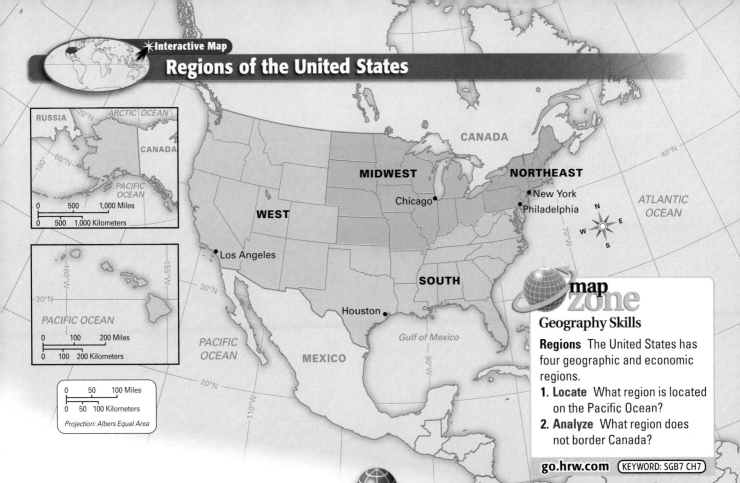

map zone

Geography Skills

Regions The United States has four geographic and economic regions.

1. **Locate** What region is located on the Pacific Ocean?
2. **Analyze** What region does not border Canada?

go.hrw.com KEYWORD: SGB7 CH7

Some natural resources of the Northeast states include rich farmland and huge pockets of coal. Used in the steelmaking process, coal remains very important to the region's economy. The steel industry helped make Pittsburgh, in western Pennsylvania, the largest industrial city in the Appalachians.

Today fishing remains an important industry in the Northeast. Major seaports allow companies to ship their products to markets around the world. Cool, shallow waters off the Atlantic coast are good fishing areas. Cod and shellfish such as lobster are the most valuable seafood.

The Northeast is the most densely populated region of the United States. Much of the Northeast is a **megalopolis**, a string of large cities that have grown together. This area stretches along the Atlantic coast from Boston to **Washington, D.C.** The three other major cities in the megalopolis are New York, Philadelphia, and Baltimore.

THE WORLD ALMANAC · **Facts about Countries**
Population of Major U.S. Cities

	City	Population
1	New York	8,143,197
2	Los Angeles	3,844,829
3	Chicago	2,842,518
4	Houston	2,016,582
5	Philadelphia	1,463,281

New York, New York

go.hrw.com KEYWORD: SGB7 CH7

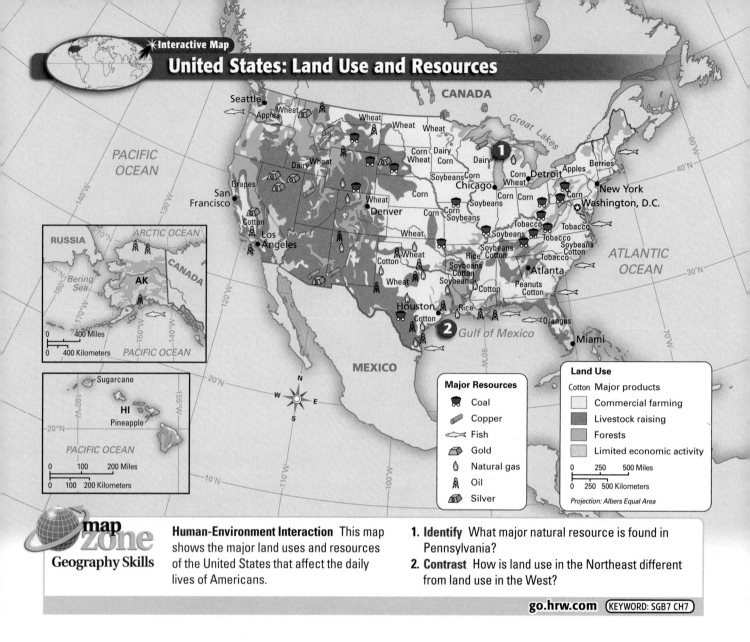

Interactive Map
United States: Land Use and Resources

CANADA

Seattle
Apples
Wheat
Wheat
Wheat
Wheat
Wheat
Corn Dairy
Wheat
Corn
Dairy
Great Lakes
Corn Wheat
Detroit
Apples
Berries
Chicago
Corn Corn
Corn
New York
Washington, D.C.
Corn
Wheat
Dairy
Grapes
San Francisco
Dairy
Soybeans Corn
Corn
Soybeans
Corn
Denver
Corn Soybeans
Soybeans
Tobacco
Tobacco
Cotton
Los Angeles
Wheat
Corn Soybeans
Tobacco
Tobacco
Cotton
ATLANTIC OCEAN
Wheat
Rice Cotton
Soybeans Cotton
Tobacco
Cotton
Wheat
Soybeans Cotton
Atlanta
Wheat
Soybeans
Cotton
Peanuts Cotton
Houston
Rice
Oranges
Cotton
Gulf of Mexico
Miami

MEXICO

PACIFIC OCEAN

RUSSIA
ARCTIC OCEAN
CANADA
AK
Bering Sea
PACIFIC OCEAN
0   400 Miles
0   400 Kilometers

Sugarcane
HI
Pineapple
PACIFIC OCEAN
0   100   200 Miles
0   100   200 Kilometers

Major Resources
- Coal
- Copper
- Fish
- Gold
- Natural gas
- Oil
- Silver

Land Use
Cotton Major products
- Commercial farming
- Livestock raising
- Forests
- Limited economic activity
0   250   500 Miles
0   250   500 Kilometers
Projection: Albers Equal Area

map zone Geography Skills

Human-Environment Interaction This map shows the major land uses and resources of the United States that affect the daily lives of Americans.

1. **Identify** What major natural resource is found in Pennsylvania?
2. **Contrast** How is land use in the Northeast different from land use in the West?

go.hrw.com **KEYWORD: SGB7 CH7**

At least 40 million people live in this urban area. All of these cities were founded during the colonial era. They grew because they were important seaports. Today these cities are industrial and financial centers.

The South

The South is a region that includes long coastlines along the Atlantic Ocean and the Gulf of Mexico. Along the coastal plains rich soils provide farmers with abundant crops of cotton, tobacco, and citrus fruit.

In recent years, the South has become more urban and industrial and is one of the country's fastest-growing regions. The

South's cities, such as Atlanta, have grown along with the economy. The Atlanta metropolitan area has grown from a population of only about 1 million in 1960 to more than 4 million today.

Other places in the South have also experienced growth in population and industry. The Research Triangle in North Carolina is an area of high-tech companies and several large universities. The Texas Gulf Coast and the lower Mississippi River area have huge oil refineries and petrochemical plants. Their products, which include gasoline, are mostly shipped from the ports of Houston and New Orleans.

1 Farms with fertile soils like this one in Wisconsin cover much of the rural Midwest.

2 Large white containers, shown here at the Port of Houston, store oil from the Gulf Coast.

Millions of Americans vacation in the South, which makes the travel industry profitable in the region. Warm weather and beautiful beaches draw many vacationers to resorts in the South. You may not think of weather and beaches when you think about industry, but you should. Resort areas are an industry because they provide jobs and help local economies grow.

Many cities in the South trade goods and services with Mexico and countries in Central and South America. This trade is possible because several of the southern states are located near these countries. For example, Miami is an important trading port and travel connection with Caribbean countries, Mexico, and South America. Atlanta, Houston, and Dallas are also major transportation centers.

The Midwest

The Midwest is one of the most productive farming regions in the world. The Mississippi River and many of its tributaries carry materials that help create the region's rich soils, which are good for farming. Midwestern farmers grow mostly corn, wheat, and soybeans. Farmers in the region also raise livestock such as dairy cows.

The core of the Midwest's corn-growing region stretches from Ohio to Nebraska. Much of the corn is used to feed livestock, such as beef cattle and hogs.

To the north of the corn-growing region is an area of dairy farms. States with dairy farms are major producers of milk, cheese, and other dairy products. This area includes Wisconsin and most of Michigan and Minnesota. Much of the dairy farm region is pasture, but farmers also grow crops to feed dairy cows.

Many of the Midwest's farm and factory products are shipped to markets by water routes, such as those along the Ohio and Mississippi rivers. The other is through the Great Lakes and the Saint Lawrence Seaway to the Atlantic Ocean.

Most major cities in the Midwest are located on rivers or the Great Lakes. As a result, they are important transportation centers. Farm products, coal, and iron ore are easily shipped to these cities from nearby farms and mines. These natural resources support industries such as automobile manufacturing. For example, **Detroit**, Michigan, is the country's leading automobile producer.

One of the busiest shipping ports on the Great Lakes is **Chicago**, Illinois. The city also has one of the world's busiest airports. Chicago's industries attracted many immigrants in the late 1800s. People moved here to work in the city's steel mills. Today Chicago is the nation's third-largest city.

FOCUS ON READING

As you read about the Midwest, sort the details into three categories.

The West

The West is the largest region in the United States. Many western states have large open spaces with few people. The West is not all open spaces, however. Many large cities are on the Pacific coast.

One state on the coast, California, is home to more than 10 percent of the U.S. population. California's mild climate and wealth of resources attract people to the state. Most Californians live in Los Angeles, San Diego, and the San Francisco Bay area. The center of the country's entertainment industry, Hollywood, is in Los Angeles. Farming and the technology industry are also important to California's economy.

The economy of other states in the West is dependent on ranching and growing wheat. Wheat is grown mostly in Montana, Idaho, and Washington.

Much of the farmland in the West must be irrigated, or watered. One method of irrigation uses long sprinkler systems mounted on huge wheels. The wheels rotate slowly. This sprinkler system waters the area within a circle. From the air, parts of the irrigated Great Plains resemble a series of green circles.

The West also has rich deposits of coal, oil, gold, silver, copper, and other minerals. However, mining these minerals can cause problems. For example, coal miners in parts of the Great Plains use a **process** called strip mining, which strips away soil and rock. This kind of mining leads to soil erosion and other problems. Today laws require miners to restore mined areas.

In Oregon and Washington, forestry and fishing are two of the most important economic activities. **Seattle** is Washington's largest city. The Seattle area is home to many important industries, including a major computer software company. More than half of the people in Oregon live in and around Portland.

Alaska's economy is largely based on oil, forests, and fish. As in Washington and Oregon, people debate over developing

ACADEMIC VOCABULARY

process a series of steps by which a task is accomplished

Olympic National Park

One of the largest sections of coastal wilderness in the United States, shown here, stretches along the Pacific coast in Washington's Olympic National Park.

these resources. For example, some people want to limit oil drilling in wild areas of Alaska. Others want to expand drilling to produce more oil.

Hawaii's natural beauty, mild climate, and fertile soils are its most important resources. The islands' major crops are sugarcane and pineapples. Millions of tourists visit the islands each year.

READING CHECK Comparing How is the economy of the West different from the economy of the South?

Economy, Military, and Terrorism

The United States is the world's only superpower. It has both the largest economy and the most powerful military in the world. Those two strengths bring great opportunities to the United States. However, they also bring great challenges.

Economic and Military Power

The United States has many valuable natural resources. Modern technology and plentiful jobs make the United States a land of opportunity. With so many opportunities, the United States can support itself without relying on other countries. This independence has helped make the United States the world's largest economy.

Even with a strong economy, the United States benefits by trading with other countries. Major trading partners include Canada, Mexico, China, Japan, and Europe. The United States trades mostly with its neighbors, Canada and Mexico. In 1992 the United States, Mexico, and Canada signed the North American Free Trade Agreement, or NAFTA. This agreement made trade easier and cheaper between the three countries.

Rebirth in New York

This artist's sketch shows the new building that will stand where the World Trade Center once stood in New York.

With so much wealth, the United States can afford a powerful military. The main job of the U.S. armed forces is to protect our country. The U.S. military also has the opportunity to help other countries defend themselves.

Terrorism

On September 11, 2001, the United States suffered the deadliest terrorist attack in the country's history. Terrorists hijacked four American jets. They crashed two into the World Trade Center and one into the Pentagon. These attacks were a violent reminder that some people do not want the United States to be strong.

They want to disrupt our country's economy with **terrorism**, or violent attacks that cause fear.

In response to the terrorist attacks, U.S. President George W. Bush declared war on terrorism. He sent forces to Afghanistan, to kill or capture members of a terrorist group called al Qaeda. The United States also helped a new democratic government take power in Afghanistan. The United States then turned its attention to Iraq. President Bush believed that Iraqi leader Saddam Hussein was another threat to Americans. In 2003 Bush ordered U.S. troops to invade Iraq and remove Saddam from power.

Today world leaders are working with the United States to combat terrorism. In the United States, the Department of Homeland Security, a government agency, coordinates efforts to protect the country from any other terrorist attacks. Many other countries have increased security within their borders, especially at international airports.

Many Americans will never forget the people who lost their lives on September 11. In New York, a permanent memorial and building will stand at the former World Trade Center site. The main building, Freedom Tower, will be 70 stories tall. When completed in 2009, the tower will serve as a symbol of hope for New York and the country as a whole.

READING CHECK **Making Connections** What is the connection between the military and economic strength of the United States and the threat of terrorism?

SUMMARY AND PREVIEW In this section, you learned about the landscapes and economic activities of the different regions of the United States. You also learned that trade and terrorism are important issues in the country. In the next chapter, you will learn about Canada, our neighbor to the north of the United States.

Section 3 Assessment

go.hrw.com
Online Quiz
KEYWORD: SGB7 HP7

Reviewing Ideas, Terms, and Places

1. **a. Define** What is a **megalopolis**? What major cities are part of the largest megalopolis in the United States?
   b. Compare and Contrast How is land use in the Midwest similar to and different from land use in the South?
   c. Elaborate How are the regions of the United States different from one another?
2. **a. Define** What is **terrorism**? What terrorist attack occurred in September 2001?
   b. Explain What makes the United States a superpower?
   c. Elaborate What steps are the United States and other countries taking in an attempt to combat world terrorism?

Critical Thinking

3. **Finding Main Ideas** Use your notes to help you list at least one main idea about the population, resources, and economy of each region.

	Northeast	South	Midwest	West
Population				
Resources				
Economy				

FOCUS ON VIEWING

4. **Thinking about the United States Today** You have read about the regions of the United States, as well as issues facing the country today. What key words, images, and objects might represent what you have learned?

CHAPTER 8

Standardized Test Practice

DIRECTIONS: *Read questions 1 through 7 and write the letter of the best response. Then read question 8 and write your own well-constructed response.*

1 The United States and Canada share which physical feature?

A Canadian Shield

B Rocky Mountains

C Hudson Bay

D Saskatchewan River

2 What resource in Canada provides pulp and newsprint?

A forests

B nickel

C potash

D fish

3 Many Canadians moved from farms to cities to find

A gold.

B good schools.

C jobs.

D better weather.

4 Canada's prime minister oversees the country's

A railroads.

B parliament.

C provincial governments.

D city governments.

5 Canada's capital, Ottawa, is located in

A Northwest Territories.

B Nova Scotia.

C Ontario.

D British Columbia.

Climate of British Columbia

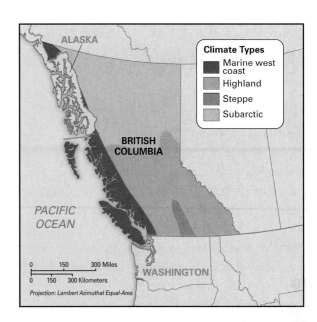

6 Based on the map above, which climate type does the Pacific coast of British Columbia experience?

A subarctic

B marine west coast

C highland

D steppe

7 About 60 percent of Canada's imported goods come from which country?

A Mexico

B Greenland

C Russia

D United States

8 **Extended Response** Look at the political map of Canada at the beginning of this chapter. Using information from the map, explain why the United States and Canada are major trading partners.

Describing a Place

Assignment
Write a paper describing one of these places in the Americas:
- a city
- a country

What are the physical features of a country? What is the weather like? What drives the economy? The answers to questions like these are often cold, hard facts and statistics. But they can bring life to a description of a place.

1. Prewrite

Identify a Topic and Big Idea

- Choose one of the topics above to write about.
- Turn your topic into a big idea, or thesis. For example, your big idea might be, "Cuba's government greatly influences life in the country."

> **TIP** **Precise Language** Describe your place with specific nouns, verbs, adjectives, and adverbs. For example, rather than writing "Buenos Aires is big," write "Buenos Aires is the largest city in Argentina."

Gather and Organize Information

- Look for information about your place in the library or on the Internet. Organize your notes in groupings such as physical features, economy, or culture. Decide which facts about the place you are describing are most important or unique.

2. Write

Use a Writer's Framework

A Writer's Framework

Introduction
- Start with an interesting fact or question.
- Identify your big idea and provide any necessary background information.

Body
- Write at least one paragraph for each category. Include facts that help explain each detail.
- Write about each detail in order of importance.

Conclusion
- Summarize your description in your final paragraph.

3. Evaluate and Revise

Review and Improve Your Paper

- Re-read your paper and use the questions below to identify ways to revise your paper.
- Make the changes needed to improve your paper.

Evaluation Questions for a Description of a Place

1. Do you begin with an interesting fact or question?
2. Does your introduction identify your big idea? Do you provide background information to help your readers better understand your idea?
3. Do you have at least one paragraph for each category?
4. Do you use order of importance to organize the details of your description?
5. Are there more details you would like to know about your place? If so, what are they?

4. Proofread and Publish

Give Your Description the Finishing Touch

- Make sure you used commas correctly when listing more than two details in a sentence.
- Check your spelling of the names of places.
- Share your description with classmates or with students in another social studies class.

5. Practice and Apply

Use the steps and strategies outlined in this workshop to write your description of a place. Share your description with classmates. With your classmates, group the descriptions by country and then identify the places you would like to visit.

References

Reading Social Studies 194

Atlas 202

Facts about the World 222

Gazetteer 226

Biographical Dictionary 231

English and Spanish Glossary 232

Economics Handbook 236

Index 238

Credits and Acknowledgments 247

Setting a Purpose

READING SOCIAL STUDIES

FOCUS ON READING

When you go on a trip, you have a purpose or a destination in mind before you start. Maps can help you get to your destination. When you read, you should also have a purpose in mind before you start. This purpose keeps you focused and moving toward your goal of understanding. Textbooks often provide "maps" to help you set a purpose for your reading. A textbook's "map" includes a chapter's headings, pictures, and study tips. To determine a purpose for your reading, look over the headings, pictures, and study tips. Then ask yourself a question that can guide you. See how looking over the chapter's first page can help you set a purpose.

What You Will Learn...

In this chapter you will learn about the location, growth, and decline of the Maya, Aztec, and Inca civilizations in the Americas.

From Early History of the Americas

SECTION 1
The Maya 14

SECTION 2
The Aztecs 20

SECTION 3
The Incas 25

Notice Headings, Pictures or Tips
Here's a tip on what I should learn about in this chapter.

Ask Questions
What do I want to learn about these three civilizations?

Set a Purpose
I've never heard of these civilizations. I wonder what they were like and why they declined. I'll read to find out.

YOU TRY IT!

You can also use the method described above to set a purpose for reading the main text in your book. Look at the heading for the following caption. Then write down one or two questions about what you will read. Finally, develop a purpose for reading about Tenochtitlán. State this purpose in one to two sentences.

Tenochtitlán

The Aztecs turned a swampy, uninhabited island into one of the largest and grandest cities in the world. The first Europeans to visit Tenochtitlán were amazed. At the time, the Aztec capital was about five times bigger than London.

From Section 2, The Aztecs

Predicting

FOCUS ON READING

Predicting is guessing what will happen next based on what you already know. In reading about geography, you can use what you know about the place you live to help you make predictions about other countries. Predicting helps you stay involved with your reading as you see whether your prediction was right. Your mind follows these four steps when you make predictions as you read:

Takes what you already know → Adds new information from your reading → Forms a prediction that makes sense → Confirms or adjusts your prediction based on what you just read

See how you might make a prediction from the following text:

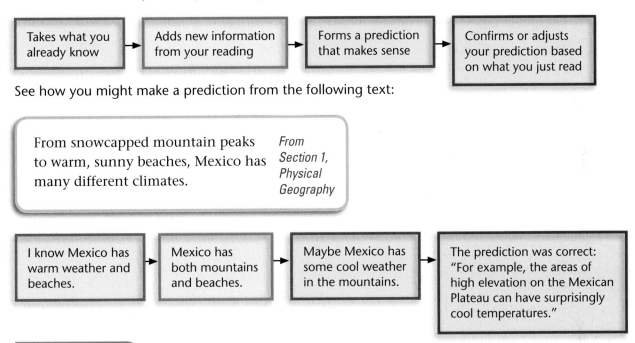

From snowcapped mountain peaks to warm, sunny beaches, Mexico has many different climates.

From Section 1, Physical Geography

I know Mexico has warm weather and beaches. → Mexico has both mountains and beaches. → Maybe Mexico has some cool weather in the mountains. → The prediction was correct: "For example, the areas of high elevation on the Mexican Plateau can have surprisingly cool temperatures."

YOU TRY IT!

Read the following sentences. Then use a graphic organizer like the one below to help you predict what you will learn in your reading. Check the text in Section 3 to see if your prediction was correct.

Mexico has a democratic government. However, Mexico is not like the United States where different political parties have always competed for power.

From Section 3, Mexico Today

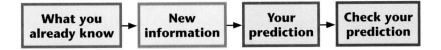

What you already know → New information → Your prediction → Check your prediction

Understanding Comparison-Contrast

FOCUS ON READING

Comparing shows how things are alike. Contrasting shows how things are different. You can understand comparison-contrast by learning to recognize clue words and points of comparison. Clue words let you know whether to look for similarities or differences. Points of comparison are the main topics that are being compared or contrasted.

> Many Caribbean islands share a similar history and culture. However, today the islands' different economies, governments, and cultural landscapes encourage many different ways of life in the Caribbean.
>
> *From Section 3, The Caribbean Islands*

Underlined words are clue words.

Highlighted words are points of comparison.

Clue Words	
Comparison	**Contrast**
share, similar, like, also, both, in addition, besides	however, while, unlike, different, but, although

YOU TRY IT!

Read the following passage to see how Haiti and the Dominican Republic are alike and different. Use a diagram like the one here to compare and contrast the two countries.

> Haiti occupies the mountainous western third of the island of Hispaniola. Port-au-Prince is the capital and center of the country's limited industry. Agricultural products such as coffee and sugarcane are the country's main exports. Most Haitians farm small plots.
>
> The Dominican Republic occupies the eastern part of Hispaniola. The Dominican Republic is not a rich country. However, its economy, health care, education, and housing are more developed than Haiti's. Agriculture is the basis of the economy
>
> *From Section 3, The Caribbean Islands*

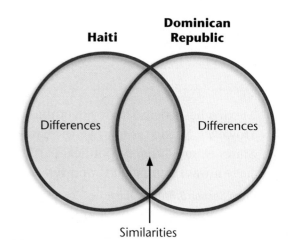

Haiti

Dominican Republic

Differences

Differences

Similarities

Identifying Supporting Details

FOCUS ON READING

Why believe what you read? One reason is because of details that support or prove the main idea. These details might be facts, statistics, examples, or definitions. In the example below, notice what kind of proof or supporting details help you believe the main idea.

> Colombia's economy relies on several valuable resources. Rich soil, steep slopes, and tall shade trees produce world-famous Colombian coffee. Other major export crops include bananas, sugarcane, and cotton. Many farms in Colombia produce flowers that are exported around the world. In fact, 80 percent of the country's flowers are shipped to the United States.
>
> *From Section 2, Colombia*

Main Idea
Colombia's economy relies on several valuable resources.

Supporting Details			
Example	**Fact**	**Fact**	**Statistic**
Colombian coffee	Other export crops	Export flowers	80 percent shipped to U.S.

YOU TRY IT!

Read the following sentences. Then identify the supporting details in a graphic organizer like the one above.

> Caribbean South America is home to some remarkable wildlife. For example, hundreds of bird species, meat-eating fish called piranhas, and crocodiles live in or around the Orinoco River. Colombia has one of the world's highest concentrations of plant and animal species. The country's wildlife includes jaguars, ocelots, and several species of monkeys.
>
> *From Section 1, Physical Geography*

Using Context Clues

FOCUS ON READING

One practical way to tackle unfamiliar words you encounter is to look at the context. Reading the words and sentences surrounding the word will often help you because they give definitions, examples, or synonyms. For example, maybe you're not sure what the word *context* means. Just from reading the previous sentences, however, you probably understood that it means the "the part of a text surrounding a word or passage that makes its meaning clear." You have relied on the context to help you define the word. In reading geography, you may forget what some of the geographical terms mean. You can use context clues to figure them out. See how this process works in the example below with the word *tributary*.

> The Amazon River is about 4,000 miles long. It extends from the Andes Mountains in Peru to the Atlantic Ocean. Hundreds of tributaries flow into it, draining an area that includes parts of most South American countries.
>
> *From Section 1, Physical Geography*

1. Look at the surrounding words or sentences.
The passage talks about the Amazon River and what flows into it.

2. Make a guess at the word's meaning.
A tributary must be a smaller river or stream that flows into a bigger river.

3. Check your guess by inserting it into the passage.
Hundreds of smaller rivers flow into it.

YOU TRY IT!

Read the following sentences, and then use the three steps described above to help you define *hydroelectric*.

> Atlantic South America also has good mineral and energy resources such as gold, silver, copper, iron, and oil. Dams on some of the region's large rivers also provide hydroelectric power.
>
> *From Section 1, Physical Geography*

Making Inferences

FOCUS ON READING

Sometimes reading effectively means understanding both what the writer tells you directly and what the writer doesn't tell you. When you fill in the gaps, you are making inferences, or educated guesses. Why worry about what the writer doesn't tell you? Making inferences can help you make connections with the text. It can also give you a fuller picture of the information. To make an inference, think about the text and what you know or can guess from the information. The example below shows you the process.

> At the southern tip of the continent, the Strait of Magellan links the Atlantic and Pacific oceans. A strait is a narrow body of water connecting two larger bodies of water. The large island south of the strait is Tierra del Fuego, or "land of fire."
>
> *From Section 1, Physical Geography*

1. Determine what the passage says:
The Strait of Magellan connects the Atlantic and Pacific oceans. There is an island south of it.

2. Determine what you know about the topic or what you can connect to your experience.
This sounds like a shortcut to me. It would keep boats from having to sail all the way around the island.

3. Make an inference.
Many ships probably use the Strait of Magellan because it is a shortcut.

YOU TRY IT!

Read the following sentences. Then use the three steps described above to make an inference about the Galápagos Islands.

> Chile and Ecuador both control large islands in the Pacific Ocean. Ecuador's volcanic Galápagos Islands have wildlife not found anywhere else in the world.
>
> *From Section 1, Physical Geography*

Categorizing

FOCUS ON READING

When you sort things into groups of similar items, you are categorizing. When you read, categorizing helps you to identify the main groups of information. Then you can find and see the individual facts in each group. Notice how the information in the paragraph below has been sorted into three main groups, with details listed under each group.

> If you were traveling across the United States, you might start on the country's eastern coast. This low area, which is flat and close to sea level, is called the Atlantic Coastal Plain. As you go west, the land gradually rises higher to a region called the Piedmont. The Appalachian Mountains, which are the main mountain range in the East, rise above the Piedmont.
>
> *From Section 1, Physical Geography*

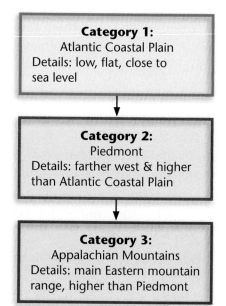

Category 1:
Atlantic Coastal Plain
Details: low, flat, close to sea level

Category 2:
Piedmont
Details: farther west & higher than Atlantic Coastal Plain

Category 3:
Appalachian Mountains
Details: main Eastern mountain range, higher than Piedmont

YOU TRY IT!

Read the following paragraph, and then use a graphic organizer like the one above to categorize the group and details in the paragraph. Create as many boxes as you need to list the main groups.

> The eastern United States has three climate regions. In the Northeast, people live in a humid continental climate with snowy winters and warm, humid summers. Southerners, on the other hand, experience milder winters and the warm, humid summers of a humid subtropical climate. Most of Florida is warm all year.
>
> *From Section 1, Physical Geography*

Understanding Lists

FOCUS ON READING

A to-do list can keep you focused on what you need to get done. Keeping lists while you read can keep you focused on understanding the main points of a text. In the example below, a list helps the reader identify and focus on the types of cold climates found in central and northern Canada.

The farther north you go in Canada, the colder it gets. The coldest areas of Canada are located close to the Arctic Circle. Much of central and northern Canada has a sub-arctic climate. The far north has tundra and ice cap climates. About half of Canada lies in these extremely cold climates.

From Section 1, Physical Geography

List of cold climates
1. subarctic
2. tundra
3. ice cap

YOU TRY IT!

Read the sentences and then list the territories that make up the Canadian North region.

Northern Canada is extremely cold due to its location close to the Arctic Circle. The region called the Canadian North includes the Yukon Territory, the Northwest Territories, and Nunavut. These three territories cover more than a third of Canada but are home to only about 100,000 people.

From Section 3, Canada Today

United States: Physical

COAST RANGES

CASCADE RANGE

ROCKY

MOUNTAINS

SIERRA NEVADA

GREAT

BASIN

COLORADO

PLATEAU

GREAT INTERIOR PLAINS

Strait of Juan de Fuca

Puget Sound

Mount Rainier
14,410 ft
(4,392 m)

Franklin D. Roosevelt Lake

Columbia River

Columbia Plateau

Bitterroot Range

Salmon River Mts.

Sawtooth Mts.

Lewis Range

CONTINENTAL

Grand Tetons

Gannett Peak
13,804 ft
(4,207 m)

Wind River Range

Milk River

Missouri River

Fort Peck Lake

Yellowstone River

Bighorn Mts.

Powder River

Lake Sakakawea

Lake Oahe

Black Hills

Cheyenne River

White River

Niobrara River

Wasatch Range

Great Salt Lake

Uinta Mts.

Uinta Lake

DIVIDE

Front Range

North Platte River

South Platte River

Platte River

Republican River

Smoky Hill River

Klamath River

Goose Lake

Shasta Lake

Pyramid Lake

Lake Tahoe

Sacramento River

Central Valley

San Joaquin River

Death Valley

Mount Whitney
14,494 ft
(4,419 m)

Mojave Desert

Cape Mendocino

San Francisco Bay

Monterey Bay

Coast Ranges

Channel Islands

Salton Sea

Imperial Valley

Lake Mead

Grand Canyon

Painted Desert

Colorado River

Lake Powell

Gila River

Sonoran Desert

Mount Elbert
14,433 ft
(4,400 m)

Pikes Peak
14,110 ft
(4,301 m)

San Luis Valley

Sangre de Cristo Mts.

Rio Grande

DIVIDE

CONTINENTAL

Canadian River

Pecos River

Colorado R.

Amistad Reservoir

Nueces Ri.

Gulf of California

PACIFIC

OCEAN

MEXICO

To understand the relative locations of Alaska and Hawaii, as well as the vast distances separating them from the rest of the United States, see the world map.

HAWAII

Kauai

Niihau

Oahu

Molokai

Maui

Lanai

Kahoolawe

Mauna Kea
13,796 ft
(4,206 m)

Hawaii

PACIFIC OCEAN

22°N

160°W

155°W

19°N

| 0 | 75 | 150 Miles |
| 0 | 75 | 150 Kilometers |

Projection: Mercator

ARCTIC OCEAN

Arctic Circle

RUSSIA

Bering Strait

BROOKS RANGE

Yukon River

Tanana River

St. Lawrence Island

St. Matthew Island

Nunivak Island

Kuskokwim River

ALASKA RANGE

Mount McKinley
20,320 ft
(6,194 m)

CANADA

Bering Sea

Attu Island

ALEUTIAN ISLANDS

Gulf of Alaska

Kodiak Island

Alexander Archipelago

55°N

50°N

170°E

180°

170°W

160°W

150°W

| 0 | 250 | 500 Miles |
| 0 | 250 | 500 Kilometers |

Projection: Albers Equal Area

PACIFIC OCEAN

CANADA

Isle Royale
Mesabi Range
Lake Superior

Minnesota River
Mississippi River
Wisconsin River
Lake Michigan
Lake Huron
Lake Ontario
Lake Erie

St. Lawrence River
St. Lawrence Seaway
St. Lawrence River
Lake Champlain
Adirondack Mts.
Green Mts.
White Mts.
Longfellow Mts.
Penobscot River
St. John River
Connecticut River
Cape Cod

Des Moines River
Missouri River
Mississippi River
Illinois River
Wabash River
Scioto River
Allegheny R.
PLATEAU
ALLEGHENY
Catskill Mts.
Susquehanna River
Delaware River
Long Island Sound
Long Island

40°N

Arkansas R.

P L A I N S

Lake of the Ozarks
OZARK PLATEAU
Keystone Lake
White River
Arkansas River
Ohio River
Cumberland River
Lake Barkley
Kentucky Lake
Cumberland Plateau
Tennessee River
Monongahela R.
Kanawha River
APPALACHIAN MOUNTAINS
BLUE RIDGE MOUNTAINS
Great Smoky Mts.
Potomac River
James River
Roanoke River

Delaware Bay
Chesapeake Bay
ATLANTIC OCEAN
70°W

Pamlico Sound
Cape Hatteras
35°N

Ouachita Mts.
Kentucky Lake

...ula Lake
...exoma

Trinity River
Saline River
Red River
Mississippi River
Pearl River
Tombigbee River
Alabama R.
Coosa River
Chattahoochee River
Oconee River
Savannah River
Altamaha River
Sea Islands

PIEDMONT

ELEVATION

Feet	Meters
13,120	4,000
6,560	2,000
1,640	500
656	200
(Sea level) 0	0 (Sea level)
Below sea level	Below sea level

0   100   200 Miles
0   100   200 Kilometers

Projection: Albers Equal Area

Toledo Bend Reservoir
GULF
COASTAL
PLAIN

Chandeleur Islands
Mississippi Delta

Okefenokee Swamp

Cape Canaveral
80°W

FLORIDA PENINSULA

N
W   E
S

Gulf of Mexico

Lake Okeechobee

BAHAMAS
25°N

The Everglades
Cape Sable
Florida Keys
Straits of Florida
75°W

95°W   90°W   85°W

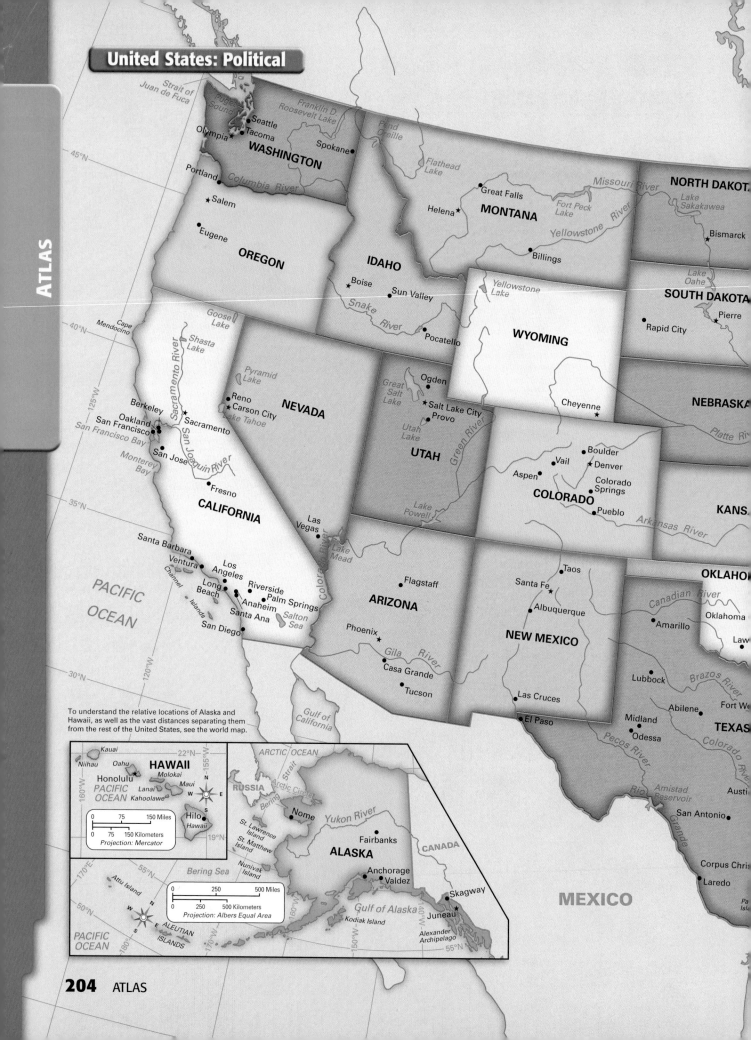

ATLAS

Strait of Juan de Fuca

Puget Sound

Seattle
Tacoma
Olympia ★
WASHINGTON
Spokane

Franklin D.
Roosevelt Lake

Pend Oreille

Flathead Lake

MONTANA
Great Falls
Helena ★
Billings

Fort Peck Lake

Missouri River

Yellowstone River

NORTH DAKOTA
Lake Sakakawea
Bismarck

Portland
Columbia River
★ Salem
Eugene
OREGON

45°N

IDAHO
Boise ★
Sun Valley
Snake River
Pocatello

Yellowstone Lake

WYOMING

Lake Oahe

SOUTH DAKOTA
Rapid City
★ Pierre

Cape Mendocino

40°N

Goose Lake

Shasta Lake

Sacramento River

Pyramid Lake

NEVADA
Reno
Carson City ★
Lake Tahoe
Sacramento ★

Great Salt Lake

Ogden
Salt Lake City ★
Provo

Utah Lake

UTAH

Green River

Cheyenne ★

NEBRASKA

Platte River

125°W

Berkeley
Oakland
San Francisco
San Francisco Bay
San Jose

San Joaquin River

Monterey Bay

Fresno

Boulder
Vail
★ Denver
Aspen
Colorado Springs
COLORADO
Pueblo

Arkansas River

KANS.

35°N

CALIFORNIA

Las Vegas

Lake Mead

Lake Powell

Santa Barbara
Ventura
Los Angeles
Long Beach
Anaheim
Santa Ana
Riverside
Palm Springs
Channel Islands
Salton Sea
San Diego

Colorado River

Flagstaff

ARIZONA

Phoenix ★

Gila River

Casa Grande

Tucson

Taos
Santa Fe ★
Albuquerque

NEW MEXICO

Canadian River

OKLAHOM.
Oklahoma ★
Amarillo
Law

PACIFIC OCEAN

30°N

120°W

Gulf of California

Las Cruces
El Paso

Lubbock
Brazos River
Abilene
Fort We
Midland
Odessa
TEXAS

Pecos River
Colorado River

Amistad Reservoir
Austin

To understand the relative locations of Alaska and Hawaii, as well as the vast distances separating them from the rest of the United States, see the world map.

Rio Grande

San Antonio

MEXICO

Corpus Christ
Laredo

Kauai
Niihau
Oahu
HAWAII
Honolulu ★
Molokai
Lanai Maui
Kahoolawe
PACIFIC OCEAN
Hilo
Hawaii

0   75   150 Miles
0   75   150 Kilometers
Projection: Mercator

22°N
19°N

155°W
160°W

ARCTIC OCEAN

Arctic Circle

RUSSIA
Bering Strait
Nome
Yukon River

St. Lawrence Island
St. Matthew Island
Nunivak Island

Fairbanks

CANADA

ALASKA

Anchorage
Valdez

Skagway

Juneau

Bering Sea

Attu Island

Aleutian Islands

0   250   500 Miles
0   250   500 Kilometers
Projection: Albers Equal Area

Kodiak Island

Gulf of Alaska

Alexander Archipelago

55°N
50°N

170°E
180°
170°W
160°W
150°W
140°W

PACIFIC OCEAN

CANADA

MINNESOTA
Grand Forks
Fargo
Duluth
Superior
Marquette
Sault Ste. Marie
MICHIGAN
Lake Superior
WISCONSIN
Green Bay
Minneapolis
St. Paul
Madison
Milwaukee
Lake Michigan
Lake Huron
Grand Rapids
Lansing
Saginaw
Detroit
Ann Arbor
Sioux Falls
Sioux City
IOWA
Cedar Rapids
Davenport
Des Moines
Rockford
Chicago
Gary
South Bend
Fort Wayne
Toledo
Cleveland
Youngstown
Akron
Lake Erie

MAINE
Augusta
Portland
Burlington
Montpelier
Lake Champlain
VT
NH
Concord
Manchester
Hudson R.
Lake Ontario
Rochester
Syracuse
Albany
Springfield
MA
Worcester
Boston
Providence
Hartford
CT
RI
New Haven
Bridgeport
Yonkers
Long Island Sound
Long Island
Cape Cod
Buffalo
NEW YORK
Jersey City
Newark
New York City
Susquehanna River
Lake Erie
PENNSYLVANIA
Allentown
Trenton
Harrisburg
Philadelphia
Camden
NJ
Atlantic City
Pittsburgh
40°N
St. Lawrence River
Connecticut R.

Missouri River
MISSOURI
Kansas City
Kansas City
Topeka
Lincoln
Omaha
Jefferson City
St. Louis
East St. Louis
Lake of the Ozarks
ILLINOIS
Peoria
Springfield
INDIANA
Indianapolis
Dayton
Cincinnati
OHIO
Columbus
Mississippi River
Illinois River

WEST VIRGINIA
Charleston
Baltimore
Washington, D.C.
MD
Annapolis
DE
Dover
Delaware Bay
Chesapeake Bay
VIRGINIA
Richmond
Newport News
Norfolk
Virginia Beach
ATLANTIC OCEAN
70°W

Wichita
Keystone Lake
Tulsa
Kaw Lake
Fayetteville
ARKANSAS
Little Rock
Pine Bluff
Springfield
KENTUCKY
Louisville
Evansville
Frankfort
Lexington
Ohio River
Lake Barkley
Nashville
Knoxville
Asheville
TENNESSEE
Chattanooga
Memphis
Huntsville
Kentucky Lake
Greensboro
Durham
Raleigh
Winston-Salem
NORTH CAROLINA
Charlotte
Greenville
Cape Hatteras
35°N

Dallas
Waco
Toledo Bend Reservoir
LOUISIANA
Shreveport
Beaumont
Houston
Galveston
Baton Rouge
New Orleans
Biloxi
Chandeleur Islands
MISSISSIPPI
Vicksburg
Jackson
Meridian
ALABAMA
Birmingham
Montgomery
Mobile
Pensacola
Red River
Mississippi River
GEORGIA
Atlanta
Columbus
Macon
Savannah
Chattahoochee River
Savannah River
SOUTH CAROLINA
Columbia
Charleston
Sea Islands
Jacksonville
30°N
80°W

Gulf of Mexico
Tallahassee
Gainesville
FLORIDA
Orlando
Tampa
St. Petersburg
Lake Okeechobee
Cape Canaveral
Fort Myers
Fort Lauderdale
Miami
Cape Sable
Florida Keys
Straits of Florida
BAHAMAS
25°N
75°W

N
W E
S

95°W
90°W
85°W

Legend:
⊛ National capital
★ State capitals
• Other cities

0   100   200 Miles
0   100   200 Kilometers

Projection: Albers Equal Area

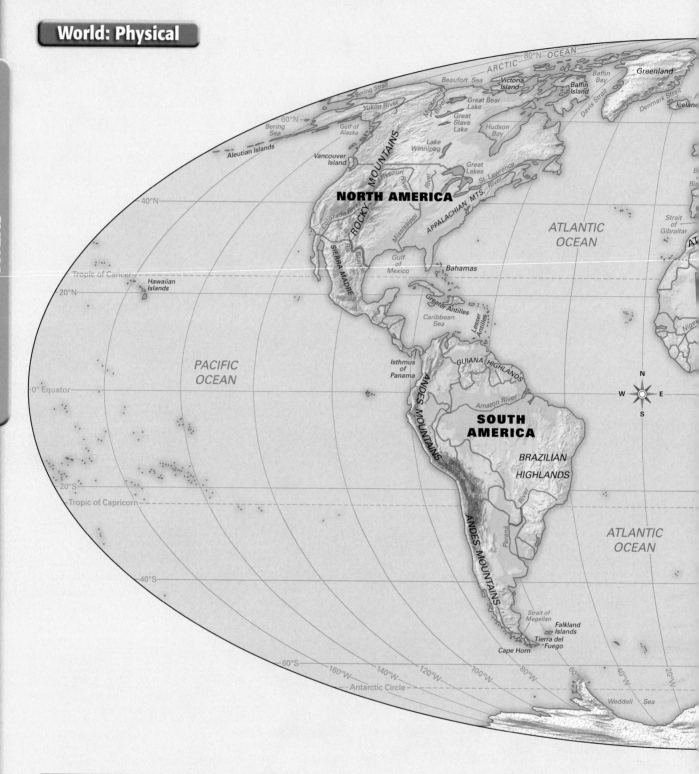

ARCTIC 80°N OCEAN

Beaufort Sea
Bering Strait
Yukon River
Bering Sea
Gulf of Alaska
Aleutian Islands
Vancouver Island
60°N
Victoria Island
Great Bear Lake
Mackenzie River
Great Slave Lake
Lake Winnipeg
Hudson Bay
Baffin Island
Davis Strait
Baffin Bay
Denmark Strait
Greenland
Iceland

ROCKY MOUNTAINS
NORTH AMERICA
Great Lakes
St. Lawrence River
APPALACHIAN MTS.
40°N
ATLANTIC OCEAN
Strait of Gibraltar

Colorado River
Missouri River
Mississippi
SIERRA MADRE
Rio Grande
Gulf of Mexico
Bahamas
Tropic of Cancer
20°N
Hawaiian Islands
Greater Antilles
Caribbean Sea
Lesser Antilles

Niger

PACIFIC OCEAN
Isthmus of Panama
GUIANA HIGHLANDS
ANDES MOUNTAINS
Amazon River
0° Equator

SOUTH AMERICA
BRAZILIAN HIGHLANDS

N
W   E
S

20°S
Tropic of Capricorn
Paraná River
ATLANTIC OCEAN

ANDES MOUNTAINS
40°S

Strait of Magellan
Falkland Islands
Tierra del Fuego
Cape Horn

60°S
160°W 140°W 120°W 100°W 80°W 60°W 40°W 20°W
Antarctic Circle
Weddell Sea

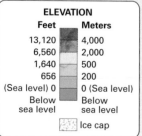

ELEVATION

Feet		Meters
13,120		4,000
6,560		2,000
1,640		500
656		200
(Sea level) 0		0 (Sea level)
Below sea level		Below sea level
	Ice cap	

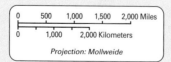

0   500   1,000   1,500   2,000 Miles
0   1,000   2,000 Kilometers

Projection: Mollweide

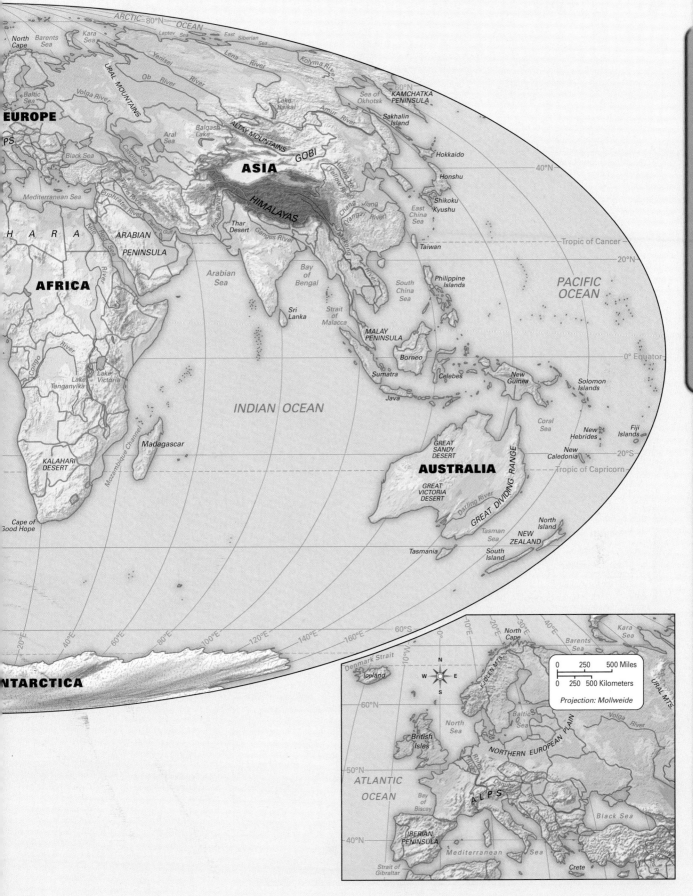

ARCTIC 80°N OCEAN
North Cape
Barents Sea
Kara Sea
Laptev Sea
East Siberian Sea

EUROPE
PS
Baltic Sea
Black Sea
Mediterranean Sea
HARA
AFRICA

URAL MOUNTAINS
Volga River
Ob River
Yenisei River
Lena River
Kolyma River
Amur River

Balqash Lake
Aral Sea
Caspian Sea
Lake Baikal
ALTAY MOUNTAINS

ASIA
GOBI

Sea of Okhotsk
KAMCHATKA PENINSULA
Sakhalin Island
60°N

Hokkaido
Honshu
Shikoku
Kyushu
40°N

Huang He
Yellow River
Chang Jiang
Yangzi River
East China Sea

Tigris River
Euphrates River
Persian Gulf

ARABIAN PENINSULA
Nile River
Red Sea

Thar Desert
HIMALAYAS
Indus River
Ganges River
Mekong River

Taiwan
Tropic of Cancer
20°N

Arabian Sea
Bay of Bengal

Philippine Islands
South China Sea

PACIFIC OCEAN

Congo River
Lake Tanganyika
Lake Victoria

Sri Lanka
Strait of Malacca

MALAY PENINSULA

Sumatra
Borneo
Celebes
Java

New Guinea
Solomon Islands

0° Equator

INDIAN OCEAN

Madagascar
Mozambique Channel

Coral Sea

New Hebrides
New Caledonia
Fiji Islands

GREAT SANDY DESERT
AUSTRALIA
GREAT VICTORIA DESERT

GREAT DIVIDING RANGE
Darling River

20°S
Tropic of Capricorn

KALAHARI DESERT

Cape of Good Hope

Tasman Sea
Tasmania
North Island
NEW ZEALAND
South Island

20°E 40°E 60°E 80°E 100°E 120°E 140°E 160°E 60°S

NTARCTICA

ATLAS

Denmark Strait
Iceland
10°W
0°
10°E 20°E 30°E 40°E
North Cape
Barents Sea
Kara Sea

60°N

0 250 500 Miles
0 250 500 Kilometers
Projection: Mollweide

ATLANTIC OCEAN
50°N

British Isles
North Sea
Baltic Sea

NORTHERN EUROPEAN PLAIN
ALPS
Volga River
URAL MTS.

Bay of Biscay
40°N
IBERIAN PENINSULA
Rhine
Danube
Black Sea

Strait of Gibraltar
Mediterranean Sea
Crete

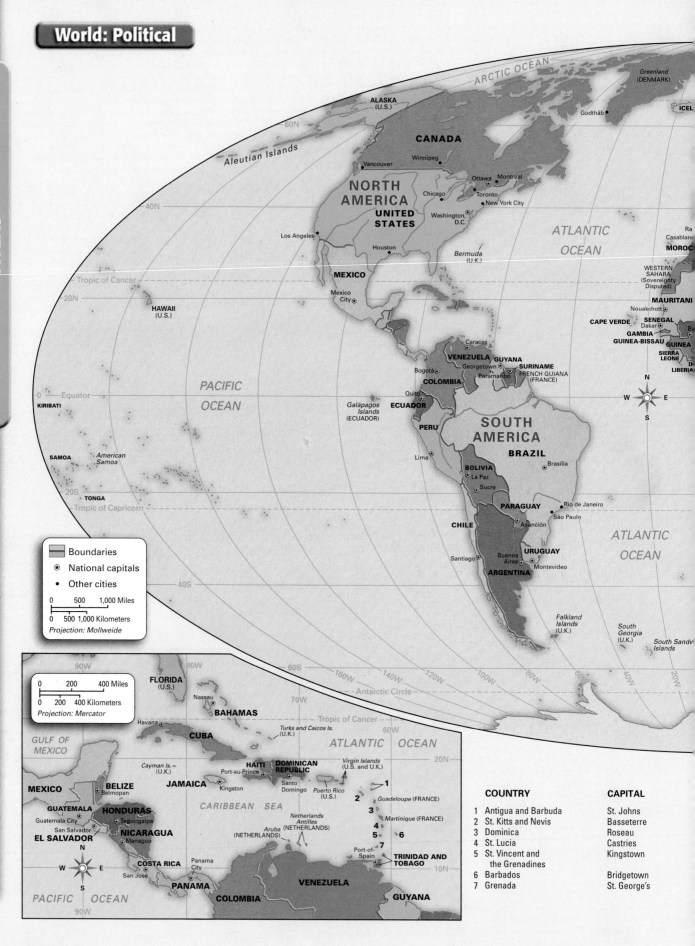

ATLAS

Boundaries
⊛ National capitals
• Other cities

0   500   1,000 Miles
0   500 1,000 Kilometers
Projection: Mollweide

0   200   400 Miles
0   200 400 Kilometers
Projection: Mercator

COUNTRY	CAPITAL
1 Antigua and Barbuda	St. Johns
2 St. Kitts and Nevis	Basseterre
3 Dominica	Roseau
4 St. Lucia	Castries
5 St. Vincent and the Grenadines	Kingstown
6 Barbados	Bridgetown
7 Grenada	St. George's

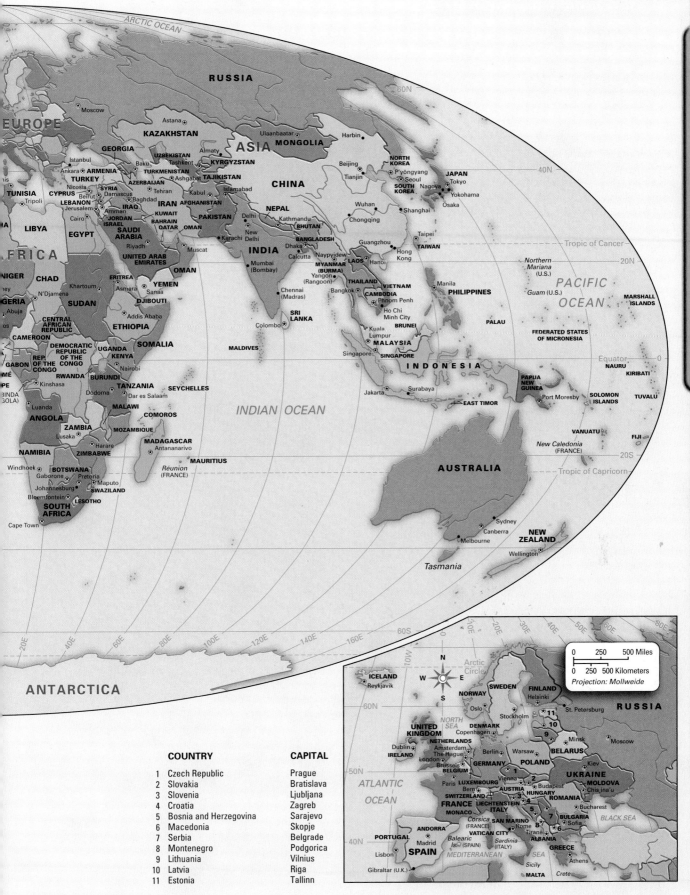

ARCTIC OCEAN

RUSSIA

Moscow

EUROPE

KAZAKHSTAN

Astana

ASIA

MONGOLIA

Ulaanbaatar

Harbin

GEORGIA

Almaty

Beijing

NORTH
KOREA

JAPAN

Istanbul

UZBEKISTAN

KYRGYZSTAN

P'yŏngyang

Tokyo

Ankara

ARMENIA

Baku

Tashkent

TAJIKISTAN

Tianjin

Seoul

SOUTH
KOREA

Nagoya

TURKEY

AZERBAIJAN

Ashgabat

Yokohama

Nicosia

SYRIA

Damascus

Tehran

CHINA

Wuhan

Osaka

TUNISIA

CYPRUS

Beirut

Baghdad

Kabul

Islamabad

Shanghai

Tripoli

LEBANON

Jerusalem

IRAQ

AFGHANISTAN

NEPAL

Chongqing

Amman

ISRAEL

JORDAN

KUWAIT

IRAN

Delhi

Kathmandu

LIBYA

Cairo

SAUDI
ARABIA

BAHRAIN

QATAR

PAKISTAN

New
Delhi

BHUTAN

Guangzhou

TAIWAN

Taipei

Tropic of Cancer

EGYPT

Riyadh

OMAN

Karachi

BANGLADESH

Dhaka

Hong
Kong

Northern
Mariana
(U.S.)

AFRICA

UNITED ARAB
EMIRATES

Muscat

INDIA

Calcutta

MYANMAR
(BURMA)

Naypyidew

LAOS

Hanoi

20N

PACIFIC
OCEAN

NIGER

CHAD

Khartoum

ERITREA

Asmara

YEMEN

OMAN

Mumbai
(Bombay)

Yangon
(Rangoon)

THAILAND

VIETNAM

Manila

Guam (U.S.)

MARSHALL
ISLANDS

GERIA

Abuja

N'Djamena

SUDAN

Sanaa

DJIBOUTI

Chennai
(Madras)

Bangkok

CAMBODIA

PHILIPPINES

os

CAMEROON

CENTRAL
AFRICAN
REPUBLIC

Addis Ababa

ETHIOPIA

SOMALIA

Colombo

SRI
LANKA

Ho Chi
Minh City

Phnom Penh

BRUNEI

PALAU

FEDERATED STATES
OF MICRONESIA

GABON

DEMOCRATIC
REPUBLIC
OF THE
CONGO

UGANDA

KENYA

MALDIVES

Kuala
Lumpur

MALAYSIA

Equator

NAURU

0

PE

REP.
OF THE
CONGO

Kinshasa

RWANDA

BURUNDI

Nairobi

Singapore

SINGAPORE

KIRIBATI

BINDA
GOLA)

Luanda

Dodoma

TANZANIA

Dar es Salaam

SEYCHELLES

INDONESIA

PAPUA
NEW
GUINEA

TUVALU

ANGOLA

ZAMBIA

MALAWI

COMOROS

INDIAN OCEAN

Jakarta

Surabaya

Port Moresby

SOLOMON
ISLANDS

VANUATU

FIJI

NAMIBIA

Lusaka

Harare

ZIMBABWE

MOZAMBIQUE

MADAGASCAR

Antananarivo

MAURITIUS

EAST TIMOR

New Caledonia
(FRANCE)

20S

Windhoek

BOTSWANA

Gaborone

Pretoria

Maputo

SWAZILAND

Réunion
(FRANCE)

AUSTRALIA

Tropic of Capricorn

Johannesburg

Bloemfontein

LESOTHO

SOUTH
AFRICA

Cape Town

Sydney

Canberra

NEW
ZEALAND

Melbourne

60S

Wellington

Tasmania

ANTARCTICA

20E

40E

60E

80E

100E

120E

140E

160E

	COUNTRY	CAPITAL
1	Czech Republic	Prague
2	Slovakia	Bratislava
3	Slovenia	Ljubljana
4	Croatia	Zagreb
5	Bosnia and Herzegovina	Sarajevo
6	Macedonia	Skopje
7	Serbia	Belgrade
8	Montenegro	Podgorica
9	Lithuania	Vilnius
10	Latvia	Riga
11	Estonia	Tallinn

0   250   500 Miles

0   250   500 Kilometers

Projection: Mollweide

ICELAND

Reykjavik

Arctic
Circle

NORWAY

SWEDEN

FINLAND

Helsinki

RUSSIA

N
W   E
S

St. Petersburg

60N

Oslo

Stockholm

11

UNITED
KINGDOM

NORTH
SEA

DENMARK

Copenhagen

10

9

Minsk

Moscow

Dublin

IRELAND

NETHERLANDS

Amsterdam

The Hague

Berlin

Warsaw

BELARUS

ATLANTIC
OCEAN

London

GERMANY

POLAND

Kiev

50N

Paris

Brussels

BELGIUM

1

UKRAINE

LUXEMBOURG

2

Budapest

MOLDOVA

Chiṣinău

FRANCE

Bern

SWITZERLAND

AUSTRIA

3

HUNGARY

ROMANIA

LIECHTENSTEIN

4

ITALY

5

7

Bucharest

MONACO

Corsica
(FRANCE)

SAN MARINO

Rome

8

BULGARIA

Sofia

BLACK SEA

PORTUGAL

ANDORRA

VATICAN CITY

Sardinia
(ITALY)

6

ALBANIA

Tirane

GREECE

40N

Madrid

Balearic
Is. (SPAIN)

SPAIN

Lisbon

MEDITERRANEAN

SEA

Sicily

Athens

Gibraltar (U.K.)

MALTA

Crete

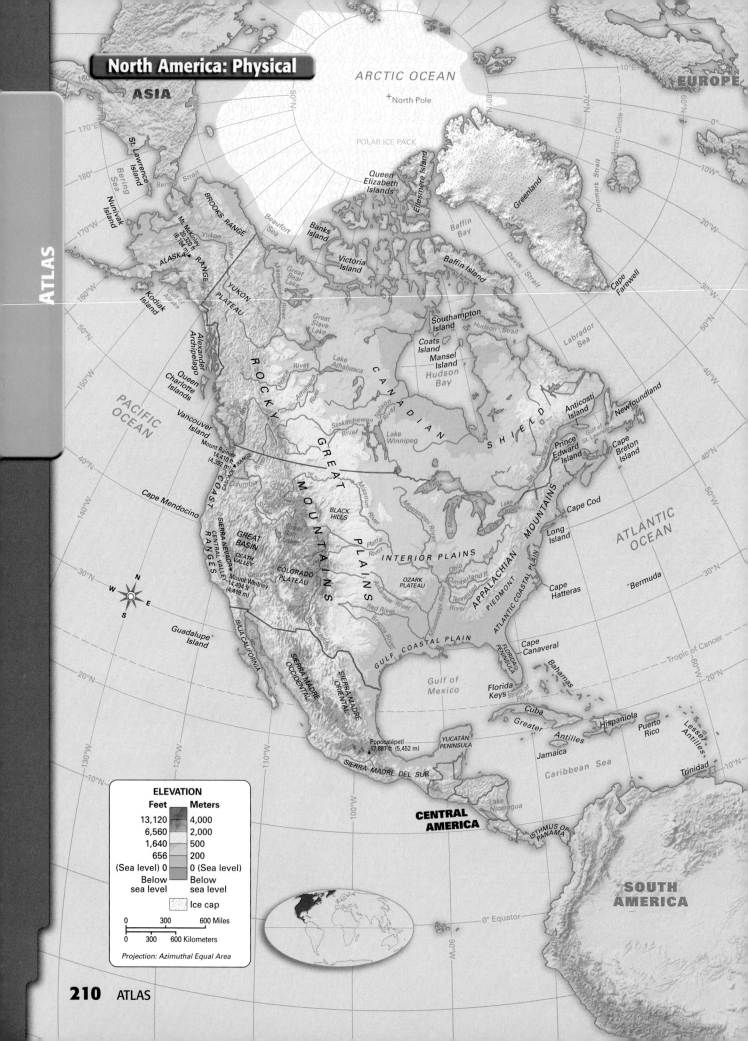

North America: Physical

ASIA

ARCTIC OCEAN

+North Pole

EUROPE

POLAR ICE PACK

10°E

80°N

St. Lawrence Island
Bering Strait
Nunivak Island
Bering Sea
170°E
180°
170°W

BROOKS RANGE
Mt. McKinley 20,320 ft (6,194 m)
ALASKA RANGE
Yukon River
Beaufort Sea
Banks Island
Victoria Island

Queen Elizabeth Islands
Ellesmere Island
Greenland

Baffin Bay
Baffin Island
Davis Strait

Arctic Circle

70°N

Denmark Strait

60°N

50°N

Cape Farewell

30°W

Kodiak Island
Gulf of Alaska
Alexander Archipelago
Queen Charlotte Islands
Vancouver Island

YUKON PLATEAU

Mackenzie River
Great Bear Lake

Great Slave Lake
Lake Athabasca

Southampton Island
Coats Island
Mansel Island
Hudson Strait

Hudson Bay

Labrador Sea

40°W

PACIFIC OCEAN

Mount Rainier 14,410 ft (4,392 m)
Columbia
Cape Mendocino

ROCKY MOUNTAINS
GREAT PLAINS

Peace River
Athabasca River
Saskatchewan River

Nelson River
Lake Winnipeg

CANADIAN SHIELD

Lake Superior

St. Lawrence River
Gulf of St. Lawrence

Anticosti Island
Prince Edward Island
Newfoundland
Cape Breton Island

50°W

40°N

Snake
CASCADE RANGE
COAST RANGES
SIERRA NEVADA
CENTRAL VALLEY
DEATH VALLEY
Mount Whitney 14,494 ft (4,419 m)

GREAT BASIN

COLORADO PLATEAU

BLACK HILLS

Missouri River
Platte River

INTERIOR PLAINS

Mississippi River

Lake Michigan
Lake Ontario
Lake Erie

APPALACHIAN MOUNTAINS

Cape Cod
Long Island

ATLANTIC OCEAN

40°N

N
W E
S

Guadalupe Island

Great Salt Lake

Colorado River
Rio Grande

OZARK PLATEAU

Ohio R.
Cumberland R.
Tennessee River

Arkansas River
Red River
Brazos River

PIEDMONT
ATLANTIC COASTAL PLAIN

Cape Hatteras

Bermuda

30°N

BAJA CALIFORNIA

SIERRA MADRE OCCIDENTAL
SIERRA MADRE ORIENTAL

GULF COASTAL PLAIN

FLORIDA PENINSULA

Cape Canaveral

Tropic of Cancer

60°W

20°N

Gulf of Mexico

Florida Keys
Straits of Florida
Bahamas

20°N

Popocatépetl 17,887 ft (5,452 m)
YUCATÁN PENINSULA

Cuba
Greater Antilles
Jamaica

Hispaniola
Puerto Rico
Lesser Antilles

SIERRA MADRE DEL SUR

Caribbean Sea

Trinidad

10°N

CENTRAL AMERICA

Lake Nicaragua
ISTHMUS OF PANAMA

0° Equator

SOUTH AMERICA

ELEVATION

Feet		Meters
13,120		4,000
6,560		2,000
1,640		500
656		200
(Sea level) 0		0 (Sea level)
Below sea level		Below sea level

Ice cap

0   300   600 Miles
0   300   600 Kilometers

Projection: Azimuthal Equal Area

North America: Political

ARCTIC OCEAN

ASIA

EUROPE

North Pole

ICELAND

Queen Elizabeth Islands

Greenland (DENMARK)

Ellesmere Island

Banks Island

Baffin Bay

Bering Strait

Point Barrow

Beaufort Sea

Victoria Island

Baffin Island

Denmark Strait

Davis Strait

Cape Farewell

St. Lawrence Island

Nunivak Island

ALASKA (U.S.)

Anchorage

Kodiak Island

Gulf of Alaska

Juneau

Alexander Archipelago

Queen Charlotte Islands

Vancouver Island

Great Bear Lake

Great Slave Lake

Southampton Island

Coats Island

Mansel Island

Hudson Strait

Labrador Sea

Hudson Bay

CANADA

Edmonton

Calgary

Vancouver

Lake Winnipeg

Anticosti Island

Newfoundland

Gulf of St. Lawrence

St. Pierre and Miquelon (FRANCE)

Seattle

Portland

Winnipeg

Lake Superior

Lake Huron

Prince Edward Island

Cape Breton Island

Quebec

Montreal

PACIFIC OCEAN

Minneapolis

Milwaukee

Detroit

Chicago

Lake Michigan

Lake Ontario

Lake Erie

Ottawa

Toronto

Boston

Cape Cod

New York City

Cleveland

Columbus

Philadelphia

Baltimore

Washington, D.C.

ATLANTIC OCEAN

San Francisco

San Jose

Great Salt Lake

Salt Lake City

Denver

Kansas City

St. Louis

Indianapolis

Norfolk

UNITED STATES

Los Angeles

San Diego

Tijuana

Phoenix

Memphis

Atlanta

Birmingham

Bermuda (U.K.)

Dallas

Austin

San Antonio

Houston

New Orleans

Jacksonville

Tropic of Cancer

Monterrey

Gulf of Mexico

Florida Keys

Miami

Nassau

BAHAMAS

Turks and Caicos Islands (U.K.)

DOMINICAN REPUBLIC

Puerto Rico (U.S.)

San Juan

ST. KITTS & NEVIS

ANTIGUA & BARBUDA

Guadeloupe (FRANCE)

DOMINICA

BARBADOS

MEXICO

Guadalajara

Mexico City

Puebla

Mérida

Straits of Florida

Havana

CUBA

Cayman Is. (U.K.)

Kingston

JAMAICA

HAITI

Port-au-Prince

Santo Domingo

Virgin Is. (U.S., U.K.)

Martinique (FRANCE)

ST. LUCIA

ST. VINCENT AND THE GRENADINES

GRENADA

Belmopan

BELIZE

Caribbean Sea

Netherlands Antilles (NETHERLANDS)

TRINIDAD AND TOBAGO

GUATEMALA

Guatemala City

San Salvador

EL SALVADOR

HONDURAS

Tegucigalpa

NICARAGUA

Managua

Aruba (NETHERLANDS)

Panama Canal

COSTA RICA

San José

PANAMA

Panama City

SOUTH AMERICA

Equator

90°W

Legend:
- National capital
- Other city

0 300 600 Miles

0 300 600 Kilometers

Projection: Azimuthal Equal-Area

South America: Physical

ATLAS

CENTRAL AMERICA

Caribbean Sea

Panama Canal

Gulf of Panama

Malpelo Island

Margarita Island

Tobago

Trinidad

Orinoco River Delta

ATLANTIC OCEAN

Devil's Island
Cape Orange

Lake Maracaibo

LLANOS

Orinoco River

Meta River

Angel Falls

GUIANA

HIGHLANDS

Cauca River

Mount Tolima
18,425 ft
(5,616 m)

Magdalena River

Orinoco River

Amazon River Delta

Galápagos Islands

0° Equator

Gulf of Guayaquil

Mount Chimborazo
20,561 ft
(6,267 m)

Caqueta River

Japurá River

Río Negro

Amazon River

AMAZON

BASIN

Tocantins River

0° Equator

Marañón River

Amazon River

Juruá River

Purus River

Ucayali River

Madeira River

Tapajós River

Xingu River

River

Mount Huascarán
22,205 ft
(6,768 m)

ANDES

PACIFIC OCEAN

Mamoré River

Beni River

MATO GROSSO
PLATEAU

BRAZILIAN

HIGHLANDS

Parnaiba River

São Francisco River

Araguaia River

Ancohuma Peak
20,958 ft
(6,388 m)

Lake Titicaca

10°S

ATACAMA DESERT

Lake Poopó

Pilcomayo River

CHACO

BRAZILIAN
PLATEAU

20°S

Tropic of Capricorn

San Félix Island

San Ambrosio Island

ANDES

Salado River

Paraguay River

Uruguay River

Paraná River

Tropic of Capricorn

Juan Fernández Islands

Mount Aconcagua
22,834 ft
(6,960 m)

Salado River

Río de la Plata

30°S

ATLANTIC OCEAN

PAMPAS

Colorado River

PATAGONIA

Gulf of San Matías

Chiloé Island

40°S

Chonos Archipelago

Gulf of San Jorge

Cape Tres Puntas

Bahía Grande

Strait of Magellan

Falkland Islands

Tierra del Fuego

South Georgia Islands

Cape Horn

50°S

ELEVATION

Feet		Meters
13,120		4,000
6,560		2,000
1,640		500
656		200
(Sea level) 0		0 (Sea level)
Below sea level		Below sea level

0   250   500 Miles

0   250   500 Kilometers

Projection: Azimuthal Equal Area

N
W   E
S

South America: Political

Caribbean Sea

CENTRAL AMERICA

Barranquilla
Cartagena
Caracas
Lake Maracaibo
VENEZUELA
Georgetown
Paramaribo
GUYANA
Cayenne
SURINAME
French Guiana (FRANCE)

ATLANTIC OCEAN

Medellín
Bogotá
COLOMBIA
Cali

Malpelo Island (COLOMBIA)

Quito
ECUADOR
Guayaquil

Galápagos Islands (ECUADOR)

0° Equator

Belém

PERU

Trujillo

Recife

BRAZIL

Callao
Lima

PACIFIC OCEAN

Lake Titicaca

Arequipa
La Paz
Lake Poopó
BOLIVIA
Sucre

Brasília

Salvador

Belo Horizonte

San Ambrosio Island (CHILE)
San Félix Island (CHILE)

PARAGUAY

Asunción
Campinas
São Paulo
Rio de Janeiro

Tropic of Capricorn

Curitiba

CHILE

Juan Fernández Islands (CHILE)

Pôrto Alegre

Córdoba

Valparaíso
Santiago
Rosario
URUGUAY
Buenos Aires
Montevideo

ATLANTIC OCEAN

ARGENTINA

National capital
Other city

0   250   500 Miles
0   250   500 Kilometers

Projection: Azimuthal Equal-Area

Strait of Magellan
Falkland Islands (U.K.)
Tierra del Fuego
South Georgia Island (U.K.)

ASIA

URAL MOUNTAINS

SOUTHWEST
ASIA

Caspian Sea

Ural River

Mt. Elbrus 18,510 ft (5,642 m)
CAUCASUS MTS.

NORTHERN EUROPEAN PLAIN

Kama River

Pechora River

Volga River

Don River

BALTIC PLAINS

Barents Sea

North Dvina River

White Sea

Lake Onega

Lake Ladoga

KOLA PENINSULA

Rybinsk Reservoir

Sea of Azov

CRIMEAN PENINSULA

Black Sea

Dnipro

Gulf of Finland

Daugava R.

Dvina River

Dnestr River

Nistru River

CARPATHIAN MTS.

TRANSYLVANIAN ALPS

Danube River

Prut River

Sea of Marmara

Aegean Sea

Rhodes

Crete

ARCTIC OCEAN

North Cape

KJOLEN MOUNTAINS

Gulf of Bothnia

Lake Vänern

Lake Vättern

Baltic Sea

Oder River

Wisla River

Elbe River

DINARIC ALPS

BALKAN
PENINSULA

Adriatic Sea

APENNINES

Tyrrhenian Sea

Sicily

Malta

Norwegian Sea

N
W E
S

Skagerrak

Kattegat

North
Sea

Tiber River

Corsica

Sardinia

Balearic Islands

Mediterranean Sea

AFRICA

Iceland

Faeroe
Islands

Shetland
Islands

Orkney
Islands

Hebrides

British
Isles

Irish Sea

PENNINES

Thames
River

English Channel

Seine River

Rhine River

Loire River

ALPS

Lake
Geneva

Mont Blanc 15,781 ft (4,810 m)

Rhône River

PYRENEES

Garonne River

Ebro River

Bay of
Biscay

Cape Finisterre

IBERIAN
PENINSULA

Douro River

Tagus River

Guadiana River

Guadalquivir River

Strait of
Gibraltar

ATLANTIC
OCEAN

Arctic Circle

Europe: Physical

ELEVATION

Feet	Meters
13,120	4,000
6,560	2,000
1,640	500
656	200
0 (Sea level)	0 (Sea level)
Below sea level	Below sea level

Ice cap

300 Miles
0 150 300 Kilometers
0 150

Projection: Azimuthal Equal Area

70°N
60°N
50°N

70°E
50°E
40°E
30°E
20°E
10°E
0°
10°W
20°W
30°W
40°W

20°E
30°E

ASIA

URAL MOUNTAINS

RUSSIA

Nizhniy Novgorod

Moscow

ARCTIC OCEAN

North Cape

Barents Sea

White Sea

St. Petersburg

FINLAND

Helsinki

ESTONIA
Tallinn

LATVIA
Riga

LITHUANIA
Vilnius

RUSSIA

BELARUS
Minsk

UKRAINE
Kiev

MOLDOVA
Chişinău

Black Sea

Caspian Sea

SWEDEN

Stockholm

Göteborg

Gulf of Bothnia

Baltic Sea

POLAND
Warsaw

Kraków

Berlin

Dresden

Prague

CZECH REPUBLIC

SLOVAKIA
Bratislava

Budapest

HUNGARY

Zagreb

CROATIA

ROMANIA
Bucharest

Sofia
BULGARIA

SERBIA
Belgrade

BOSNIA AND HERZEGOVINA
Sarajevo

MONTENEGRO
Podgorica

MACEDONIA
Skopje

ALBANIA
Tirana

GREECE
Athens

Aegean Sea

Rhodes

Crete

SOUTHWEST ASIA

NORWAY
Oslo

Bergen

DENMARK
Copenhagen

Hamburg

GERMANY

Amsterdam
THE NETHERLANDS

Cologne
Bonn

Luxembourg
LUXEMBOURG

BELGIUM
Brussels

Munich

AUSTRIA
Vienna

LIECHTENSTEIN
Vaduz

SWITZERLAND
Bern

ALPS

SLOVENIA
Ljubljana

Milan

SAN MARINO

ITALY

VATICAN CITY
Rome

Naples

Monaco
MONACO

Adriatic Sea

Sicily

MALTA
Valletta

Ionian Sea

ICELAND
Reykjavík

Faeroe Islands
(DENMARK)

Shetland Islands

SCOTLAND
Edinburgh

NORTHERN IRELAND
Belfast

IRELAND
Dublin

WALES

ENGLAND
London

Liverpool

British Isles

Channel Islands
(U.K.)

English Channel

UNITED KINGDOM

FRANCE
Paris

Lyon

Geneva
Lausanne

Marseille

Bay of Biscay

PYRENEES
Andorra la Vella
ANDORRA

Barcelona

Valencia

SPAIN
Madrid

Seville

Gibraltar
(U.K.)

Strait of Gibraltar

PORTUGAL
Lisbon

Corsica
(FRANCE)

Sardinia
(ITALY)

Balearic Islands
(SPAIN)

Mediterranean Sea

AFRICA

ATLANTIC OCEAN

North Sea

Gulf of Finland

Arctic Circle

Arctic Circle

N
W   E
S

10°W   0°   10°E   20°E   30°E

70°N

60°N

50°N

40°N

70°E
60°E
50°E
40°E
30°E
20°E
10°E

30°W   20°W   10°W

Asia: Physical

ELEVATION

Feet	Meters
13,120	4,000
6,560	2,000
1,640	500
656	200
0 (Sea level)	0 (Sea level)
Below sea level	Below sea level

Ice cap

0 250 500 750 Miles
0 250 500 750 Kilometers

Projection: Two-Point Equidistant

PACIFIC OCEAN

AUSTRALIA

EUROPE

AFRICA

North Pole

Aleutian Islands

KAMCHATKA PENINSULA

Bering Sea

Sea of Okhotsk

Sakhalin Island

Kuril Islands

Hokkaido

CENTRAL RANGE

KOLYMA MTS.

CHERSKIY RANGE

VERKHOYANSKY RANGE

STANOVOY MOUNTAINS

Aldan River

Lena River

Amur River

Shilka River

YABLONOVY RANGE

GREATER KHINGAN RANGE

MONGOLIAN PLATEAU

G O B I

S I B E R I A

CENTRAL SIBERIAN PLATEAU

TAYMYR PENINSULA

Wrangel Island

New Siberian Islands

North Land

Yenisey River

Lower Tunguska

Angara River

SAYAN MOUNTAINS

ALTAY MOUNTAINS

TIAN SHAN

TAKLIMAKAN DESERT

TARIM BASIN

KUNLUN MOUNTAINS

QIN LING

Yellow River

Huang He

NORTH CHINA PLAIN

BOHAI HILLS

Xi River

Yellow Sea

Sea of Japan (East Sea)

Korea Strait

Honshu

Shikoku

Kyushu

Ryukyu Islands

Okinawa

East China Sea

Taiwan

Luzon Strait

Hainan

South China Sea

Philippines

Luzon

Mindanao

Celebes Sea

Celebes

Borneo

MAKDE MOUNTAINS

New Guinea

Arafura Sea

Banda Sea

Moluccas

Java Sea

Java

Bangka

Sumatra

Mentawai Islands

MALAY PENINSULA

INDOCHINA PENINSULA

Gulf of Thailand

Chao Phraya River

Mekong River

Hong River

Gulf of Tonkin

Andaman Sea

Nicobar Islands

Andaman Islands

Bay of Bengal

Brahmaputra River

Ganges River

INDO-GANGETIC PLAIN

H I M A L A Y A S

PLATEAU OF TIBET

Mount Everest 29,035 ft (8,850 m)

Chang (Yangtze) River

DECCAN PLATEAU

EASTERN GHATS

WESTERN GHATS

Godavari River

THAR DESERT

HINDU KUSH

KARA KUM

KYZYL KUM

TURAN LOWLAND

Amu Darya

Syr Darya

Aral Sea

Balqash Lake

KAZAKH UPLANDS

Irtysh River

Ob River

WEST SIBERIAN PLAIN

Ishim River

Tobol River

URAL MOUNTAINS

Ural River

USTYURT PLATEAU

Caspian Sea

GREAT SALT DESERT

Novaya Zemlya

Franz Josef Land

Barents Sea

Kara Sea

Arctic Circle

CAUCASUS MTS.

Mount Ararat 16,945 ft (5,165 m)

ANATOLIAN PLATEAU

Black Sea

Bosporus

Cyprus

Mediterranean Sea

SINAI PENINSULA

Red Sea

AN-NAFUD

SYRIAN DESERT

Tigris River

Euphrates River

Persian Gulf

ZAGROS MTS.

Gulf of Oman

RUB' AL-KHALI

Gulf of Aden

Socotra Island

Arabian Sea

Lakshadweep Islands

Maldives

Sri Lanka

INDIAN OCEAN

Tropic of Cancer

Equator

Asia: Political

National capitals
Other cities

| 0 | 250 | 500 | 750 Miles |
| 0 | 250 | 500 | 750 Kilometers |

Projection: Two-Point Equidistant

AUSTRALIA

New Guinea

PACIFIC OCEAN

Equator

Arafura Sea

EAST TIMOR

Dili

Celebes Sea

PHILIPPINES

Manila

INDONESIA

Ujung Pandang

Surabaya

Jakarta

Bandung

Java Sea

BRUNEI

Bandar Seri Begawan

MALAYSIA

SINGAPORE

Singapore

Kuala Lumpur

Medan

Gulf of Thailand

South China Sea

Macao

Hong Kong

Hainan (CHINA)

VIETNAM

Ho Chi Minh City

CAMBODIA

Phnom Penh

THAILAND

Bangkok

LAOS

Vientiane

Hanoi

Guangzhou

TAIWAN

Taipei

East China Sea

Tropic of Cancer

RYUKYU ISLANDS (JAPAN)

Nagasaki

Hiroshima

Pusan

SOUTH KOREA

Seoul

NORTH KOREA

Pyongyang

Osaka

Kyoto

Tokyo

Yokohama

JAPAN

Sapporo

Kuril Islands (RUSSIA)

Sakhalin Island

Vladivostok

Sea of Okhotsk

Bering Sea

Aleutian Islands

MYANMAR (BURMA)

Yangon (Rangoon)

Naypyidaw

Andaman Islands (INDIA)

Andaman Sea

Nicobar Islands (INDIA)

Bay of Bengal

SRI LANKA

Colombo

Male

MALDIVES

INDIAN OCEAN

Chennai (Madras)

Bangalore

Lakshadweep Islands (INDIA)

INDIA

Mumbai (Bombay)

Ahmadabad

Jaipur

New Delhi

Delhi

BHUTAN

Thimphu

BANGLADESH

Dhaka

Kolkata (Calcutta)

NEPAL

Kathmandu

Lahore

PAKISTAN

Karachi

Masqat (Muscat)

Arabian Sea

Socotra (YEMEN)

Gulf of Aden

YEMEN

Sanaa

AFRICA

Red Sea

Mecca

Jidda

Jerusalem

Tel Aviv

ISRAEL

LEBANON

Beirut

CYPRUS

Nicosia

JORDAN

Amman

Damascus

SYRIA

TURKEY

Ankara

Izmir

Istanbul

Mediterranean Sea

EUROPE

Black Sea

GEORGIA

Tbilisi

ARMENIA

Yerevan

AZERBAIJAN

Baku

Mosul

Baghdad

IRAQ

Basra

Kuwait City

KUWAIT

SAUDI ARABIA

Riyadh

BAHRAIN

Manama

QATAR

Doha

UNITED ARAB EMIRATES

Abu Dhabi

OMAN

Persian Gulf

IRAN

Tehran

Shiraz

Caspian Sea

TURKMENISTAN

Ashgabat

AFGHANISTAN

Kabul

Islamabad

TAJIKISTAN

Dushanbe

KYRGYZSTAN

Bishkek

UZBEKISTAN

Tashkent

Almaty

KAZAKHSTAN

Astana

Aral Sea

Lake Balkhash

Omsk

Yekaterinburg

Chelyabinsk

URAL MOUNTAINS

Novosibirsk

MONGOLIA

Ulaanbaatar

Irkutsk

Lake Baykal

Harbin

Fushun

Beijing

Shenyang

Dalian

Qingdao

Yellow Sea

Shanghai

Nanjing

Wuhan

CHINA

Chengdu

Chongqing

Yakutsk

Moscow

RUSSIA

Barents Sea

Kara Sea

Laptev Sea

North Pole

Arctic Circle

ATLAS **217**

EUROPE

SOUTHWEST
ASIA

ATLAS

40°N

Azores

Madeira
Islands

30°N

Strait of
Gibraltar

Mediterranean Sea

Gulf of
Sidra

Suez Canal

Persian Gulf

ATLAS MOUNTAINS

QATTARA
DEPRESSION

Canary
Islands

LIBYAN DESERT

Tropic of Cancer

Nile River

Cape
Blanc

EL DJOUF

S A H A R A

AHAGGAR
MOUNTAINS

Lake
Nasser

NUBIAN
DESERT

Red Sea

20°N

TIBESTI
MOUNTAINS

AIR MTS.

Cape Verde
Islands

Niger River

S   A   H   E   L

Senegal R.

Cape
Verde

S   U   D   A   N

CHAD
BASIN

Lake
Chad

Lake
Tana

Blue Nile

White Nile

Gulf of Aden

10°N

FOUTA
DJALLON

White Volta R.

Black Volta R.

Benue River

SUDAN
BASIN

ETHIOPIAN
HIGHLANDS

HORN OF AFRICA

SOMALI
PENINSULA

10°N

Cape
Palmas

Lake
Volta

ADAMAWA
MTS.

Ubangi
River

RIFT VALLEY

Gulf of
Guinea

Congo River

Lake
Albert

Lake
Turkana

Mount Kenya
17,058 ft
(5,199 m)

0° Equator

Cape
Lopez

CONGO

BASIN

Kasai River

Lake
Edward

Lake
Victoria

Mount Kilimanjaro
19,340 ft
(5,895 m)

INDIAN

OCEAN

0° Equator

N

W   E

S

Ascension

ATLANTIC

OCEAN

MITUMBA MOUNTAINS

WESTERN RIFT VALLEY

Lake
Kivu

Lake
Tanganyika

SERENGETI
PLAIN

EASTERN RIFT VALLEY

MASAI
STEPPE

Zanzibar

Seychelles

Lake Rukwa

10°S

Cuanza
River

Lake
Mweru

Lake Malawi
(Nyasa)

Cape Delgado

Comoro
Islands

10°S

Mozambique Channel

Madagascar

Lake
Kariba

Zambezi River

Okavango
Delta

Victoria
Falls

Limpopo River

Mauritius

20°S

NAMIB DESERT

KALAHARI BASIN

KALAHARI
DESERT

Réunion

Tropic of Capricorn

Tropic of Capricorn

Vaal River

ELEVATION	
Feet	Meters
13,120	4,000
6,560	2,000
1,640	500
656	200
(Sea level) 0	0 (Sea level)
Below
sea level	Below
sea level

Orange River

DRAKENSBERG MOUNTAINS

30°S

GREAT
KARROO

Cape of
Good Hope

30°S

0   250   500 Miles

0   250   500 Kilometers

Projection: Azimuthal Equal-Area

40°S

40°S

Africa: Political

EUROPE

SOUTHWEST
ASIA

40°N

Azores
(PORTUGAL)

Strait of
Gibraltar

Madeira
(PORTUGAL)

Algiers   Tunis
Casablanca   Rabat

Mediterranean Sea

30°N

Canary Islands
(SPAIN)

TUNISIA
Tripoli

Alexandria

MOROCCO

El Aaiún

Giza   Cairo

WESTERN
SAHARA
(Claimed by
Morocco)

ALGERIA

LIBYA

EGYPT

Tropic of Cancer

20°N

**CAPE
VERDE**

MAURITANIA

Nouakchott

MALI

NIGER

CHAD

Khartoum

ERITREA

Asmara

Red Sea

Gulf of Aden

Praia

SENEGAL

Dakar

GAMBIA

Banjul

Bissau

**GUINEA
BISSAU**

Conakry

Freetown

SIERRA LEONE

Monrovia

LIBERIA

Bamako

GUINEA

**BURKINA
FASO**

Ouagadougou

**CÔTE
D'IVOIRE**

Yamoussoukro

Abidjan

Niamey

**BENIN
TOGO**

GHANA

Lomé
Accra

Porto-
Novo

NIGERIA

Abuja

Lagos

SUDAN

N'Djamena

Lake
Chad

**CENTRAL AFRICAN
REPUBLIC**

Bangui

DJIBOUTI

Djibouti

ETHIOPIA

Addis Ababa

10°N

SOMALIA

10°N

CAMEROON

Malabo

EQUATORIAL GUINEA

Yaoundé

UGANDA

Kampala

KENYA

Nairobi

Mogadishu

0° Equator

SÃO TOMÉ AND PRÍNCIPE

São Tomé

Gulf of
Guinea

Libreville

GABON

**REPUBLIC
OF THE
CONGO**

Kisangani

RWANDA

Kigali

BURUNDI

Bujumbura

0° Equator

**INDIAN
OCEAN**

Victoria

SEYCHELLES

Brazzaville

CABINDA
(ANGOLA)

**DEMOCRATIC
REPUBLIC
OF THE CONGO**

Kinshasa

TANZANIA

Dodoma

Mombasa

Pemba

Zanzibar

Dar es Salaam

Lake
Victoria

Lake
Tanganyika

Luanda

10°S

**ATLANTIC
OCEAN**

Lubumbashi

ANGOLA

ZAMBIA

Lusaka

MALAWI

Lilongwe

Lake Malawi
(Nyesa)

COMOROS

Moroni

10°S

St. Helena
(U.K.)

Harare

ZIMBABWE

Bulawayo

MOZAMBIQUE

Antananarivo

MAURITIUS

Port Louis

20°S

NAMIBIA

Windhoek

BOTSWANA

Gaborone

Pretoria

Maputo

MADAGASCAR

Réunion
(FRANCE)

Tropic of Capricorn

Johannesburg

Bloemfontein

Mbabane

SWAZILAND

Maseru

LESOTHO

N
W   E
S

30°S

SOUTH AFRICA

Cape Town

✪ National capital
• Other city

0   250   500 Miles
0   250   500 Kilometers

Projection: Azimuthal Equal-Area

The Pacific: Political

NORTH AMERICA

ASIA

AUSTRALIA

NEW ZEALAND

National capital
• Other city

1,000 Miles
1,000 Kilometers
500
500
0
0

Projection: Azimuthal Equal-Area

NORTH PACIFIC OCEAN

SOUTH PACIFIC OCEAN

INDIAN OCEAN

Tropic of Cancer

Equator

Tropic of Capricorn

International Date Line

30°N
15°N
0°
15°S
30°S
45°S

135°W
150°W
165°W
180°
165°E
150°E
135°E
120°E
120°W

POLYNESIA

MICRONESIA

MELANESIA

KIRIBATI

Easter Island (CHILE)

Pitcairn (U.K.)
Pitcairn Island
Ducie Island

Marquesas Islands (FRANCE)

Tuamotu Archipelago (FRANCE)

Rapa Island (FRANCE)

French Polynesia

Tubuai Islands (FRANCE)

Society Islands (FRANCE)

Tahiti (FRANCE)
Papeete

Starbuck Island

Manihiki Island

Cook Islands (NEW ZEALAND)

Rarotonga Island

Hawaiian Islands

Hawaii (U.S.)

Kingman Reef
Palmyra Island (U.S.)
Washington Island
Fanning Island

Jarvis I. (U.S.)

Phoenix Islands

Howland I. (U.S.)
Baker I. (U.S.)

McKean I.
Gardner

Tokelau (N.Z.)

SAMOA
Apia
American Samoa
Pago Pago

Niue (N.Z.)

TONGA
Nuku'alofa

Midway Island (U.S.)

Johnston Island (U.S.)

Wallis & Futuna (FR. FR.)

TUVALU
Funafuti

FIJI
Suva

Kermadec Islands (N.Z.)

Chatham Islands (N.Z.)

Auckland
North Island
Wellington
Christchurch
South Island

Bounty Islands (N.Z.)

Auckland Islands (NEW ZEALAND)

NEW ZEALAND

Wake Island (U.S.)

MARSHALL ISLANDS
Eniwetok I.
Kwajalein Island
Majuro

Tarawa

Gilbert Islands

NAURU

SOLOMON ISLANDS
Honiara
Guadalcanal I.

Espiritu Santo I.
Malekula I.
VANUATU
Port Vila

New Caledonia (FRANCE)
Noumea

Loyalty Islands (FRANCE)

Norfolk Island (AUSTRALIA)

Palikir
FEDERATED STATES OF MICRONESIA

Truk Is.

Bismarck Archipelago

PAPUA NEW GUINEA
Port Moresby

New Guinea

Coral Sea

Northern Marianas (U.S.)

Guam (U.S.)
Agana

Bonin Islands (JAPAN)

Volcano Islands (JAPAN)

Koror
PALAU

Philippine Sea

South China Sea

Arafura Sea

Timor Sea

Darwin

Christmas Island (AUSTRALIA)

AUSTRALIA

Perth

Adelaide

Melbourne

Hobart

Sydney
Canberra

Brisbane

Tasman Sea

N
E
S
W

220 ATLAS

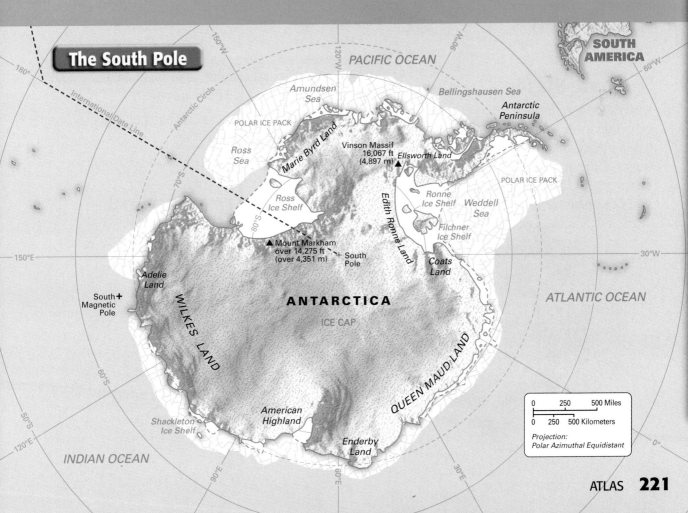

The North Pole

0 200 400 Miles
0 200 400 Kilometers

Projection:
Polar Azimuthal Equidistant

Kara Sea

Barents Sea

EUROPE

Norwegian Sea

Laptev Sea

90°E

60°E

30°E

Arctic Circle

ASIA

ARCTIC OCEAN

+ North Pole

Greenland Sea

0°

Greenland (DENMARK)

ATLANTIC OCEAN

30°W

150°E

80°N

International Date Line

POLAR ICE PACK

North Magnetic Pole +

Baffin Bay

120°E

150°W

90°W

60°W

Beaufort Sea

60°N

180°

Bering Sea

Bering Sea

60°N

NORTH AMERICA

50°N

The South Pole

180°

International Date Line

150°W

120°W

PACIFIC OCEAN

90°W

SOUTH AMERICA

60°W

Antarctic Circle

Amundsen Sea

Bellingshausen Sea

Antarctic Peninsula

POLAR ICE PACK

Ross Sea

Marie Byrd Land

Vinson Massif
16,067 ft
(4,897 m) ▲

Ellsworth Land

POLAR ICE PACK

70°S

Ross Ice Shelf

Edith Ronne Land

Ronne Ice Shelf

Weddell Sea

80°S

▲ Mount Markham
over 14,275 ft
(over 4,351 m)

+ South Pole

Filchner Ice Shelf

30°W

150°E

Adelie Land

South + Magnetic Pole

WILKES LAND

ANTARCTICA

ICE CAP

Coats Land

ATLANTIC OCEAN

60°S

Shackleton Ice Shelf

American Highland

QUEEN MAUD LAND

0°

120°E

INDIAN OCEAN

90°E

Enderby Land

60°E

30°E

0 250 500 Miles
0 250 500 Kilometers

Projection:
Polar Azimuthal Equidistant

ATLAS

The Physical World

Inside the Earth

Earth's interior has several different layers. Deep inside the planet is the core. The inner core is solid, and the outer core is liquid. Above the core is the mantle, which is mostly solid rock with a molten layer on top. The surface layer of Earth includes the crust, which is made up of rocks and soil. Finally, the atmosphere extends from the crust into space. It supports much of the life on Earth.

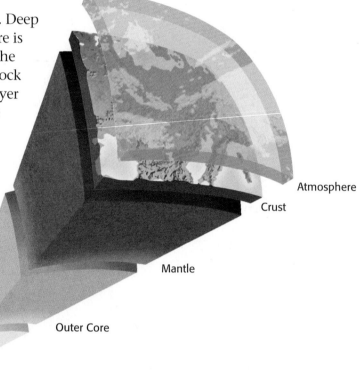

Atmosphere

Crust

Mantle

Outer Core

Inner Core

Tectonic Plates

Earth's crust is divided into huge pieces called tectonic plates, which fit together like a puzzle. As these plates slowly move, they collide and break apart, forming surface features like mountains, ocean basins, and ocean trenches.

Earth Facts	
Age:	4.6 billion years
Mass:	5,974,000,000,000,000,000,000 metric tons
Distance around the equator:	24,902 miles (40,067 km)
Distance around the poles:	24,860 miles (40,000 km)
Distance from the sun:	about 93 million miles (150 million km)
Earth's speed around the sun:	18.5 miles a second (29.8 km a second)
Percent of Earth's surface covered by water:	71%
What makes Earth unique:	large amounts of liquid water, tectonic activity, and life

The Continents

Geographers identify seven large landmasses, or continents, on Earth. Most of these continents are almost completely surrounded by water. Europe and Asia, however, are not. They share a long land boundary.

The world's continents are very different. For example, much of Australia is dry and rocky, while Antarctica is cold and icy. The information below highlights some key facts about each continent.

North America

- Percent of Earth's land: 16.5%
- Percent of Earth's population: 5.1%
- Lowest point: Death Valley, 282 feet (86 m) below sea level

South America

- Percent of Earth's land: 12%
- Percent of Earth's population: 8.6%
- Longest mountains: Andes, 4,500 miles (7,240 km)

Asia

- Percent of Earth's land: 30%
- Percent of Earth's population: 60.7%
- Highest point: Mount Everest, 29,035 feet (8,850 m)

Europe

- Percent of Earth's land: 6.7%
- Percent of Earth's population: 11.5%
- People per square mile: 187

Africa

- Percent of Earth's land: 20.2%
- Percent of Earth's population: 13.6%
- Longest river: Nile River, 4,160 miles (6,693 km)

Australia

- Percent of Earth's land: 5.2%
- Percent of Earth's population: 0.3%
- Oldest rocks: 3.7 billion years

Antarctica

- Percent of Earth's land: 8.9%
- Percent of Earth's population: 0%
- Coldest place: Plateau Station, -56.7°C (-70.1°F) average temperature

The Human World

World Population

More than 6 billion people live in the world today, and that number is growing quickly. Some people predict the world's population will reach 9 billion by 2050. As our population grows, it is also becoming more urban. Soon, as many people will live in cities and in towns as live in rural areas.

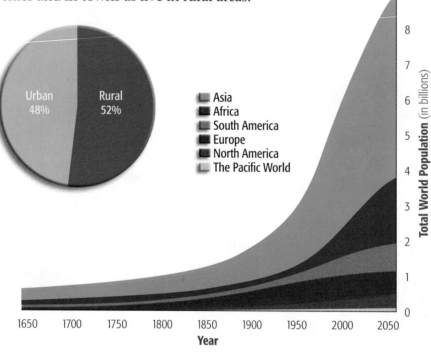

Urban 48%
Rural 52%

Asia
Africa
South America
Europe
North America
The Pacific World

Total World Population (in billions)

1650 1700 1750 1800 1850 1900 1950 2000 2050
Year

As the world's population grows, people are moving to already large cities such as Shanghai (above) and Hong Kong (right) in China.

Geographers divide the world into developed and less developed regions. In general, developed countries are wealthier and more urban, have lower population growth rates and higher life expectancies. As you can imagine, life is very different in developed and less developed regions.

Developed and Less Developed Countries

	Population	Rate of Natural Increase	Life Expectancy	Percent Urban	Per Capita GNI (U.S. $)
Developed Countries	1.2 billion	0.1%	77	77%	$27,790
Less Developed Countries	5.3 billion	1.5%	65	41%	$4,950
The World	6.5 billion	1.2%	67	48%	$9,190

World Religions

A large percentage of the world's people follow one of several major world religions. Christianity is the largest religion. About 33 percent of the world's people are Christian. Islam is the second-largest religion with about 20 percent. It is also the fastest-growing religion. Hinduism and Buddhism are also major world religions.

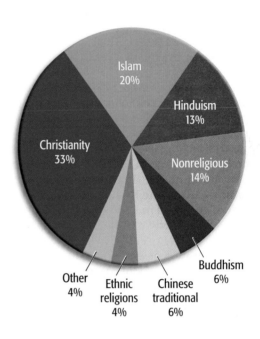

Islam 20%

Hinduism 13%

Christianity 33%

Nonreligious 14%

Buddhism 6%

Other 4%

Ethnic religions 4%

Chinese traditional 6%

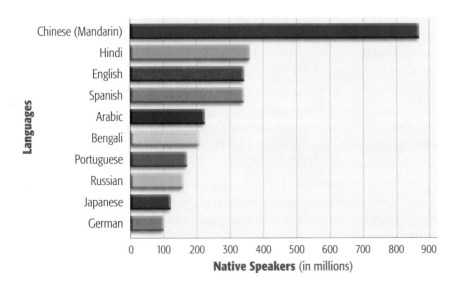

Languages

Chinese (Mandarin)
Hindi
English
Spanish
Arabic
Bengali
Portuguese
Russian
Japanese
German

0   100   200   300   400   500   600   700   800   900
Native Speakers (in millions)

World Languages

Although several thousand languages are spoken today, a handful of major languages have the largest numbers of native speakers. Chinese (Mandarin) is spoken by nearly one in six people. Hindi, English, Spanish, and Arabic are next, with native speakers all over the world.

Gazetteer

A

Acapulco (17°N, 100°W) a resort on the Pacific Ocean in southwest Mexico (p. 37)

Alabama (AL) a state in the southern United States; admitted in 1819 (pp. 204–205)

Alaska (AK) a state in northwestern North America; admitted in 1959 (pp. 204–205)

Alberta a province in western Canada (p. 171)

Amazon Basin a huge basin in the heart of South America (p. 212)

Amazon River the major river in South America (p. 212)

Andes Mountains (AN-deez) a long mountain range along the west coast of South America (p. 212)

Appalachian Mountains a mountain system in eastern North America (p. 145)

Argentina a country in South America (p. 101)

Arizona (AZ) a state in the southwestern United States; admitted in 1912 (pp. 204–205)

Arkansas (AR) a state in the south-central United States; admitted in 1836 (pp. 204–205)

Asunción (ah-soon-SYOHN) (25°N, 58°W) the capital of Paraguay (p. 116)

Atacama Desert a desert located in northern Chile near the border with Peru (p. 125)

Atlanta (33°N, 84°W) capital of Georgia (p. 143)

Atlantic Ocean the ocean between the continents of North and South America and the continents of Europe and Africa (p. 206)

B

Bahamas a country and group of islands located east of Florida in the Atlantic Ocean (p. 59)

Baja California a peninsula in Mexico (p. 39)

Baltimore (39°N, 76°W) a large city in Maryland northeast of Washington, D.C. (p. 143)

Barbados island country in the Caribbean (p. 57)

Basse-Terre (16°N, 62°W) the capital of Saint Kitts and Nevis (p. 57)

Belize a country in Central America (p. 57)

Belmopan (17°N, 90°W) capital of Belize (p. 57)

Bogotá (4°N, 72°W) capital of Colombia (p. 81)

Bolivia a country in South America (p. 123)

Boston (42°N, 71°W) the capital of Massachusetts (p. 143)

Brasília (10°S, 55°W) the capital of Brazil (p. 109)

Brazil a country in South America (p. 101)

Brazilian Highlands a region of rugged, old, eroded mountains in eastern Brazil (p. 103)

British Columbia a province in Canada (p. 171)

Buenos Aires (BWAY-nuhs y-reez) (36°S, 60°W) the capital of Argentina (p. 101)

C

Calgary (51°N, 114°W) a large city in the province of Alberta in Canada (p. 170)

California (CA) a state in the western United States; admitted in 1850 (pp. 204–205)

Callao (kah-YAH-oh) (12°S, 77°W) a port city in Peru west of Lima (p. 136)

Canada a country in North America (p. 170)

Canadian Shield a region of ancient rock that covers more than half of Canada (p. 173)

Cancún (21°N, 87°W) a popular resort on Mexico's Caribbean coast (p. 37)

Caracas (11°N, 67°W) the capital of Venezuela (p. 81)

Caribbean Islands a group of islands in the Caribbean Sea (p. 57)

Caribbean Sea an arm of the Atlantic Ocean between North and South America (p. 57)

Cartagena (kahr-tah-HAY-nuh) (10°N, 74°W) a coastal city in northern Colombia (p. 80)

Cascade Range a mountain range in western North America (p. 145)

Cauca River a river in Colombia (p. 83)

Cayenne (4°N, 53°W) the capital of French Guiana (p. 81)

Central America a region in North America south of Mexico (p. 56–57)

Chicago (42°N, 88°W) a major U.S. city and port in northeastern Illinois on Lake Michigan (p. 143)

Chile (CHEE-lay) a country in western South America (p. 123)

Coast Mountains a mountain range in North America along the Pacific coast (p. 173)

Colombia a country in South America (p. 80)

Colorado (CO) a state in the southwestern United States; admitted in 1876 (pp. 204–205)

Connecticut (CT) a state in the northeastern United States; admitted in 1788 and one of the original 13 colonies (pp. 204–205)

Costa Rica a country in Central America (p. 56)

Cuba an island country in the Caribbean Sea south of Florida (p. 57)

Cuzco (KOO-skoh) (14°S, 72°W) a city in Peru and the former capital of the Inca Empire (p. 26)

Dallas (33°N, 97°W) a major U.S. city and transportation and financial center in Texas (p. 143)

Delaware (DE) a state in the eastern United States; admitted in 1787 and one of the original 13 colonies (pp. 204–205)

Detroit (42°N, 83°W) a large U.S. city in Michigan (p. 143)

District of Columbia (39°N, 77°W) a federal district between Maryland and Virginia; the capital of the United States (p. 143)

Dominican Republic a country in the Caribbean (p. 57)

Ecuador a country in South America (p. 123)

El Salvador a country in Central America (p. 56)

equator the imaginary line of latitude that circles the globe halfway between the North and South Poles (p. 206–207)

Florida (FL) a state in the southeastern United States; admitted in 1845 (p. 204–205)

French Guiana (gee-A-nuh) a region of France in northern South America (p. 81)

Galápagos Islands a group of islands in the Pacific Ocean that are part of Ecuador (p. 122)

Georgetown (5°N, 59°W) capital of Guyana (p. 81)

Georgia (GA) a state in the southeastern United States; admitted in 1788 and one of the original 13 colonies (pp. 204–205)

Gran Chaco (grahn CHAH-koh) a region of lowlands in South America (p. 103)

Grand Banks (47°N, 52°W) a rich fishing ground near Newfoundland, Canada (p. 173)

Greater Antilles an island group in the Caribbean that includes Cuba, Jamaica, Hispaniola, and Puerto Rico (p. 59)

Great Lakes a group of five large freshwater lakes in North America; they are Lake Superior, Lake Michigan, Lake Huron, Lake Erie, and Lake Ontario (p. 145)

Great Plains a large region of plains and grasslands in central North America (p. 145)

Greenland a large island in North America that was settled by the Vikings (p. 210)

Guadalajara (21°N, 103°W) the second-largest city in Mexico (p. 37)

Guadeloupe a group of islands in the Caribbean that are part of France (p. 57)

Guatemala a country in Central America (p. 56)

Guatemala City (15°N, 91°W) the capital of Guatemala (p. 56)

Guayaquil (gwah-ah-KEEL) (2°S, 80°W) a city in Ecuador (p. 123)

Guiana Highlands (gee-YAH-nah) a large plateau region in northern South America (p. 83)

Guianas (gee-AH-nuhz) a term used to refer to Guyana, Suriname, and French Guiana (p. 81)

Gulf of Mexico a large gulf off the southeastern coast of North America (p. 37)

Guyana (gy-AH-nuh) a country in northern South America (p. 81)

Haiti a country in the Caribbean (p. 57)

Havana (23°N, 82°W) the capital of Cuba (p. 57)

Hawaii (HI) state in the Pacific Ocean comprised of the Hawaiian Islands; admitted in 1959 (pp. 204–205)

Hispaniola (ees-pah-nee-O-lah) an island in the Caribbean (p. 59)

Honduras a country in Central America (p. 56)

Houston (30°N, 95°W) a major U.S. port city in Texas (p. 143)

Hudson Bay a large bay in central Canada (p. 173)

Idaho (ID) a state in the northwestern United States; admitted in 1890 (pp. 204–205)

Illinois (IL) a state in the north-central United States; admitted in 1819 (pp. 204–205)

Indiana (IN) a state in the north-central United States; admitted in 1816 (pp. 204–205)

Interior Plains a large plains region of North America (p. 145)

Iowa (IA) a state in the north-central United States; admitted in 1846 (pp. 204–205)

J, K

Jamaica an island country in the Caribbean (p. 58)

Kansas (KS) a state in the central United States; admitted in 1861 (pp. 204–205)

Kentucky (KY) a state in the east-central United States; admitted in 1792 (pp. 204–205)

L

Lake Maracaibo (mah-rah-KY-boh) (10°N, 72°W) an oil-rich body of water in Venezuela (p. 83)

Lake Texcoco (tays-KOH-koh) an ancient lake in Mexico; it was the site of Tenochtitlán (p. 21)

La Paz (17°S, 65°W) the capital of Bolivia (p. 123)

Latin America a region in the Western Hemisphere; it includes countries where Spanish, Portuguese, or French culture shaped life (p. 38)

Lesser Antilles a group of small islands in the Caribbean; they stretch from the Virgin Islands in the north to Trinidad in the south (p. 59)

Lima (10°S, 75°W) the capital of Peru (p. 123)

Llanos a plains region in South America (p. 83)

Louisiana (LA) a state in the southeastern United States; admitted in 1812 (pp. 204–205)

M

Machu Picchu (MAH-choo PEEK-choo) (13°S, 73°W) a sacred city and fortress of the Incas (p. 26)

Magdalena River a river in Colombia (p. 83)

Maine (ME) a state in the northeastern United States; admitted in 1820 (pp. 204–205)

Manaus (3°S, 60°W) a major port and industrial city in Brazil's Amazon rain forest (p. 101)

Manitoba a province in central Canada (p. 171)

Martinique a group of islands in the Caribbean that are part of France (p. 57)

Maryland (MD) a state in the eastern United States; admitted in 1788 and one of the original 13 colonies (pp. 204–205)

Massachusetts (MA) a state in the northeastern United States; admitted in 1788 and one of the original 13 colonies (pp. 204–205)

Mato Grosso Plateau a high plateau area in Brazil (p. 103)

Mesoamerica a region in North America; the first permanent farming settlements in the Americas developed in Mesoamerica (p. 14)

Mexican Plateau a high, mostly rugged region covering much of the interior of Mexico (p. 39)

Mexico a country in North America (p. 36–37)

Mexico City (23°N, 104°W) the capital of Mexico (p. 37)

Michigan (MI) a state in the north-central United States; admitted in 1837 (pp. 204–205)

Minnesota (MN) a state in the north-central United States; admitted in 1858 (pp. 204–205)

Mississippi (MS) a state in the southeastern United States; admitted in 1817 (pp. 204–205)

Mississippi River a major river in the United States (p. 145)

Missouri (MO) a state in the central United States; admitted in 1821 (pp. 204–205)

Montana (MT) a state in the northern United States; admitted in 1889 (pp. 204–205)

Monterrey (26°N, 100°W) a large city and industrial center in northern Mexico (p. 37)

Montevideo (mawn-tay-vee-DAY-oh) (35°S, 56°W) the capital of Uruguay (p. 101)

Montreal (46°N, 74°W) a major Canadian city in Quebec; founded by the French in 1642 (p. 171)

Mount Saint Helens (46°N, 122°W) a volcano in Washington state that erupted in 1980 (p. 146)

N

Nassau (25°N, 77°W) the capital of the Bahamas (p. 57)

Nebraska (NE) a state in the central United States; admitted in 1867 (pp. 204–205)

Nevada (NV) a state in the western United States; admitted in 1864 (pp. 204–205)

New Brunswick a province in Canada (p. 171)

Newfoundland and Labrador an island province in eastern Canada (p. 171)

New Hampshire (NH) a state in the northeastern United States; admitted in 1788 and one of the original 13 colonies (pp. 204–205)

New Jersey (NJ) a state in the northeastern United States; admitted in 1787 and one of the original 13 colonies (pp. 204–205)

New Mexico (NM) a state in the southwestern United States; admitted in 1912 (pp. 204–205)

New Orleans (30°N, 90°W) a major U.S. port city located in southeastern Louisiana (p. 162)

New York (NY) a state in the northeastern United States; admitted in 1788 and one of the original 13 colonies (pp. 204–205)

New York City (41°N, 74°W) the largest city in the United States (p. 143)

Niagara Falls waterfall on the border of the United States and Canada (p. 172)

Nicaragua a country in Central America (p. 56)

North America a continent including Canada, the United States, Mexico, Central America, and the Caribbean islands (p. 210)

North Carolina (NC) a state in the southeastern United States; admitted in 1789 and one of the original 13 colonies (pp. 204–205)

North Dakota (ND) a state in the north-central United States; admitted in 1889 (pp. 204–205)

Northern Hemisphere the northern half of the globe, between the equator and the North Pole (p. H7)

Northwest Territories a territory in Canada (p. 170)

Nova Scotia (noh-vuh SKOH-shuh) a province in eastern Canada (p. 170)

Nunavut (NOO-nah-VOOT) a territory in northern Canada created as a homeland for Canada's Inuit people (p. 170)

Ohio (OH) a state in the north-central United States; admitted in 1803 (pp. 204–205)

Oklahoma (OK) a state in the south-central United States; admitted in 1890; admitted in 1907 (pp. 204–205)

Ontario a province in east-central Canada (p. 170)

Oregon (OR) a state in the northwestern United States; admitted in 1859 (pp. 204–205)

Orinoco River (OHR-ee-NOH-koh) a major river in Venezuela (p. 83)

Ottawa (45°N, 76°W) capital of Canada (p. 171)

Pacific Ocean the world's largest ocean; located between Asia and the Americas (p. 206)

Palenque (pay-LENG-kay) (18°N, 92°W) an ancient Maya city in southern Mexico (p. 15)

Pampas a fertile plains region in southern South America located mainly in Argentina (p. 103)

Panama a country in Central America (p. 57)

Panama Canal (26°N, 80°W) a canal built by the United States in the early 1900s across the Isthmus of Panama (p. 68)

Panama City (8°N, 81°W) capital of Panama (p. 57)

Paraguay a country in South America (p. 116)

Paraguay River a river in South America (p. 103)

Paramaribo (6°N, 55°W) the capital of Suriname (p. 81)

Paraná River a river in South America (p. 103)

Patagonia a region of dry plains and plateaus east of the Andes in southern Argentina (p. 103)

Pennsylvania (PA) a state in the eastern United States; admitted in 1787 and one of the original 13 colonies (pp. 204–205)

Peru a country in western South America (p. 123)

Philadelphia (40°N, 75°W) a major U.S. city located in southeastern Pennsylvania; it was the capital of the United States from 1790 to 1800 (p. 143)

Pittsburgh (40°N, 80°W) a major U.S. city in Pennsylvania (p. 205)

Popocatépetl (poh-poh-cah-TE-pet-uhl) (19°N, 99°W) a volcano near Mexico City (p. 39)

Port-au-Prince (pohr-toh-PRINS) (19°N, 72°W) the capital of Haiti (p. 57)

Port of Spain (11°N, 61°W) the capital of Trinidad and Tobago (p. 57)

Prince Edward Island (46°N, 64°W) a small province in eastern Canada (p. 171)

Puerto Rico an island east of Cuba and southeast of Florida; it is a U.S. territory (p. 57)

Quebec a province in eastern Canada (p. 171)

Quito (2°S, 78°W) the capital of Ecuador (p. 123)

Rhode Island (RI) a state in the northeastern United States; admitted in 1790 and one of the original 13 colonies (pp. 204–205)

Río Bravo the Mexican name for the river known as the Rio Grande in the United States; it forms the border between Mexico and Texas (p. 37)

Rio de Janeiro (23°N, 43°W) the second-largest city in Brazil; it is a major port city and Brazil's former capital (p. 101)

Rio de la Plata (REE-oh day lah PLAH-tah) a body of water in South America (p.103)

Rocky Mountains a major mountain range in western North America (p. 145)

St. Kitts and Nevis country in the Caribbean (p. 57)

St. Lawrence River a river in North America that flows from the Great Lakes to the Atlantic Ocean (p. 173)

St. Lawrence Seaway a shipping waterway in North America built in the 1950s to connect the Great Lakes with the Atlantic Ocean (p. 205)

San Francisco (37°N, 122°W) a major U.S. port city in Northern California (p. 143)

San Jose (10°N, 84°W) capital of Costa Rica (p. 56)

San Salvador (14°N, 89°W) the capital of El Salvador (p. 56)

Santiago (33°S, 71°W) the capital of Chile (p. 123)

Santo Domingo (19°N, 71°W) the capital of the Dominican Republic (p. 57)

São Paulo (24°S, 47°W) the largest city in Brazil and South America (p. 101)

Saskatchewan a province in Canada (p. 171)

Seattle (48°N, 122°W) a major U.S. port and city in Washington state (p. 143)

Sierra Madre (SYER-rah MAH-dray) the chief mountain range in Mexico (p. 39)

Sierra Nevada a large mountain range mainly in California (p. 145)

South America a continent in the Western and Southern hemispheres (p. 212)

South Carolina (SC) a state in the southeastern United States; admitted in 1788 and one of the original 13 colonies (pp. 204–205)

South Dakota (SD) a state in the north-central United States; admitted in 1889 (pp. 204–205)

Southern Hemisphere the southern half of the globe, between the equator and the South Pole (p. H7)

Spain a country in Southern Europe; it colonized much of the Americas (p. 215)

Strait of Magellan a waterway through the southern tip of South America (p. 125)

Sucre (SOO-kray) (19°S, 65°W) the capital of Bolivia (p. 123)

Suriname (soohr-uh-NAHM) a country in northern South America (p. 81)

Tegucigalpa (15°N, 87°W) the capital of Honduras (p. 56)

Tennessee (TN) a state in the south-central United States; admitted in 1796 (pp. 204–205)

Tenochtitlán (tay-nawch-teet-LAHN) the capital of the Aztec Empire (p. 21)

Texas (TX) a state and former independent republic in the south-central United States; admitted in 1845 (pp. 204–205)

Tierra del Fuego a group of islands in southern South America (p. 125)

Toronto (44°N, 79°W) Canada's largest city (p. 171)

Trinidad and Tobago a country in the Caribbean just north of Venezuela (p. 57)

United States of America a country in North America located between Canada and Mexico (p. 204–205)

Uruguay a country in South America (p. 101)

Utah (UT) a state in the western United States; admitted in 1896 (pp. 204–205)

Valley of Mexico a large plateau region in central Mexico (p. 39)

Valparaiso (bahl-pah-rah-EE-soh) (33°S, 72°W) a city and major port in Chile (p. 123)

Vancouver (49°N, 123°W) a city in western Canada just north of the U.S. border (p. 170)

Venezuela a country in South America (p. 81)

Vermont (VT) a state in the northeastern United States; admitted in 1791 (pp. 204–205)

Virginia (VA) a state in the eastern United States; admitted in 1788 and one of the original 13 colonies (pp. 204–205)

Virgin Islands a group of small islands in the Caribbean (p. 57)

Washington (WA) a state in the northwestern United States; admitted in 1889 (pp. 204–205)

Washington, D.C. (39°N, 77°W) the capital of the United States (p. 143)

West Indies a group of more than 1,200 islands in the Caribbean Sea (p. 70)

West Virginia (WV) a state in the east-central United States; admitted in 1863 (pp. 204–205)

Western Hemisphere the half of the globe between 180° and the prime meridian that includes North and South America and the Pacific and Atlantic oceans (p. H7)

Windsor (42°N, 83°W) a city in Canada near the U.S. border (p. 171)

Wisconsin (WI) a state in the north-central United States; admitted in 1848 (pp. 204–205)

Wyoming (WY) a state in the northwestern United States; admitted in 1890 (pp. 204–205)

Yucatán Peninsula (yoo-kah-TAHN) a large peninsula that separates the Caribbean Sea from the Gulf of Mexico (p. 39)

Yukon Territory a territory in Canada (p. 170)

Biographical Dictionary

A, B

Atahualpa (ah-tah-WAHL-pah) (c.1502–1533) The last Inca king, he was captured by the Spanish conquistador Francisco Pizarro (p. 29)

Bolivar, Simón (1783–1830) Latin American revolutionary leader, he inspired revolutionary movements in Bolivia, Colombia, Ecuador, and Venezuela. (p. 91)

C

Castro, Fidel (1926–) Premier of Cuba, his revolutionary movement overthrew Cuba's government in 1959 and established the first Communist government in the Western Hemisphere. (p. 74)

Chavez, Hugo (1954–) President of Venezuela, he was elected to office in 1998. He successfully changed the country's constitution to give the president more power and survived a military coup in 2002 and a recall election in 2004. (p. 93)

Cortés, Hernán (er-NAHN kawr-TAYS) (c.1485–1547) Spanish conquistador, he went to Mexico in search of riches and captured the Aztec capital of Tenochtitlán, causing the collapse of the Aztec Empire. (p. 24)

F

Fox, Vicente (1942–) President of Mexico, his election in 2000 ended 71 years of one-party rule in Mexico. A populist leader, he has worked to strengthen Mexico's economy and fight poverty. (p. 48)

H

Hidalgo, Miguel (1753–1811) Mexican priest and revolutionary leader, he led a revolt against Spain that eventually led to Mexico's independence in 1821. He is known as the Father of Mexican Independence. (p. 44)

J

Juárez, Benito (1806–1872) President of Mexico, he helped to establish democracy in the country and was Mexico's first president of Indian descent. He is a national hero in Mexico. (p. 45)

L, M

L'Ouverture, Toussaint (too-sahn loo-ver-toor) (c.1743–1803) Haitian leader, he was a former slave who became a revolutionary general and government leader in Haiti and fought for his people's freedom. (p. 71)

Moctezuma II (MAWK-tay-SOO-mah) (1466–1520) Last Aztec emperor, he was captured by the Spanish conquistador Hernán Cortés. (p. 24)

P

Pacal (puh-KAHL) (603–683) Maya king of Palenque, he had a temple built in the city to record his achievements. During his reign, Palenque became an important Maya ceremonial center. (p. 17)

Pachacuti (pah-chah-KOO-tee) (died 1471) Inca ruler, he greatly expanded the Incas' territory. (p. 25)

Perón, Eva (1919–1952) Argentine political leader, she was the wife of Argentina's president Juan Perón. Known as Evita, she was a popular figure who worked to improve the lives of women, workers, and the poor. (p. 113)

Pizarro, Francisco (c.1475–1541) Spanish conquistador, he conquered the Inca Empire and captured the Inca ruler Atahualpa. (p. 29)

W

Washington, George (1732–1799) Revolutionary general and first American president, he led American troops in their fight for independence from Britain. After the war, he served two terms as president and is known as the Father of His Country. (p. 153)

English and Spanish Glossary

MARK	AS IN	RESPELLING	EXAMPLE
a	alphabet	a	*AL-fuh-bet
ā	Asia	ay	AY-zhuh
ä	cart, top	ah	KAHRT, TAHP
e	let, ten	e	LET, TEN
ē	even, leaf	ee	EE-vuhn, LEEF
i	it, tip, British	i	IT, TIP, BRIT-ish
ī	site, buy, Ohio	y	SYT, BY, oh-HY-oh
	iris	eye	EYE-ris
k	card	k	KAHRD
kw	quest	kw	KWEST
ō	over, rainbow	oh	OH-vuhr, RAYN-boh
ů	book, wood	ooh	BOOHK, WOOHD
ò	all, orchid	aw	AWL, AWR-kid
òi	foil, coin	oy	FOYL, KOYN
aů	out	ow	OWT
ə	cup, butter	uh	KUHP, BUHT-uhr
ü	rule, food	oo	ROOL, FOOD
yü	few	yoo	FYOO
zh	vision	zh	VIZH-uhn

*A syllable printed in small capital letters receives heavier emphasis than the other syllable(s) in a word.

Phonetic Respelling and Pronunciation Guide

Many of the key terms in this textbook have been respelled to help you pronounce them. The letter combinations used in the respelling throughout the narrative are explained in this phonetic respelling and pronunciation guide. The guide is adapted from *Merriam-Webster's Collegiate Dictionary, Eleventh Edition; Merriam-Webster's Geographical Dictionary;* and *Merriam-Webster's Biographical Dictionary.*

A

altiplano a broad, high plateau that lies between the ridges of the Andes (p. 125)
altiplano meseta amplia y elevada que se extiende entre las cadenas montañosas de los Andes (pág. 125)
archipelago (ahr-kuh-PE-luh-goh) a large group of islands (p. 59)
archipiélago grupo grande de islas (pág. 59)

B

bilingual a term used to describe people who speak two languages (p. 156)
bilingüe término utilizado para describir a las personas que hablan dos idiomas (pág. 156)

C

cash crop a crop that farmers grow mainly to sell for a profit (p. 49)
cultivo comercial cultivo que los agricultores producen principalmente para vender y obtener ganancias (pág. 49)
causeway a raised road across water or wet ground (p. 20)
carretera elevada camino construido sobre agua o terreno pantanoso (pág. 20)
civil war a conflict between two or more groups within a country (p. 66)
guerra civil conflicto entre dos o más grupos dentro de un país (pág. 66)
cloud forest a moist, high-elevation tropical forest where low clouds are common (p. 60)
bosque nuboso bosque tropical de gran elevación y humedad donde los bancos de nubes son muy comunes (pág. 60)

colony a territory inhabited and controlled by people from a foreign land (p. 152)
colonia territorio habitado y controlado por personas de otro país (pág. 152)

commonwealth a self-governing territory associated with another country (p. 73)
mancomunidad o estado libre asociado territorio autogobernado asociado con otro país (pág. 73)

conquistadors (kahn-KEES-tuh-dohrs) Spanish soldiers in the Americas who explored new lands, searched for gold and silver, and tried to spread Christianity (p. 24)
conquistadores soldados españoles en América que exploraron nuevas tierras, buscaron oro y plata e intentaron difundir el cristianismo (pág. 24)

continental divide an area of high ground that divides the flow of rivers towards opposite ends of a continent (p. 146)
línea divisoria de aguas zona de terreno elevado que divide el flujo de los ríos en dos direcciones, hacia los extremos opuestos de un continente (pág. 146)

cooperative an organization owned by its members and operated for their mutual benefit (p. 74)
cooperativa organización cuyos miembros son los propietarios y que es operada para beneficio de todos (pág. 74)

cordillera (kawr-duhl-YER-uh) a mountain system made up of roughly parallel ranges (p. 82)
cordillera sistema de cadenas montañosas aproximadamente paralelas entre sí (pág. 82)

coup (KOO) a sudden overthrow of a government by a small group of people (p. 137)
golpe de estado derrocamiento repentino de un gobierno por parte de un grupo reducido de personas (pág. 137)

Creole an American-born descendant of Europeans (p. 132)
criollo persona de ascendencia europea y nacida en América (pág. 132)

deforestation the clearing of trees (p. 105)
deforestación tala de árboles (p. 105)

dialect a regional variety of a language (p. 72)
dialecto variedad regional de un idioma (pág. 72)

ecotourism the practice of using an area's natural environment to attract tourists (p. 66)
ecoturismo uso de regiones naturales para atraer turistas (pág. 66)

El Niño an ocean and weather pattern that affects the Pacific coast of the Americas; about every two to seven years, it warms normally cool ocean water and causes extreme ocean and weather events (p. 127)
El Niño patrón oceánico y del tiempo que afecta a la costa del Pacífico de las Américas; aproximadamente cada dos a siete años, calienta las aguas normalmente frías del océano, y provoca sucesos oceánicos y climatológicos extremos (pág. 127)

empire a land with different territories and peoples under a single ruler (p. 43)
imperio zona que reúne varios territorios y pueblos bajo un solo gobernante (pág. 43)

estuary a partially enclosed body of water where freshwater mixes with salty seawater (p. 103)
estuario masa de agua parcialmente rodeada de tierra en la que el agua de mar se combina con agua dulce (pág. 103)

favela (fah-VE-lah) a huge slum in Brazil (p. 109)
favela enorme barriada en Brasil (pág. 109)

gaucho (GOW-choh) an Argentine cowboy (p. 113)
gaucho vaquero argentino (pág. 113)

guerrilla a member of an irregular military force (p. 89)
guerrillero miembro de una fuerza militar irregular (pág. 89)

hacienda (hah-see-en-duh) a huge expanse of farm or ranch land in the Americas (p. 44)
hacienda granja o rancho de gran tamaño en las Américas (pág. 44)

inflation a rise in prices that occurs when currency loses its buying power (p. 48)
inflación aumento de los precios que ocurre cuando la moneda de un país pierde poder adquisitivo (pág. 48)

informal economy a part of the economy that is based on odd jobs that people perform without government regulation through taxes (p. 115)
economía informal parte de la economía basada en trabajos pequeños que se realizan sin el pago de impuestos regulados por el gobierno (pág. 115)

isthmus a narrow strip of land that connects two larger land areas (p. 58)
istmo franja estrecha de tierra que une dos zonas más grandes (pág. 58)

landlocked completely surrounded by land with no direct access to the ocean (p. 116)
sin salida al mar completamente rodeado de tierra, sin acceso directo al océano (pág. 116)

llanero (yah-NAY-roh) Venezuelan cowboy (p. 92)
llanero vaquero venezolano (pág. 92)

maize corn (p. 14)
maíz cereal también conocido como elote o choclo (pág. 14)

maquiladora (mah-kee-lah-DORH-ah) a U.S. or other foreign-owned factory in Mexico (p. 51)
maquiladora fábrica estadounidense o de otro país establecida en México (pág. 51)

maritime on or near the sea (p. 183)
marítimo en o cerca del mar (pág. 183)

masonry stonework (p. 27)
mampostería obra de piedra (pág. 27)

megacity a giant urban area that includes surrounding cities and suburbs (p. 108)
megaciudad zona urbana enorme que incluye los suburbios y ciudades de alrededor (pág. 108)

megalopolis a string of large cities that have grown together (p. 161)
megalópolis serie de ciudades grandes que han crecido hasta unirse (pág. 161)

Mercosur an organization that promotes trade and economic cooperation among the southern and eastern countries of South America (p. 114)
Mercosur organización que promueve el comercio y la cooperación económica entre los países del sur y el este de América del Sur (pág. 114)

mestizo (me-STEE-zoh) a person of mixed European and Indian ancestry (p. 44)
mestizo persona de origen europeo e indígena (pág. 44)

mission a church outpost (p. 44)
misión asentamiento de la Iglesia (pág. 44)

newsprint cheap paper used mainly for newspapers (p. 175)
papel de prensa papel económico utilizado principalmente para imprimir periódicos (pág. 175)

observatory a building from which people study the sky (p. 18)
observatorio edificio desde el cual las personas estudian el cielo (pág. 18)

peninsula a piece of land surrounded on three sides by water (p. 38)
península pedazo de tierra rodeado de agua por tres lados (pág. 38)

pioneer an early settler; in the United States, people who settled the interior and western areas of the country were known as pioneers (p. 154)
　pionero poblador; en Estados Unidos, las personas que se establecieron en el interior y el oeste del país se llamaron pioneros (pág. 154)

plantation a large farm that grows mainly one crop (p. 153)
　plantación granja muy grande en la que se produce principalmente un solo tipo de cultivo (pág. 153)

province an administrative division of a country (p. 178)
　provincia división administrativa de un país (pág. 178)

pulp softened wood fibers; used to make paper (p. 175)
　pulpa fibras ablandadas de madera; usadas para hacer papel (pág. 175)

Q

Quechua (ke-chuh-wuh) the official Inca language (p. 26)
　quechua idioma oficial de los incas (pág. 26)

R

referendum a recall vote (p. 94)
　referéndum voto para quitar a alguien de su cargo (pág. 94)

refugee someone who flees to another country, usually for political or economic reasons (p. 73)
　refugiado persona que escapa a otro país, generalmente por razones económicas o políticas (pág. 73)

regionalism the strong connection that people feel toward the region in which they live (p. 183)
　regionalismo gran conexión que las personas sienten con la región en la que viven (pág. 183)

S

slash-and-burn agriculture the practice of burning forest in order to clear land for planting (p. 49)
　agricultura de tala y quema práctica de quemar los bosques para despejar el terreno y sembrar en él (pág. 49)

smog a mixture of smoke, chemicals, and fog (p. 50)
　smog mezcla de humo, sustancias químicas y niebla (pág. 50)

soil exhaustion the process of soil becoming infertile because it has lost nutrients needed by plants (p. 105)
　agotamiento del suelo proceso por el cual el suelo se vuelve estéril porque ha perdido los nutrientes que necesitan las plantas (pág. 105)

strait a narrow passageway that connects two large bodies of water (p. 125)
　estrecho paso angosto que une dos grandes masas de agua (pág. 125)

strike a work stoppage by a group of workers until their demands are met (p. 94)
　huelga interrupción del trabajo por parte de un grupo de trabajadores hasta que se cumplan sus demandas (pág. 94)

T

terrorism violent attacks that cause fear (p. 166)
　terrorismo ataques violentos que provocan miedo (pág. 166)

tributary a smaller stream or river that flows into a larger stream or river (p. 145)
　tributario río o corriente más pequeña que fluye hacia un río o una corriente más grande (pág. 145)

V

viceroy governor (p. 131)
　virrey gobernador (pág. 131)

ENGLISH AND SPANISH GLOSSARY

Economics Handbook

What Is Economics?

Economics may sound dull, but it touches almost every part of your life. Here are some examples of the kinds of economic choices you may have made yourself:

- Which pair of shoes to buy—the ones on sale or the ones you really like, which cost much more
- Whether to continue saving your money for the DVD player you want or use some of it now to go to a movie
- Whether to give some money to a fundraiser for a new park or to housing for the homeless

As these examples show, we can think of economics as a study of choices. These choices are the ones people make to satisfy their needs or their desires.

Glossary of Economic Terms

Here are some of the words we use to talk about economics:

ECONOMIC SYSTEMS

capitalism See market economy.

command economy an economic system in which the central government makes all economic decisions

communism a political system in which the government owns all property and runs a command economy

free enterprise a system in which businesses operate with little government involvement, as in a market economy

market economy an economic system based on free trade and competition; the government has little to say about what, how, or for whom goods are produced

mixed economy an economy that is a combination of command, market, and traditional economies

traditional economy an economy in which production is based on customs and tradition

THE ECONOMY AND MONEY

consumer one who buys goods or services for personal use

currency paper or coins that a country uses for its money supply

demand the amount of goods and services that consumers are willing and able to buy at a given time

economy the structure of economic life in a country

investment the purchase of something with the expectation that it will gain in value; usually property, stocks, etc.

productivity the amount of goods or services that a worker or workers can produce within a given amount of time

standard of living how well people are living; determined by the amount of goods and services they can afford

INTERNATIONAL TRADE

comparative advantage the ability of a company or country to produce something at a lower cost than other companies or countries

competition rivalry between businesses selling similar goods or services; a condition that often leads to lower prices or improved products

exports goods or services that a country sells and sends to other countries

free trade trade among nations that is not affected by financial or legal barriers; trade without barriers

gross domestic product (GDP) total market value of all goods and services produced in a country in a given year; per capita GDP is the average value of goods and services produced per person in a country in a given year

imports goods or services that a country brings in or purchases from another country

interdependence a relationship between countries in which they rely on one another for resources, goods, or services

market clearing price the price of a good or service at which supply equals demand

opportunity cost a trade-off; the value lost when producing or consuming one thing prevents producing or consuming another

profit the gain or excess made by selling goods or services over their costs

scarcity a condition of limited resources and unlimited wants by people

specialization a focus on only one or two aspects of production in order to produce a product more quickly and cheaply; for example, one worker washes the wheels of the car, another cleans the interior, and another washes the body

supply the amount of goods and services that are available at a given time

trade barriers financial or legal limitations to trade; prevention of free trade

PERSONAL ECONOMICS

barter the exchange of one good or service for another

credit a system that allows consumers to pay for goods and services over time

income a gain of money that comes typically from labor or capital

interest the money that a borrower pays to a lender in return for a loan

money any item, usually coins or paper currency, that is used in payment for goods or services

savings money or income that is not used to purchase goods or services

tax a required payment to a local, state, or national government; different kinds of taxes include sales taxes, income taxes, and property taxes

wage the payment a worker receives for his or her labor

RESOURCES

capital generally refers to wealth, in particular wealth that can be used to finance the production of goods or services

goods objects or materials that humans can purchase to satisfy their wants and needs

human capital sometimes used to refer to human skills and education that affect the production of goods and services in a company or country

natural resource any material in nature that people use and value

producer a person or group that makes goods or provides services to satisfy consumers' wants and needs

services any activities that are performed for a fee

Activities

1. On a separate sheet of paper, fill in the blanks in the following sentences:

    A. The total value of all the goods and services produced in the United States in one year is its _____.

    B. The amount of goods and services that consumers are willing and able to buy at any given time is known as _____.

    C. _____are objects or materials that humans can buy to satisfy their needs and wants.

    D. The money we don't spend on goods or services is our _____.

    E. Businesses are able to operate with little government involvement in a _____system.

2. Interview someone of your parents' generation and your grandparents' generation. Ask each one what the following things cost when they were in sixth or seventh grade: shoes for school, a typical lunch at school, a movie ticket. Compare the prices. How would you account for any differences?

Index

KEY TO INDEX

c = chart	*m* = map
f = feature	*p* = photo

Academic Words, H4
Acapulco, 49
Active Reading, H3
Africa: Africa: Physical, 218m; Africa: Political, 219m
African Americans: in United States, 156, 157m
agriculture: Canada, 185; Caribbean Islands, 61; cash crop, 49; Central America, 61, 66–67; Chile, 138; climate in Andes and, 126–27; Colombia, 88; colonial Mexico, 44; Inca Empire, 27; Maya civilization, 15; Mexico, 44, 49, 51, 52; Midwest region of United States, 163; one-crop economies of Central America, 63p; Ontario, Canada, 175p; Paraguay, 117; slash-and-burn agriculture, 49, 49p; United States, 148; Uruguay, 116; vegetation in Mexico, 40–41; Venezuela, 92; in West region of United States, 164
Alaska, 164–65
Alberta, 174, 185
altiplano, 125, 125p, 127
Amazon Basin, 101p, 103, 103m; climate of, 105; oil deposits in Ecuador, 135
Amazon rain forest, 104f, 109–10; deforestation, 105, 110f; as natural resource, 105
Amazon River, 102, 103m
American Indians: in colonial Mexico, 44; culture of Pacific South America and, 132–33, 133p; language, 45; native Canadians, 177; in North America, 30–31f; Spanish rule of, in Pacific South America, 132–33
Americas, The Americas: 500 BC–AD 1537, 13m; climate map of, 7m; Early Civilizations of the Americas, 35m; early history of, 12–32; facts about countries, 8–10c; Geographical Extremes: The Americas, 3c; largest cities and urban populations, 10c; major food exports of, 11c; North America: Political, 4m; physical

map of, 2m; population map of, 6m; regional atlas of, 2–7m; Size Comparison: The United States and the Americas, 3m; South America: Political, 5m
Andes, 82, 83m, 122p, 139p; climate zones in, 126–27, 126p; land-scape of, 124–25
Antigua: facts about, 8c
Appalachian Mountains, 144–45, 145m, 145p
archipelago, 59
architecture: Aztec Empire, 23; Inca Empire, 27; Maya civilization, 15–16, 16–17f, 18
Arctic Circle, 124, 174, 186
Argentina: Argentina's Largest Cities, 114m; Buenos Aires, 114, 114c, 115p; climate of, 105; colonial rule of, 112–13; culture of, 114; Dirty War, 113; economy of, 114–15; Eva Perón, 113f; facts about, 8c; food/eating habits, 114; gauchos, 113; government of, 113; history of, 112–13; informal economy, 115; people of, 114; physical features of, 102–3, 103m; population of, 114m; today, 114–15; trade, 114; urban population of, 10c
art: Aztec Empire, 23, 23p; Caribbean Islands, 73f; Inca Empire, 27, 28p; Maya civilization, 18
Asia: Asia: Physical, 216m; Asia: Political, 217m
Asian Americans: in United States, 156, 157m
Asian immigrants: to Canada, 180
astronomy: Aztec Empire, 23; Maya civilization, 18, 18f
Atacama Desert, 127, 127p
Atahualpa (Inca King), 28–29, 29p
Atlanta, 162, 163
Atlantic Ocean: Panama Canal, 67, 68–69f
Atlantic South America: climate of, 105; natural resources, 105; physical geography of, 102–3, 103m; political map of, 100–101m; vegetation of, 105
Atlas: Africa: Physical, 218m; Africa: Political, 219m; The Americas Regional Atlas, 2–7m; Asia: Physical, 216m; Asia: Political, 217m; Europe: Physical, 214m; Europe: Political, 215m; North America: Physical, 210m; North America: Political, 211m; The North Pole, 221m; The Pacific: Political,

220m; The Poles, 221m; South America: Physical, 212m; South America: Political, 213m; The South Pole, 221m; United States: Physical, 202–3m; United States: Political, 204–5m; World: Physical, 206–7m; World: Political, 208–9m
Aztec Empire, 20–24; architecture, 23; art, 23, 23p; astronomy, 23; The Aztec Empire, 1519, 21m; building empire, 20–21; calendar, 23; Cortés conquers, 24, 44; in history of Mexico, 43–44; Moctezuma II, 24; religion, 23; social structure, 21, 23; Tenochtitlán, 20–21, 21p, 22f; warfare, 23

Bahamas, 59, 59m; facts about, 8c
Baja California, 38, 39m; climate of, 41
Banff National Park, Canada, 174p
Barbados, 72; facts about, 8c
Barbuda: facts about, 8c
bay: defined, H14
Bearstone (Will Hobbs), 159f
Belize, 58, 59m, 66; ecotourism, 66, 66p; facts about, 8c; as Great Britain colony, 62; independence of, 63; language of, 64; Maya civilization and, 62
bilingual, 156
Biography: Atahualpa, 29; Bolívar, Simon, 91; Juárez, Benito, 45; Pacal, 17; Pachacuti, 26; Perón, Eva, 113; Pizarro, Francisco, 29; Toussaint-L'Ouverture, 71; Washington, George, 153
Bogotá, 88
Bolívar, Simon, 91, 91p
Bolivia, 91p; Andes, 124–25; climate and vegetation in, 126–27, 126p; economy of, 135; elevation and, 126–27; El Niño, 127; facts about, 8c; government of, 135; Inca empire, 130; independence, 132; Indian heritage and, 132; languages in, 132, 132m; natural resources of, 127–28, 128m, 135; physical geography of, 124–25, 125m; poverty in, 135; Spanish rule, 131–32; today, 135
Boston, 152
Brasília, 109

Brazil: Amazon region, 109–10, 109p; Brazil's Urban and Rural Population, 121c; climate of, 105; colonialization of, 106–7; culture of, 107–8; facts about, 8c; festivals and foods of, 108; government of, 107; history of, 106–7; interior region, 109; language, 107; northeast region, 109, 109p; people of, 107; physical features of, 102–3, 103m; population of, 106; poverty in, 109; regions of, 108–10, 108m; religion, 108; since independence, 107; soccer in, 107p; southeast region, 108–9, 108p; today, 108–10; urban population of, 10c

Brazilian Highlands, 103, 103m

British Columbia, 178p, 185–86; climate of, 174, 191m; immigration to, 180

Buenos Aires, 114, 114c, 115p

Bush, George W., 166

calendar: Aztec Empire, 23; Maya civilization, 18

Callao, Peru, 136, 136m

Canada: agriculture in, 185; British conquest, 178; climate of, 174; creation of, 178–79; culture of, 179–81; Eastern Provinces of, 183–84; economy of, 186–87; ethnic groups of, 179c; European settlement in, 177; facts about, 8c; French and Indian War, 178; government of, 182; Heartland region, 184–85; history of, 176–79; immigration, 179–80; industries of, 186–87; language of, 179m, 183, 184, 185; movement to cities, 180–81; native Canadians, 177; natural resources of, 174–75; New France, 177; North American Free Trade Agreement (NAFTA), 49; Northern region of, 186; parliament, 171p, 182; physical geography of, 172–75, 173m; political map of, 149m, 170p–171p; regionalism in, 183; regions of, 183–86, 183m; trade, 187, 187c; trade with United States, 187, 187c; Upper and Lower Canada, 178; urban population of, 10c; Western Provinces of, 185–86

Canadian Pacific Railway, 178–79, 178p

Canadian Shield, 173, 173m, 174

Canaima National Park, 84p

Cancún, 36p, 49

canyon: defined, H15

Caracas, 93, 94p

Caribbean Islands: climate and vegetation, 60–61; colonialization, 70, 71m; Cuba, 74p; culture of, 72; Dominican Republic, 74; early history of, 70; European Colonies in Caribbean, 1763, 71m; festivals and food of, 72; Haiti, 73; independence of, 71; languages of, 72, 72c; music of, 73f; physical geography of, 59–60, 59m; political map of, 56–57m; Puerto Rico, 73; religion, 72; resources of, 61; today, 73–75; tourism, 75, 75p; Toussaint-L'Ouverture, 71f; volcanic activity of, 60, 60m

Caribbean Sea, 58, 59m; Panama Canal, 67, 68–69f

Caribbean South America: climate of, 85; Colombia, 86–89; French Guiana, 95; Guyana, 94–95; mountains and highlands, 82–83, 83p; physical geography of, 82–84, 83m, 84p; plains, rivers, and wildlife of, 83–84; political map of, 80–81m, H12; resources of, 85; Suriname, 95; vegetation of, 85; Venezuela, 90–94, 93m

Carnival, 72, 100p, 108, 133p

Cartagena, 80p, 87, 87p

Casa Rosada, Buenos Aires, 101p

Cascade Range, 146

Case Study: Natural Hazards in the United States, 150–51f, 150m

cash crop, 49

Castro, Fidel, 74

Categorizing, 142, 200

Catholic Church: Colombia's independence from Spain and, 87; colonial Mexico and, 44

Catholics: in Brazil, 108; in Caribbean Islands, 72; in Central America, 65; in Mexico, 45; in Pacific South America, 132–33; in Uruguay, 115

Cauca River, 84, 88

causeways, 20

Central America: agriculture, 63, 66–67; Belize, 66; climate and vegetation, 60–61; cloud forest, 60; colonization in, 62; Costa Rica, 67; culture of, 64–65; early history of, 62; El Salvador, 66; festivals of, 65; food, 65; Guatemala, 64–65f, 66; history of, 62–63; Honduras, 66; languages of, 64, 79m; Maya civilization, 14–19; Nicaragua, 66–67; one-crop economies, 63p; Panama, 67; people of, 64; physical geography of, 58, 59m; political map of, 56–57m; religion, 65; resources of, 61; since independence, 63; today, 66–67; volcanic activity of, 60, 60m

Central Mexico, 50p, 51

charts and graphs: Argentina's Largest Cities, 114c; Brazil's Urban and Rural Population, 121c; Canadian Ethnic Groups, 179c; Chile's Exports to the United States, 2004, 141c; Climate Graph: Nassau, Bahamas, 78c; Climate Graph: Tegucigalpa, Honduras, 76c; Developed and Less Developed Countries, 224c; Earth Facts, 222c; Ecuador: Elevation Profile, 129; Facts about Countries: The Americas, 8–10c; Geographical Extremes: The Americas, 3c; Languages in Pacific South America, 132c; Languages of the Caribbean, 72c; Major Food Exports of the Americas, 11c; Mexico's Trading Partners, 55c; Population of Major U.S. Cities, 161c; Trade with the United States, 187c; Urban Populations in the Americas, 10c; World Languages, 225c; World's Largest Cities, 10c; World Population, 224c; World Religions, 225c; World's Top Oil Exporters, 93c

Chart and Graph Skills: Interpreting a Climate Graph, 76; Reading an Elevation Profile, 129; Using Latitude and Longitude, 96

Chavez, Hugo, 93–94

Chibcha, 86–87

Chicago, 163; population of, 161c

Chichén Itzá, 18p

Chile: agriculture in, 138; Andes, 124–25; Atacama Desert, 127, 127p; Chile's Exports to the United States, 2004, 141m; climate and vegetation in, 126–27, 126p; economy of, 138; elevation and, 126–27; El Niño, 127; facts about, 8c; government of, 137; Inca empire, 131, 131p; independence, 132; languages in, 132, 132m; natural resources of, 127–28, 138; physical geography of, 124–25, 125m; Spanish rule, 131–32; today, 137–38; trade and, 138; urban population of, 10c

chinampas, 21

Chinatown: Vancouver, British Colombia, 181p
Christianity, 37p; Central America, 65; spreading in colonial Mexico, 44; in United States, 156
cities: Argentina, 114–15; Brazil, 108–9; Canada, 180–81; 181f; Lima, 136, 136m; Maya civilization, 14, 15; megacity, 108; Mexico, 50; Tenochtitlán, 22f; United States, 161–65, 161c; Urban Populations in the Americas, 10c; Venezuela, 93–94; World's Largest Cities, 10c
citizenship: in United States, 155
civil war, 66; Colombia, 89; El Salvador, 66; Nicaragua, 66–67
climate: Andes, 126–27, 126p; Atlantic South America, 105; Canada, 174; Caribbean Islands, 60–61; Caribbean South America, 85; Central America, 60–61; El Niño, 127; Mexico, 40, 40m; Pacific South America, 126–27; United States, 147–48, 147m, 147p
climate maps: Americas, 7m; Mexico, 40m; United States, 147m; West Africa, H13
coast: defined, H15; Mexico, 40
Cold War, 155
Colombia, 86–89; agriculture, 88; Bogotá, 88; Chibcha, 86–87; civil war, 89; as colony, 87; culture of, 88; daily life in, 88–89p; economy of, 88; facts about, 8c; history of, 86–87; independence from Spain, 87; mountains of, 82, 83m; natural resources, 85, 88; people of, 88; Spanish conquest of, 87; today, 88–89; Volcanoes in Colombia, 99m; wildlife of, 84
colonialization: Argentina, 112–13; Brazil, 106–7; Caribbean Islands, 70–71, 71m; Central America, 62; Colombia, 87; Mexico, 44; United States, 152; Venezuela, 90
colony, 152
Columbus, Christopher, 70
commonwealth, 73
communism: Cuba, 74
compass rose, H11
conic projection, H9
conquistadors, 24, 44
Constitution, U.S., 155f
Continental Divide, 146
continents, H7
cooperative, 74
coral reef: defined, H14
cordillera, 82
Córdoba, Argentina, 114c
Cortés, Hernán, 24, 44

Costa Rica, 58, 59m, 67; facts about, 8c; independence of, 63
coup, 137
Cree, 177
Creole, 72, 72c, 95, 95p, 132
Critical Thinking Skills: Analyzing Information, 32; Connecting Ideas, 111
Cuba, 59, 59m, 59p, 74, 74p; facts about, 8c; government of, 74; independence of, 71
cultural regions: of Mexico, 50–51m, 50–52
culture: Argentina, 114; Brazil, 107–8; Canada, 179–81; Caribbean Islands, 72; Central America, 64–65; Colombia, 88; Day of the Dead, 45–46; Feast of Corpus Christi, 92f; Maya civilization, 16–18; Mexico, 45–46; Pacific South America, 132–33; popular in United States, 158; soccer in Brazil, 107f; United States, 156, 158; Venezuela, 91
Cuzco, 25
cylindrical projection, H8

Dallas, 163
Day of the Dead, 45–46, 46f
Declaration of Independence, 153
deforestation, 105, 110, 110p
degrees: defined, H6
delta: defined, H14
demography. *See* population
deserts: in Andes, 127; defined, H15; in Pacific South America, 127, 127p
Detroit, 163
developed countries: 224c
developing countries: 224c
Dirty War, 113
Dominica: facts about, 8c
Dominican Republic, 74; facts about, 8c; independence of, 71; music of, 73f
dune: defined, H15

Earth: facts about, 222c; mapping, H6–H7
earthquakes: Caribbean Islands, 60; Pacific South America, 124; United States, 150, 150m
Eastern Hemisphere: defined, H7; map of, H7

Eastern Provinces of Canada, 183–84
Eastern states of United States: climate of, 147, 147m; physical features of, 144–45, 145m
economics: of Argentina, 114–15; of Bolivia, 135; of Canada, 186–87; of Chile, 138; of Colombia, 88; Economics Handbook, 236–37; of Ecuador, 135; of Inca Empire, 26; informal economy, 115, 135f; of Mexico, 48–49; of Midwest United States, 163; of Northeast United States, 161; one-crop economies of Central America, 63p; Paraguay, 117; of Peru, 136–37; of South region of United States, 162–63; of United States, 165–66; of Uruguay, 116; of Venezuela, 92–93; of West region of United States, 164
economics connection: The Informal Economy, 135f
ecotourism, 66, 66p
Ecuador: Andes, 124–25; climate and vegetation of, 126–27, 126p; economic regions of, 135; elevation and, 126–27; El Niño, 127; facts about, 8c; government, 134; Inca empire, 131, 131p; independence, 132; independence from Spain, 87; languages in, 132, 132c, 132m; natural resources of, 127–28, 135; oil in, 128, 135; physical geography of, 124–25, 125m; Spanish rule, 131–32; today, 134–35
elevation profile: reading, 129
Ellesmere Island, 173, 173m
El Niño, 127
El Salvador, 58, 59m, 66; civil war, 66; facts about, 9c; independence of, 63
empire, 43
equator: defined, H6
essential elements of geography, H16–H17
ethnic groups: Brazil, 107; Canada, 179c; Central America, 64; Paraguay, 117; United States, 156, 157m; Uruguay, 115; Venezuela, 91
Europe: Europe: Physical, 214m; Europe: Political, 215m

favelas, 109
Feast of Corpus Christi, 92f

festivals: of Brazil, 108; Caribbean Islands, 72; Carnival, 72, 100p, 108, 133p; Central America, 65; Day of the Dead, 45–46; Feast of Corpus Christi, 92f

First Nations, 177

five themes of geography, H16–H17

flat-plane projection, H9

Florida: climate of, 147p

food/eating habits: Argentina, 114; of Brazil, 108; Caribbean Islands, 72; Central America, 65; in United States, 158

forests: Amazon rain forest, 104f; in Canada, 175; cloud, 60; defined, H14; deforestation, 105, 110; slash-and-burn agriculture, 49

Fox, Vicente, 48

France: colonization of Canada, 177; colony in Caribbean Islands, 71; French and Indian War, 178

French and Indian War, 178

French Guiana, 95

Galápagos Islands, 125, 125m

Gaucho Martín Fierro, The **(José Hernández),** 118

gauchos, 113, 113p

Geographic Dictionary, H14–H15

Geography and History: North America's Native Cultures, 30–31f; The Panama Canal, 68–69f

Geography and Map Skills Handbook: Geographic Dictionary, H14–H15; Map Essentials, H10–H11; Mapmaking, H8–H9; Mapping the Earth, H6–H7; Themes and Essential Elements of Geography, H16–H17; Working with Maps, H12–H13

Geography Skills: Interpreting a Climate Graph, 76; Interpreting an Elevation Profile, 129; Using Latitude and Longitude, 96; Using Mental Maps and Sketch Maps, 188; Using a Political Map, 149

Georgetown, Guyana, 94

glaciers: Andean, 125; defined, H15

globe, H6

gold: Mexico, 41, 44

government: of Argentina, 113; of Bolivia, 135; of Brazil, 107; of Canada, 182; of Chile, 137; of Cuba, 74; of Ecuador, 134; of Inca Empire, 26; of Mexico, 48; of Paraguay, 116; of Peru, 137; of United States, 155; of Uruguay, 115; of Venezuela, 91, 93–94

Gran Chaco, 103, 103m; climate of, 105

Gran Colombia, 87, 91p

Grand Banks, 174

Grand Canyon, 143p

Great Britain: colonies in United States, 152–53; colonization in Central America, 62; colonization of Canada, 178; French and Indian War, 178

Greater Antilles, 59

Greater Mexico City, 50, 51p

Great Lakes, 145, 145m, 173

Great Plains, 146, 147, 164

Grenada: facts about, 9c

Grenadines: music of, 73f

grid, H6

Guadalajara, Mexico, 51

Guadeloupe, 71, 71m

Guaraní, 117

Guatemala, 58, 59m, 66; facts about, 9c; independence of, 63; market in, 64–65f; Maya civilization, 14–19, 62

Guayaquil, 135

guerrillas, 89

Guiana Highlands, 83, 83m, 93

Guianas, 94–95

gulf: defined, H14

Gulf of Mexico, 38, 39m

Gulf Stream, 174

Guyana, 94–95; facts about, 9c; mountains of, 83, 83m

haciendas, 44

Haiti, 73; facts about, 9c; independence of, 71; Toussaint-L'Ouverture, 71p

Halifax, Nova Scotia, 177p, 184

Hamilton, Ontario, 185

Havana, 74

Hawaii, 146, 165

Heartland of Canada, 184–85

hemispheres: defined, H7

Hernández, José, 118

Hidalgo, Miguel, 44p, 45

highlands: of Caribbean South America, 82–83

hill: defined, H15

Hispanic Americans: in United States, 156, 157m

Hispaniola, 59, 59m; Dominican Republic, 74; Haiti, 73

history: of Argentina, 112–13; of Brazil, 106–7; of Canada, 176–79; of Caribbean Islands, 70–71; of Central America, 62–63; of Colombia, 86–87, 87f; early history of Americas, 12–32; of Mexico, 42–45; of Native Americans, 30–31f; of Pacific South America, 130–32; of Panama Canal, 68–69f; of United States, 152–55; of Venezuela, 90–91

history connection: Catagena's Spanish Fort, 87

Hollywood, 164

Homeland Security, Department of, 166

Honduras, 58, 59m, 66; facts about, 9c; independence of, 63

Houston, 162, 163, 163p; population of, 161c

Huáscar, 28

Hudson Bay, 173, 173m

Hurricane Isabel, 61p

hurricanes: Central America and Caribbean Islands, 61, 61p; in United States, 150, 150m

Hussein, Saddam, 166

hydroelectric power, 116, 117

Identifying Supporting Details, 80, 197

Iguazú Falls, 103p

immigration: to Canada, 179–80

Inca Empire, 25–29, 131, 131p; agriculture, 27; architecture, 27; art, 27, 28p; Atahualpa, 28–29; central rule of, 26; creating empire, 25; government, 26; The Inca Empire, 1530, 26m; labor tax in, 26; language, 26; Pachacuti, 25, 26; Pizarro conquers, 28–29; religion, 27; social structure of, 27; as well-organized economy, 26; written and oral history of, 28

India: physical map of, H13

industry: Canada, 186–87; Mexico, 49

inflation, 48

informal economy, 115, 135p

Interior Plains of United States: climate of, 147, 147m; physical features of, 145–46

Internet Activities: Analyzing Climate, 140; Creating a Poster, 120; Making a Brochure, 168; Making Diagrams, 34; Taking an Ecotour, 78; Writing a Description, 54; Writing a Journal Entry, 98; Writing Newspaper Articles, 190

Inuit, 177; Nunavut, 186, 186p

Iran: oil exports of, 93c

islands: defined, H7, H14
isthmus: Central America as, 58; defined, H14

jade: Maya civilization, 15, 33p
Jamaica, 59, 59m, 75; facts about, 9c; music of, 73f
Juárez, Benito, 45, 45p
Judaism: in United States, 156

Korean War, 155
Kuna, 57p

Labrador, 174, 183, 183m
Labrador Sea, 174, 183m
Lake Erie, 173, 173m
Lake Maracaibo: oil reserves and, 92, 93m
Lake Ontario, 173
lakes: defined, H14
Lake Texcoco, 20
Lake Titicaca, 125
landforms, examples of, H14–H15
landlocked, 116
language: American Indians, 45; Belize, 64; bilingual, 156; Brazil, 107; Canada, 178, 179m, 183, 184, 185; Caribbean Islands, 72, 72c; Central America, 64, 79m; Inca Empire, 26; Mexico, 45; Pacific South America, 132, 132m; Paraguay, 117; United States, 156; Uruguay, 115; of the world, 225c
La Paz, 135
Latin America, 38
latitude: defined, H6; using, 96
legend, H11
Lesser Antilles, 59, 59m
Lima, 136–37p, 136m
Literature: *Bearstone* (Will Hobbs), 159; *Gaucho Martín Fierro, The* (José Hernández), 118
llaneros, 81p, 92
llanos, 83
locator map, H11
longitude: defined, H6; using, 96
Los Angeles, 164; population of, 161c
Lower Canada, 178

Machu Picchu, 27, 131p
macumba, 108
Magdalena River, 84, 88
maize, 14
Making Inferences, 122, 199
Manaus, 109
Manitoba, 185
map projections, H8–H9; conic projection, H9; cylindrical projection, H8; flat-plane projection, H9; Mercator projection, H8
maps. *See also* **Map Skills**
    The Americas: 500 BC–AD 1537, 13m
    The Aztec Empire, 1519, 21m
    Bolivia: Resources, 128m
    Canada's Major Languages, 179m
    Canaima National Park, 84m
    climate maps: The Americas, 7m; Mexico, 40m; United States, 147m; West Africa, H13
    Climate of British Columbia, 191m
    Conic Projections, H9
    defined, H8
    Distribution of Selected Ethnic Groups, 2000, 157m
    Early Civilizations of the Americas, 35m
    Eastern Hemisphere, H7
    European Colonies in the Caribbean, 1763, 71m
    The First Crusade, 1096, H10
    Flat-plane Projections, H9
    The Inca Empire, 1530, 26m
    Languages in Pacific South America, 132m
    Languages of Central America, 79m
    Map Activity, 34m, 54m, 78m, 98m, 120m, 140m, 168m, 190m
    Maya Civilization, c. 900, 15m
    Mental Maps and Sketch Maps, 188
    Mercator Projection, H8
    Mexico's Cultural Regions, 50–51m
    Native Americans, 30–31m
    Natural Hazards in the United States, 150m
    Northern Hemisphere, H7
    Paraguay and Uruguay, 116m
    physical maps: Africa, 218m; The Americas, 2m; Asia, 216m; Atlantic South America, 103m; Canada, 173m; Central America and the Caribbean, 59m; defined, H13; Europe, 214m; The Indian

Subcontinent, H13; Mexico, 39m; North America, 210m; The North Pole, 221m; The Pacific, 220m; Pacific South America, 125m; Paraguay, 116m; South America, 212m; The South Pole, 221m; United States, 145m, 202–3m; Uruguay, 116m; World, 206–7m
    political maps: Africa, 219m; Asia, 217m; Atlantic South America, 100–101m; Canada, 149m, 170–71m; Caribbean South America, 80–81m, H12; Central America and the Caribbean, 56–57m; defined, H12; Europe, 215m; Mexico, 36–37m, 149m; North America, 4m, 211m; The Pacific, 220m; Pacific South America, 123m; South America, 5m, 213m; United States, 142–43m, 149m, 204–5m; using, 149; World, 208–9m
    population maps: Americas, 6m; Argentina, 114m
    Regions of Brazil, 108m
    Regions of Canada, 183m
    Regions of the United States, 161m, 169m
    Routes Before and After the Panama Canal, 68m
    Settlements around Lima, 136m
    Size Comparison: The United States and the Americas, 3m
    Sketch Map of the World, 188m
    Southern Hemisphere, H7
    United States: Land Use and Resources, 162m
    Venezuela's Major Resources, 93m
    Volcanic Activity in Central America and Caribbean, 60m
    Volcanoes of Colombia, 99m
    Western Expansion of the United States, 154m
    Western Hemisphere, H7
Map Skills: Interpreting an Elevation Profile, 129; interpreting maps, 2m, 4m, 5m, 6m, 7m, 15m, 21m, 37m, 39m, 40m, 57m, 59m, 60m, 71m, 83m, 93m, 103m, 114m, 116m, 125m, 128m, 132m, 136m, 145m, 147m, 154m, 157m, 161m, 162m, 173m, 179m, 183m; Understanding Map Projections, H8–H9; Using Latitude and Longitude, 96, H6–H7; Using Mental Maps and Sketch Maps, 188; Using a Political Map, 149; Working With Different Kinds of Maps, H12–H13

maquiladoras, 51
maritime, 183
Maritime Provinces, 183
Martinique, 71m
masonry, 27
mathematics: Maya civilization, 18
Mato Grosso Plateau, 103, 103m
Maya civilization, 14–19; achievements of, 18; agriculture, 15; architecture, 15–16, 16–17f, 18; art, 18; Chichén Itzá, 18p; cities, 15, 15m; Classic Age of, 15–16; culture of, 16–18; decline of, 19; geography and, 14; in history of Central America, 62; in history of Mexico, 43; jade and obsidian, 15, 15m; mathematics, 18; observatories, 18; Pacal, 15, 17p; Palenque, 15, 16–17f; religion, 17; social structure, 16–17; trade, 15, 15m; writing system, 18
megacity, 108
megalopolis, 161
mental maps, 188
Mercator projection, H8
Mercosur, 114
meridians: defined, H6
Mesoamerica, 14
mestizos, 44, 64, 66, 117
Mexican-American War, 45
Mexican Plateau, 39, 39m; climate of, 40
Mexican Revolution, 45
Mexico, 38–52; agriculture, 44, 49, 51, 52; Aztec Empire, 20–24, 43–44; Baja California, 38, 39m; Benito Juárez, 45; bodies of water, 38, 39m; Central Mexico, 50p, 51; climate, 40, 40m; coastal lowlands of, 40; colonial times of, 44; cultural regions of, 50–51m, 50–52; culture of, 45–46; Day of the Dead, 45–46, 46f; early cultures of, 42–43; economy of, 48–49; facts about, 9c; government, 48; Greater Mexico City, 50, 51p; hacienda, 44; independence from Spain, 45; industry, 49; language, 45; maquiladoras, 51; Maya civilization, 14–19, 43; Mexican-American War, 45; Mexican Revolution, 45; Mexico's Trading Partners, 55c; Miguel Hidalgo, 44p, 45; natural resources of, 41; North American Free Trade Agreement (NAFTA), 49; Northern Mexico, 50p, 51–52; oil, 41, 49, 52; Olmec, 42p, 43; physical geography of, 38–41; physical map of, 39m; plateaus and mountains of, 39, 39m; political map of, 36–37m, 149m; religion, 45; Rio Bravo River, 38, 39m; Sierra Madre, 39, 39m; Southern Mexico, 51p, 52; tourism, 49, 52; urban population of, 10c; vegetation and animals of, 40–41; Yucatán Peninsula, 38, 39m
Mexico City, 10c, 39, 50, 51p
Miami, 163
Midwest region of United States, 161m, 163
military power: of United States, 165–66
mining, 164
minutes: defined, H6
missions, 44, 65
Mississippi River, 145, 145m, 163; delta of, 146, 146p
Missouri River, 146
mita, 26
Moctezuma II, 24
Monterrey, 51
Montevideo, Uruguay, 115
Montreal, 181, 184
mountains: of Caribbean South America, 82–83, 83m; climate of Andes, 126–27, 126p; cordillera, 82; defined, H15; Mexico, 39, 39m
Mount McKinley, 146
Mount Saint Helens, 146
movement: to cities in Canada, 180–81; immigration to Canada, 179–80
mulattoes, 44
Mumbai, 10c
music: in United States, 158
Muslims: in United States, 156

N

NAFTA. *See* North American Free Trade Agreement (NAFTA)
Native Americans: in Canada, 176p; in North America, 30–31f; in United States, 156, 157m
natural hazards in United States, 150–51f, 150m
natural resources: Amazon rain forest as, 105; of Atlantic South America, 105; of Bolivia, 127–28, 128m, 135; of Canada, 174–75; of Caribbean South America, 85; of Central America and Caribbean Islands, 61; of Chile, 127–28, 138; of Colombia, 88; of Ecuador, 127–28, 135; of Mexico, 41; of Midwest United States, 163; of Northeast United States, 161; of Pacific South America, 127–28; of Peru, 127–28, 137; of South region of United States, 162–63; of United States, 148; of Venezuela, 92–93, 93m; of West region of United States, 164
Nazca Lines, 130
Nevis, 75; facts about, 9c
New Brunswick, 178, 183–84
Newfoundland, 174, 183m
Newfoundland Island, 177
New France, 176p, 177
New Granada: independence from Spain, 87
New Orleans, 162
newsprint, 175
New York City, 10c, 152, 161p; climate of, 147p; population of, 161c
Niagara Falls, 172–73, 173p
Nicaragua, 58, 59m, 66–67; civil war, 66–67; facts about, 9c; as Great Britain colony, 62; independence of, 63
North America: Native Americans of, 30–31f; physical map of, 210m; political map of, 4m, 211m
North American Free Trade Agreement (NAFTA), 49, 165
Northeast region of United States, 160–62, 161m
Northern Hemisphere: defined, H7; map of, H7
Northern Mexico, 50p, 51–52
North Pole: 221m
Northwest Territories, 183m, 186
Norway: oil exports of, 93c
note-taking skills, 20, 25, 38, 42, 48, 58, 62, 70, 82, 86, 90, 102, 106, 112, 124, 130, 134, 144, 152, 172, 176, 182
Nova Scotia, 178, 183–84, 183m
number system: Maya civilization, 18
Nunavut, 186, 186p

O

oasis: defined, H15
observatories, 18, 18p
obsidian: Maya civilization, 15
oceans: defined, H14
O'Gorman, Juan, 44p
Ohio River, 145, 146, 163
oil. *See* petroleum
Olmec, 42p, 43
Olympic National Park, 164p
Ontario, 181, 184–85; agriculture in, 175p
oral history: Inca Empire, 28

INDEX

oral tradition: Aztec Empire, 23
Oregon Trail, 154
Organization of Petroleum Exporting Countries (OPEC), 92–93
Orinoco River, 83p, 84; oil reserves and, 92, 93m
Ottawa, 171m, 171p, 181, 185

Pacal (Maya King), 15, 17p
Pachacuti (Inca ruler), 25, 26, 26p
Pacific Ocean: El Niño, 127; Panama Canal, 67, 68–69f
Pacific South America: Bolivia today, 135; Chile today, 137–38; climate and vegetation of, 126–27; culture of, 132–33; deserts in, 127; Ecuador today, 134–35; elevation and, 126–27; El Niño, 127; history of, 130–32; informal economy, 135f; languages in, 132, 132m; natural resources of, 127–28, 128m; Peru today, 136–37; physical geography of, 124–25, 125m; political map of, 123m; religion and, 132–33
Palenque, 15, 16–17f
Pampas, 103, 103m, 103p, 113, 113p; climate of, 105
Panama, 58, 59m, 67; facts about, 9c; independence from Spain, 87; independence of, 63
Panama Canal, 67; Routes Before and After the Panama Canal, 68m
Paraguay, 116m; agriculture, 117; economy of, 117; facts about, 9c; government of, 116; language, 117; people of, 117; physical features of, 102–3, 103m; physical map of, 116m; religion, 117; as Spanish colony, 116
parallels: defined, H6
Paramaribo, 95, 95p
Paraná River, 103, 103m, 117
Patagonia, 103, 103m; climate, 105
peninsula, 38; Baja California, 38, 39m; defined, H14; Yucatán Peninsula, 38, 39m
Perón, Eva, 113, 113p
Persian Gulf War, 155
Peru: Andes, 124–25; climate and vegetation in, 126–27, 126p; desert climate of, 127; early civilizations of, 130; elevation and, 126–27; El Niño, 127; facts about, 9c; government, 137; Inca empire, 131, 131p; independence,

132; languages in, 132, 132m; Lima, 136–37p; natural resources of, 127–28, 137; physical geography of, 124–25, 125m; political violence, 137; Spanish rule, 131–32; today, 136–37; urban population of, 10c
petroleum: in Alaska, 164–65; in Caribbean South America, 85; in Colombia, 88; in Ecuador, 128, 135; in Mexico, 41, 49, 52; United States and, 148; in Venezuela, 91, 92–93, 93m; World's Top Oil Exporters, 93c
Philadelphia: population of, 161c
physical features: H14–H15
physical geography: of Canada, 172–73, 173m; of Caribbean Islands, 59–60, 59m; of Caribbean South America, 82–84, 83m; of Central America, 58, 59m; of Mexico, 38–40, 39m; of Pacific South America, 124–25, 125m; of United States, 144–46, 145m; of the world, 222–23
physical maps: Africa, 218m; The Americas, 2m; Asia, 216m; Atlantic South America, 103m; Canada, 173m; Central America and the Caribbean, 59m; defined, H13; Europe, 214m; The Indian Subcontinent, H13; Mexico, 39m; North America, 210m; Pacific South America, 125m; Paraguay, 116m; The Poles, 221m; South America, 212m; United States, 145m, 202–3m; Uruguay, 116m; World, 206–7m
pioneers, 154
Pizarro, Francisco, 28–29, 29m, 131
plains: of Atlantic South America, 103, 103m; of Caribbean South America, 83; defined, H15
plantation, 153
plateau: of Atlantic South America, 103, 103m; defined, H15; Mexico, 39, 39m
plate tectonics: Central America and the Caribbean, 60, 60m; Pacific South America, 124; of the world, 222c
political maps: Africa, 219m; Asia, 217m; Atlantic South America, 100–101m; Canada, 149m, 170–71m; Caribbean South America, 80–81m, H12; Central America and the Caribbean, 56–57m; defined, H12; Europe, 215m; Mexico, 36–37m, 149m; North America, 4m, 211m; The Pacific, 220m; Pacific South America,

123m; South America, 5m, 213m; United States, 142–43m, 149m, 204–5m; using, 149; World, 96m, 208–9m
pollution: in Mexico City, 50
Popocatépetl, 39, 39p
popular culture: in United States, 158
population: of Argentina, 114m; of Brazil, 106; of Chicago, 161c; of Houston, 161c; of Los Angeles, 161c; of New York City, 161c; of Northeast United States, 161; of Philadelphia, 161c; Population of Major U.S. Cities, 161c
population maps: The Americas, 6m; Argentina, 114m
Port-au-Prince, 73
Portugal: colonization of Brazil, 106–7
poverty: in Bolivia, 135; in Brazil, 109; in Lima, Peru, 136–37p; in Mexico City, 50; in Venezuela, 92, 93, 94
Predicting, 36, 195
Primary Sources: *Florentine Codex,* 23; *U.S. Constitution,* 155
prime meridian, H6
prime minister, 182
Prince Edward Island, 183, 183m
projections. *See* map projections
Protestantism: in Brazil, 108
provinces, 178
Puerto Rico, 56p, 59, 73
pulp, 175

Quebec, Canada, 178, 184–85; winter carnival, 184–85p
Quebec City, 177
Quebecois, 184
Quechua, 26
Quetzalcoatl, 24
Quick Facts: Atlantic South America visual summary, 119; Canada visual summary, 189; Caribbean South America visual summary, 97; Central America and the Caribbean visual summary, 77; Early History of the Americas visual summary, 33; Mexico visual summary, 53; Pacific South America visual summary, 139; United States visual summary, 167
quipus, 28
Quito, 135, 135p

rain forest: Amazon, 104f
Reading Skills: Categorizing, 142, 200; Identifying Supporting Details, 80, 197; Making Inferences, 122, 199; Predicting, 36, 195; Reading Social Studies, H1–H3; Setting a Purpose, 12, 194; Understanding Comparison-Contrast, 56, 196; Understanding Lists, 170, 201; Using Context Clues, 100, 198
referendum, 94
refugee, 73, 74p
regionalism, 183
regions: in Brazil, 108–109p; in Canada, 183–86, 183m; in United States, 160–65, 161m
religion. *See also* Catholics/Catholic Church: Aztec Empire, 23; Brazil, 108; Caribbean Islands, 72; Central America, 65; Inca Empire, 27; Maya civilization, 17; Mexico, 45; Pacific South America, 132–33; Paraguay, 117; United States, 156; Uruguay, 115; of the world, 225c
Research Triangle, North Carolina, 162
Revolutionary War, 153
Rio Bravo River, 38, 39m
Rio de Janeiro, 108, 108p
Río de la Plata, 103, 115
rivers: of Atlantic South America, 102–3, 103m; of Caribbean South America, 83–84; defined, H14; tributary, 145
Rocky Mountains, 146, 172, 178p, 185
Roman Catholic Church. *See* Catholic Church
Rosario, Argentina, 114c
Russia: oil exports of, 93c

St. Lawrence River, 172
Saint Kitts and Nevis, 75; facts about, 9c
Saint Lawrence Seaway, 163
Saint Lucia: facts about, 9c
Saint Vincent and the Grenadines: facts about, 9c
San Diego, California, 164
Sandinistas, 67
San Francisco Bay, 164
San Francisco de Yare, 92f
San Miguel, Argentina, 114c
Santiago, 138
Santo Domingo, 74

São Paulo, 10c, 108
Saskatchewan, 174, 185
Saudi Arabia: oil exports of, 93c
scale, map, H11
Scavenger Hunt, H20
science and technology: of Aztec civilization, 20–21, 43f; of Inca civilization, 27; of Maya civilization, 18; Panama Canal, 68–69f
Seattle, Washington, 164
Setting a Purpose, 12, 194
Shining Path, 137
Sierra Madre, 39, 39m
Sierra Nevada, 146
silver: colonial Mexico, 44; Mexico, 41
sinkhole: defined, H14; Yucatán Peninsula, 40
sketch maps, 188
slash-and-burn agriculture, 49, 49f
slaves: Aztec empire, 23; Brazil, 107; Caribbean Islands, 70–71, 71f, 72; Central America, 62; Maya civilization, 17; Venezuela, 90
smallpox, 24, 44
smog, 50
soccer: in Brazil, 107f
social structure: in Aztec Empire, 21, 23; in Inca Empire, 27; in Maya civilization, 16–17
Social Studies Skills
  Chart and Graph Skills: Interpreting a Climate Graph, 76; Interpreting an Elevation Profile, 129; Using Latitude and Longitude, 96
  Critical Thinking Skills: Analyzing Information, 32; Connecting Ideas, 111
  Geography Skills: Interpreting a Climate Graph, 76; Interpreting an Elevation Profile, 129; Using Latitude and Longitude, 96; Using Mental Maps and Sketch Maps, 188; Using a Political Map, 149
  Study Skills: Analyzing Information, 32; Connecting Ideas, 111; Taking Notes, 47
Social Studies Words, H4
soil exhaustion, 105
South America. *See also* Atlantic South America; Caribbean South America; Pacific South America: political map of, 5m, 213m; physical map of, 212m
Southern Hemisphere: defined, H7; map of, H7
Southern Mexico, 51p, 52
Southern states of United States, 161m, 162–63; climate of, 147, 147p, 147m; physical features of, 144–45

South Pole: 221m
Spain: colonization of Argentina, 112–13; colonization in Central America, 62; colonization of Colombia, 87; colonization of Paraguay, 116; colonization of Venezuela, 90; Cortés conquers Aztecs, 24, 44; Mexico's independence from, 45; Pizarro conquers Incas, 28–29, 29p, 131
Spanish: in Caribbean, 72; in Central America, 64; in Mexico, 45; in Pacific South America, 132, 132c; in United States, 156; in Venezuela, 91
Speaking Skills: Creating a Radio Ad, 170; Interviewing, 122
special-purpose maps, H13
Standardized Test Practice, 35, 55, 79, 99, 121, 141, 169, 191
Statue of Liberty, 143p
strait, 125; defined, H14
Strait of Magellan, 125, 125m
strike, 94
Study Skills: Analyzing Information, 32; Connecting Ideas, 111; Taking Notes, 47
Sucre, 135
Suriname, 95, 95p; facts about, 10c; mountains of, 83, 83m

Tarabuco, Bolivia, 133p
technology. *See* science and technology
tectonic plates: Caribbean Islands and, 60, 60m
Tenochtitlán, 20–21, 21p, 22f, 33p
tepuís, 83
terrorism: United States and, 165–66
Tiahuanaco, 130
Tierra del Fuego, 125, 125m
Tijuana, 51
time measurement: Maya civilization, 18
Tokyo, 10c
tornadoes: in United States, 150–51, 150m
Toronto, Canada, 180–181, 180p, 185
tourism: Canada, 186–87; Caribbean Islands, 75; Central America and the Caribbean, 61; ecotourism, 66, 66p; Mexico, 49, 52; South region of United States, 163
Toussaint-L'Ouverture, 71p
trade: Argentina, 114; Canada, 187, 187c; Chile and, 138; Cuba, 74; Maya civilization, 14, 15, 15m;

Mercosur, 114; Native Canadians and European settlers, 177; North American Free Trade Agreement (NAFTA), 49, 165; South region of United States and Mexico, 163; United States and, 165

tributary, 145

Trinidad and Tobago, 59, 59m; facts about, 10c; music of, 73f

Understanding Comparison-Contrast, 56, 196

Understanding Lists, 170, 201

United Arab Emirates: oil exports of, 93c

United Fruit Company, 63, 63p

United Nations, 155

United States: agriculture, 148; American colonies, 152–53; Chile's Exports to the United States, 2004, 141m; climate of, 147–48, 147m; culture in, 156, 158; Distribution of Selected Ethnic Groups, 2000, 157m; Eastern states, 144–45, 147, 161m; economic and military power of, 165; ethnic groups in, 156, 157m; facts about, 8c, 9c; food in, 157; George Washington and, 153p; government and citizenship, 155; independence, 153; Interior Plains, 145–46, 147, 145m; language in, 156; Mexican-American War, 45; Midwest region, 161m, 163; music in, 158; natural hazards in, 150–51f, 150m; natural resources and land use of, 148, 160–65, 162m; North American Free Trade Agreement (NAFTA), 49; Northeast region, 160–62, 161m; oil and, 148; Panama Canal, 67; physical geography of, 144–46, 145m; physical map of, 145m, 202–3m; political map of, 142–43m, 149m, 204–5m; popular culture, 158; Population of Major U.S. Cities, 161c; Puerto Rico and, 73; regions in, 160–65, 161m, 169; religion in, 156; Revolutionary War, 153; rights and responsibilities, 155; Size Comparison: The United States and the Americas,

3m; Southern states, 144–45, 147, 161m, 162–63; terrorism, 165–66; trade with Canada, 187, 187c; urban population of, 10c; wars and peace, 155; Western expansion and industrial growth, 153–54, 154m; Western states, 146, 148, 161m, 164–65

Upper Canada, 178

urbanization: in Canada, 180–81

Uruguay, 115–16, 116m; agriculture, 116; economy of, 116; facts about, 10c; government of, 115; language of, 115; people of, 115; physical features of, 102–3, 103m; physical map of, 116m; religion of, 115; urban population of, 10c

U.S. Constitution, 155

Using Context Clues, 100, 198

Uxmal, 43p

valley: defined, H15

Valley of Mexico, 39

Valparaíso, 138

Vancouver, 181, 186; Chinatown in, 181f

vegetation: Andes, 126–27, 126p; Atlantic South America, 105; Caribbean South America, 85; Central America and the Caribbean, 60; Mexico, 40–41; Pacific South America, 126–27

Venezuela: agriculture and ranching, 92; Canaima National Park, 84m, 84p; Caracas, 93, 94p; Chavez as president, 93–94; culture of, 91; economy of, 92–93; facts about, 10c; government of, 91, 93–94; history of, 90–91; independence and self-rule, 91; independence from Spain, 87; llaneros, 92; mountains of, 83, 83m; natural resources of, 85, 92–93, 93m; oil exports of, 93c; oil in, 91, 92–94, 93m; Orinoco River, 83p, 84; people of, 91; Simon Bolívar, 91f; Spanish settlement and colonial rule of, 90; today, 92–93

viceroy, 131

Vietnam War, 155

Viewing Skills: Creating a Collage, 142

Virgin Islands, 59, 75, 75p

Vocabulary, H4

volcanoes: Central America and the Caribbean, 60; defined, H15; Hawaii, 146; Mount Saint Helens, 146; Pacific South America, 124; United States, 150, 150m; Volcanoes of Colombia, 99m

warfare: Aztec Empire, 23

Washington, D.C., 161

Washington, George, 153p

water: Mexico, 41

wealth: in Mexico City, 50; in Venezuela, 92

weather: El Niño, 127; tornadoes, 150–51, 150m

West Africa: climate map of, H13

Western Hemisphere: defined, H7; map of, H7

Western Provinces of Canada, 185–86

Western United States: 161m, 164–65; climate of, 147m, 148; physical features of, 146; Western expansion, 153–54, 154m

West Indies, 70

wetland: defined, H14

wildfires: in United States, 150–51f, 150m

wildlife: of Caribbean South America, 84

World Trade Center, 165–66

World War I, 155

World War II, 155

Writing Skills: Creating a Travel Guide, 56; Creating a Web Site, 100; Describing a Place, 192; Writing an "I Am" Poem, 36; A Newspaper Article, 12; Writing a Letter, 80

writing system: Inca Empire, 28; Maya civilization, 18

young towns, 136, 137p

Yucatán Peninsula, 19, 38, 39m, 40, 52

Yukon Territory, 180, 186

Credits and Acknowledgments

Acknowledgments

For permission to reproduce copy-righted material, grateful acknowl-edgment is made to the following sources:

Atheneum Books for Young Readers, an imprint of Simon & Schuster Children's Publishing Division: From *Bearstone* by Will Hobbs. Copyright ©1989 by Will Hobbs. All rights reserved.

Sources used by The World Almanac® for charts and graphs:

Geographical Extremes: The Americas: *The World Almanac and Book of Facts, 2005; The World Factbook, 2005;* U.S. Bureau of the Census; The Americas: *The World Factbook, 2005;* U.S. Bureau of the Census, International Database; United Nations Statistical Yearbook; World's Largest Cities: United Nations Population Division National Censuses; Urban Populations in the Americas: United Nations Population Division; Major Food Exports of the Americas: Food and Agriculture Organization of the United Nations; Languages of the Caribbean: Joshua Project; World's Top Oil Exporters: Energy Information Administration of the U.S. Department of Energy; Argentina's Largest Cities: National Institute of Statistics and Censuses, Argentina, 2001 Census; Languages in Pacific South America: Ethnologue: Languages of the World, 15th Edition; Population of Major U.S. Cities: U.S. Census Bureau; Canadian Ethnic Groups: The World Factbook, 2005

Illustrations and Photo Credits

Cover: (l), Ray Boudreau; (r), Chris Rennie/Robert Harding World Imagery/Getty Images.

Frontmatter: ii, Victoria Smith/HRW; iv, Sally Brown/Index Stock Imagery, Inc.; v, Juan Silva/The Image Bank/Getty Images; vi, Superstock; vii, Index Stock Imagery, Inc.; viii, CORBIS; H16 (t), Earth Satellite Corporation/Science Photo Library; H16 (tc), Frans Lemmens/Getty Images; H16 (c), London Aerial Photo Library/Corbis; H16 (bc), Harvey Schwartz/Index Stock Imagery; H16 (b), Tom Nebbia/Corbis

Introduction: A, Taxi/Getty Images; B (bl) Stephen Frink/Digital Vision/Getty Images; B (cr), Frans Lemmens/The Image Bank/Getty Images; 1 (bc), Robert Harding/Digital Vision/Getty Images; B–1 (background satellite photos), Planetary Visions.

Chapter 1: 12 (br), Justin Kerr; 13 (bl), Trustees of the British Museum; 13 (br), Kevin Schafer/Corbis; 15 (bl), Justin Kerr, k4809/Kerr Associates; 15 (br), Erich Lessing/Art Resource, NY; 17 (c), Scala/Art Resource, NY; 18 (tl), Robert Frerck/Odyssey Productions, Inc.; 18 (tr), © Trustees of the British Museum, London; 21 (tr), Mexican National Museum, Mexico City/DDB Stock Photography; 23 (tl), © Trustees of the British Museum, London; 25 (b), Robert Frerck/Odyssey/Chicago; 26 (tl), New York Historical Society, New York, USA/Bridgeman Art Library; 27 (tr), The Granger Collection, New York; 28 (tl), American Museum of Natural History, New York/Bridgeman Art Library; 28 (tc), Stuart Franklin/Magnum Photos; 28 (tr), Museo del Banco Central de Ecuador/DDB Stock Photograph; 29 (t), Museo Pedro de Osma Lima/Mireille; 29 (c), Musée du Chateau de Versailles/Dagli Orti/The Art Archive; 33 (t), Erich Lessing/Art Resource, NY; 33 (b), Museo del Banco Central de Ecuador/DDB Stock Photograph.

Chapter 2: 36, Rommel/Masterfile; 37 (bl), Age Fotostock/SuperStock; 37 (br), Danny Lehman/CORBIS; 39, Charles & Josette Lenars/CORBIS; 40-41, Sally Brown/Index Stock Imagery, Inc.; 42, Kevin Schafer/CORBIS; 43 (bl), Fred Lengnick/Imagestate; 43 (br), Werner Forman/Art Resource, NY; 44, Schalkwijk/Art Resource, NY; 46, Liba Taylor/CORBIS; 49, NASA; 50 (tl), Edward Degginger/Bruce Coleman, Inc.; 50 (c), Robert Frerck/Odyssey/Chicago; 51 (tc), Age Fotostock/SuperStock; 51 (cr), Macduff Everton/CORBIS; 53 (tl), Charles & Josette Lenars/CORBIS; 53 (tc), Schalkwijk/Art Resource, NY; 53 (tr), Age Fotostock/SuperStock.

Chapter 3: 56, Robert Frerck/Odyssey/Chicago; 57 (br), Taxi/Getty Images; 57 (bl), Robert Frerck/Odyssey/Chicago; 59, Peter Treanor/Pictures Colour Library Ltd.; 60, Galen Rowell/CORBIS; 61, CORBIS; 63 (tl), David Alan Harvey/Magnum Photos; 63 (cr), Bettmann/CORBIS; 66, Look GMBH/eStock Photo; 72, Stuart Cohen/The ImageWorks; 73, Dave Bartruff/DanitaDelimont.com; 74 (b), AFP/NewsCom; 74 (cr), Hans Deryk/AP/Wide World Photos; 75, Picture Finders/Pictures Colour Library Ltd.; 77 (l), Peter Treanor/Pictures Colour Library Ltd.; 77 (r), Dave Bartruff/DanitaDelimont.com.

Chapter 4: 80, Krzysztof Dydynski/Lonely Planet Images; 81 (bl), Kevin Schafer/kevinschafer.com; 81 (br), Olivier Grunewald/Photolibrary; 83 (cr), MedioImages/SuperStock; 83 (cl), Robert Caputo/Aurora Photos; 84 (bc), Juan Silva/The Image Bank/Getty Images; 84 (bl), Ed Darack/D. Donne Bryant Photography; 84 (r), James Marshall/CORBIS; 86, Bridgeman Art Library; 87, Jane Sweeney/Lonely Planet Images; 88, Stone/Getty Images; 89 (tr), Krzysztof Dydynski/Lonely Planet Images; 89 (tl), Robert Frerck/Odyssey/Chicago; 91 (tl), Jorge Silva/Reuters/NewsCom; 92, Chico Sanchez/EPA/Landov; 93, John Van Hasselt/CORBIS; 94, Pablo Corral V/CORBIS; 95, Larry Luxner; 97 (l), James Marshall/CORBIS; 97 (c), Bridgeman Art Library; 97 (tr), Jorge Silva/Reuters/NewsCom.

Chapter 5: 100, Dario Lopez-Mills/AP/Wide World Photos; 101(bl), Steve Vidler/eStock Photo; 101 (br), Robert Frerck/Odyssey/Chicago; 103 (cr), Kit Houghton/CORBIS; 103 (tr), George Hunter/Pictures Colour Library Ltd.; 106, Stuart Cohen/The Image Works; 107, Renzo Gostoli/AP/Wide World Photos; 108, SIME s.a.s/eStock Photo; 109 (tl), Moacyr Lopes Jr./UNEP/Peter Arnold, Inc.; 109 (tr), Wolfgang Kaehler/CORBIS; 110, Science Photo Library/Photo Researchers, Inc.; 113 (t), The British Library/Topham-HIP/The

Image Works; 113 (br), Bettmann/CORBIS; 115, Marcel & Eva Malherbe/The Image Works; 116 (br), Wayne Walton/Lonely Planet Images; 116 (cr), Julio Etchart/Peter Arnold, Inc.; 118, Andrea Booher/Stone/Getty Images; 119 (cl), SIME s.a.s/eStock Photo; 119 (bl), Julio Etchart/Peter Arnold, Inc.

Chapter 6: 122, Francesc Muntada/CORBIS; 123 (br), Darrell Gulin/DanitaDelimont.com; 123 (bl), Robert Frerck/Odyssey/Chicago; 125, Graham Neden; Ecoscene/CORBIS; 127, CNES, Distribution Spot Image/Science Photo Library; 131 (t), Robert Frerck/Odyssey/Chicago; 131 (tr), Ric Ergenbright; 133, SuperStock; 135, Robert Fried/Robert Fried Photography; 136, Photodisc/Fotosearch Stock Photography; 137 (tl), Art Directors/Warren Jacobs; 137 (tr), Ron Giling/Peter Arnold, Inc.; 138, Randa Bishop/DanitaDelimont.com; 139 (tl), Graham Neden; Ecoscene/CORBIS; 139 (tc), SuperStock; 139 (tr), Art Directors/Warren Jacobs.

Chapter 7: 142, eStock Photo/PictureQuest; 143 (br), Rommel Pecson/The Image Works; 143 (bl), Ron Watts/CORBIS; 145, Altrendo/Getty Images; 146, NASA/Photo Researchers, Inc.; 147(br), Dallas and John Heaton/Stock Connection/IPN; 147 (cr), Alan Schein/CORBIS; 151 (tl), Stone/Getty Images; 153(b), Metropolitan Museum of Art, New York/ Bridgeman Art Library; 155, *The Signing of the Constitution of the United States in 1787,* 1940, Christy, Howard Chandler (1873-1952), Hall of Representatives, Washington D.C., USA/www.bridgeman.co.uk; 157, Jeff Greenberg/The Image Works; 159, Sam Dudgeon/HRW; 161, Alan Schein Photography/CORBIS; 163 (tl), Royalty Free/CORBIS; 163 (cl), Ray Soto/CORBIS; 164, Art Wolfe/DanitaDelimont.com; 165, LMDC/ZUMA/CORBIS; 167 (tl), Altrendo/Getty Images; 167 (bl), Alan Schein Photography/CORBIS.

Chapter 8: 170, Workbook/Photolibrary; 171 (br), Tom Bean/CORBIS; 171 (bl), Steve Vidler/eStock Photo; 173, Joseph Sohm; Visions of America/CORBIS; 174, Simon Harris/eStock Photo; 175, CNES, Distribution Spot Image/Photo Researchers, Inc.; 176 (bl), Steve Vidler/eStock Photo; 176 (br), AKG-Images; 177 (bl), Photocanada Digital Inc.; 177 (br), Photocanada Digital Inc.; 178, PhotoDisc Green, Inc./HRW; 180, Robert Frerck/Odyssey Productions, Inc.; 181, Albert Normandin/Masterfile; 186 (tr), Index Stock Imagery, Inc.; 186 (t), Bryan & Cherry Alexander/arcticphoto.co.uk; 187, Joseph Sohm; Visions of America/CORBIS; 189 (tl), Simon Harris/eStock Photo; 189 (tc), Steve Vidler/eStock Photo.

Backmatter: 223, Planetary Visions; 224-225 (t), Oriental Touch/Robert Harding; 225 (cl), Amanda Hall/Robert Harding; 236 (tr), Tom Stewart/Corbis.

Staff Credits

The people who contributed to *Holt Social Studies: The Americas* are listed below. They represent editorial, design, production, emedia, and permissions.

Melanie Baccus, Ed Blake, Henry Clark, Grant Davidson, Nina Degollado, Rose Degollado, Michelle Dike, Lydia Doty, Chase Edmond, Susan Franques, Bob Fullilove, Matthew Gierhart, Janet Harrington, Wendy Hodge, Tim Hovde, Cathy Jenevein, Kadonna Knape, David Knowles, Aylin Koker, Laura Lasley, Sean McCormick, Joe Melomo, Richard Metzger, Andrew Miles, Joeleen Ornt, Jarred Prejean, Shelly Ramos, Curtis Riker, Michael Rinella, Beth Sample, Annette Saunders, Jenny Schaeffer, Kay Selke, Chris Smith, Jeannie Taylor, Joni Wackwitz, Mary Wages, Diana Holman Walker, Nadyne Wood, Robin Zaback